# A-Z

HANDBOOK 3RD EDITION

## Accounting

Ian Harrison

DIGITAL EDITION

**PHILIP ALLAN**
UPDATES

Philip Allan Updates, an imprint of Hodder Education, an Hachette UK company, Market Place, Deddington, Oxfordshire OX15 0SE

**Orders**

Bookpoint Ltd, 130 Milton Park, Abingdon, Oxfordshire OX14 4SB
tel: 01235 827720
fax: 01235 400454
e-mail: uk.orders@bookpoint.co.uk

Lines are open 9.00 a.m.–5.00 p.m., Monday to Saturday, with a 24-hour message answering service. You can also order through the Philip Allan Updates website: www.philipallan.co.uk

ISBN 978-0-340-99105-3

First published 1998
Second edition 2003
Third edition 2009

Impression number   5   4   3   2   1
Year   2014   2013   2012   2011   2010   2009

Typeset by Macmillan, India.

Printed by Antony Rowe, Chippenham, Wiltshire.

**Environmental information**

Hachette UK's policy is to use papers that are natural, renewable and recyclable products and made from wood grown in sustainable forests. The logging and manufacturing processes are expected to conform to the environmental regulations of the country of origin.

# Contents

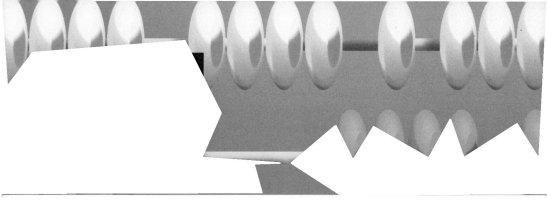

# How to use this book

The *A–Z Accounting Handbook* aims to provide a quick point of reference for students studying a wide variety of accounting courses (GCSE, GCE AS and A-level and IB). Each entry begins with a simple definition of the word or term in question and a more detailed explanation follows if necessary. In some cases, a worked example is included and, depending on the type of course being studied, students may then wish to refer to a more detailed course text in order to determine the specific skill level required for their course.

This book is not an exhaustive list of all accounting terms but it does encompass the main terms and concepts currently employed by the majority of bodies validating accounting qualifications.

This edition of the handbook has been updated to include recent changes in terminology used in the preparation of financial statements. While at the moment the terminology used in international accounting standards applies in the main to limited companies, the terminology has been applied to all business organisations throughout this book. In this way, we hope to help both students and teachers by presenting them with only one set of terminology to remember.

Accounting is studied at many different levels. For example, in the majority of AS examinations students are required to understand financial statements but do not need to construct the more complex of these. They must have knowledge of the underlying accounting concepts and bookkeeping entries. However, at A-level, knowledge is required of how to construct financial statements and students must have a knowledge of the underlying accounting concepts and bookkeeping entries.

Those studying the subject at a professional level will need a much more detailed knowledge of very specific areas of accounting such as taxation; a detail not required in AS and A-level examinations. The Association of Accounting Technicians course requires a practical knowledge of a wide variety of accounting activities, for example payroll and VAT. It is the intention of this book to give useful references for all these purposes and to aim explanations at the general reader rather than a specific one.

There are various ways in which students can benefit from this book. Some sections can be used to check the accepted format for certain aspects of accounting while others will help to develop understanding and the application of commonly used terms. In AS and A-level examinations, written rather than purely numerical answers are increasingly being assessed and some of the definitions included in this handbook provide clear and precise explanations suitable for answering this type of narrative question.

In order to help readers find their way around the book, entries have been cross-referenced in bold italic where necessary.

Revision lists of key words, terms and abbreviations have been included at the end of the book, together with some useful tips for examinations. This section is designed to help you to avoid the pitfalls that so many people fall into when taking examinations. On the website that accompanies this handbook, you can access revision lists specific to your exam board.

## A–Z Online

This new digital edition of the *A–Z Accounting Handbook* includes free access to a supporting website and a free desktop widget to make searching for terms even quicker. Log on to **www.philipallan.co.uk/a-zonline** and create an account using the unique code provided on the inside front cover of this book.

Once you are logged on, you will be able to:

- search the entire database of terms in this handbook
- print revision lists specific to your exam board
- get expert advice from examiners on how to get an A* grade
- create a personal library of your favourite terms
- expand your vocabulary with our word of the week

You can also add the other *A–Z Handbooks (digital editions)* that you own to your personal library on A–Z Online.

I hope that you will find this handbook useful to help you through your learning and as an invaluable time-saving reference during revision.

*Ian Harrison*

## Acknowledgements

Writing a book of this type is extremely time consuming and requires many hours of research. I must thank the team at Philip Allan Updates for the patience shown when awaiting my drafts. On a personal level, I must thank my wife Sandie for her proof reading, word processing and comments and most of all for her patience.

Every effort has been made to be as accurate as possible but there may be occasions when a critical reader could feel that I have oversimplified some entries. I have done this in order to make the book as accessible to as many people as possible and I therefore hope that the 'experts' will be forgiving.

*Ian Harrison*

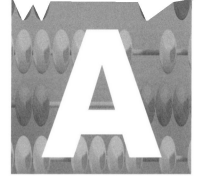

**AAT:** see *Association of Accounting Technicians*

**ABC classification of inventories:** a method that classifies inventories held into categories of importance. Businesses can then apply the most elaborate procedures in the control of inventory only to the items deemed to be most important. It is used when a business has large inventories of many different items.

**abnormal losses** are losses that occur during the production process but which should be avoided if normal efficient procedures are adopted and followed. They occur when a machine goes wrong or a worker wastes some material or component which ordinarily should not be wasted. The bookkeeping entries are:

**Debit:** Abnormal loss account    **Credit:** Process account

At the financial year end the abnormal loss account is treated as a *period cost*:

**Debit:** Income statement    **Credit:** Abnormal loss account

**above the line:** income and expenditure that appear in the *income statement* before the deduction of taxation.

**absorption:** when all *production overheads* have been allocated and *apportioned* to a product *cost centre*, the total has to be charged to specific units of production. This process is known as absorption. The main methods of absorption are:
- direct labour hour rate
- direct labour cost percentage rate
- machine hour rate

> **Worked example**
>
> Saluts are manufactured in department J of S M Neal & Co. Ltd. The budgeted overhead costs of department J are estimated to be £200 000 for the next accounting period.
>
> Budgeted direct labour hours for department J for the next accounting period are expected to be 10 000 hours.
>
> Budgeted costs of direct labour in department J for the next accounting period are expected to be £80 000.
>
> Budgeted machine hours to be worked in department J for the next accounting period are expected to be 2450 hours.

**Required:**

Calculate the overhead absorption rate for department J using the following bases of absorption:

a) direct labour hour rate

b) direct labour cost rate, and

c) machine hour rate

**Solution:**

a) direct labour hour rate: $\dfrac{£200\,000}{10\,000}$ = £20 per direct labour hour

b) direct labour cost percentage rate: $\dfrac{200\,000}{80\,000}$ = 250% of direct labour cost

c) machine hour rate: $\dfrac{£200\,000}{2450}$ = £81.63 per machine hour

**absorption costing:** the system of absorbing factory overheads into the total product cost for each saleable unit produced in a factory. **CIMA** (the Chartered Institute of Management Accountants) defines absorption costing as 'the process which charges fixed as well as variable overheads to cost units'.

**abstract:** a shortened form, or an extract from a document or a report.

**ACA:** an Associate of the Institute of Chartered Accountants in England and Wales.

**ACCA:** an Associate of the Chartered Association of Certified Accountants.

**accept a bill of exchange:** to sign a bill of exchange indicating that the person signing will pay that bill when it falls due.

**account:** a record of financial transactions. Financial data are initially entered into a *book of prime entry*. From there the information is recorded in the *double-entry bookkeeping* system in a book called the *ledger*. The ledger is made up of individual accounts which show in detail every financial transaction undertaken by the business. Generally, each account is shown on a separate page in the ledger. Every account has two sides: the *debit* (left side) and the *credit* (right side). Each piece of financial information is recorded in two accounts: one entry is made on the debit of one account, the other entry is made on the credit of another account.

### Worked example

Mary purchases goods for resale paying cash £34.

**Required:**

Show this transaction in Mary's ledger.

**Solution:**

| Purchases | | Cash | |
|---|---|---|---|
| Cash    34 | | | Purchases    34 |

**accountancy** is the profession whose members are engaged in the collection of financial data, summarising that data and then presenting it to the *users of financial reports*.

**accountant:** a person compiling financial records. Anyone can call themselves an accountant and set up in business offering their services. However, some work undertaken by accountants is restricted to those who are members of one of the major accounting bodies.

**accounting:** the term applied to the use of financial information once it has been extracted from the basic *books of account*. The function of accounting is to record this information and classify it. The information is then summarised and prepared in a format which is designed to be accessible to the many *users of financial reports*.

The American Accounting Association describes accounting as 'the process of identifying, measuring and communicating economic information to permit informed judgements and decisions by users of the information'.

**accounting bases:** methods that have been developed in order to apply, generally, accounting concepts to particular accounting transactions. With the issue of *International Accounting Standards (IASs)* the number of alternative bases available has been reduced. (See also *accounting policies*.)

**accounting concepts and conventions:** assumptions that are generally recognised when *financial statements* are being prepared.

Financial statements are prepared on the assumption that:
- the business will continue to trade into the foreseeable future (*going-concern concept*)
- revenues and costs are recorded when they are incurred, not when the cash is received or paid (*accruals concept*)
- they are prepared following the same principles that were used in the previous sets of financial statements (concept of *consistency*)
- only transactions that can be given a monetary value are recorded in the *books of account* (*money measurement concept*)
- as far as accounting is concerned, the business unit is distinct from all other units including the owner(s) (*business entity concept*)
- all financial transactions should be shown separately if a user of the financial statements would be misled by not revealing that transaction (concept of *materiality*)
- if there is any doubt of the value of any transaction then a conservative approach should be adopted (concept of *prudence*)

**accounting entity:** this can be a *sole trader*, a *partnership*, a *limited company* or some form of non-trading organisation.

**accounting equation:** the accounting equation recognises that the assets owned by an organisation are always equal to the claims against the organisation.

One side of the accounting equation shows in monetary terms the resources (assets) that are owned by the organisation. The other side of the equation shows how these resources have been financed by funds provided by the owner(s) and borrowings.

The accounting equation can be stated as:

$$\textit{FORMULA:} \quad \frac{\text{non-current}}{\text{assets}} + \frac{\text{current}}{\text{assets}} = \text{capital} + \frac{\text{non-current}}{\text{liabilities}} + \frac{\text{current}}{\text{liabilities}}$$

3

**accounting packages** are computer software programs specifically designed to record the financial transactions of a business. They may be specific to certain tasks, for example payroll and inventory recording packages, or they may be generalised so that a multitude of tasks can be undertaken, culminating in the preparation of financial statements.

**accounting period:** *financial statements* are prepared for a finite period of time – usually one year, although many businesses will also prepare financial statements monthly, quarterly or half yearly. The use of an accounting period enables financial statements of one accounting period to be compared with those of another accounting period for *stewardship* and *management accounting* purposes.

**accounting policies:** *accounting bases* that the managers of a business have selected to use because they are appropriate to their specific business, e.g. the managers of a quarry may choose to use the *depletion method* of depreciating their quarry; the managers of a fleet of delivery vans may decide to use a *reducing balance method* of depreciating their delivery vans. The name given to the fundamental *accounting concepts* used to prepare the financial statements of *limited companies* in the *Companies Act 1985*.

**accounting policies, changes in accounting estimates and errors IAS8:** the standard defines accounting policies and provides details on:

*accounting principles* – concepts applied in the preparation of accounting statements, e.g. *prudence, accruals, consistency*.

*accounting bases* – methods used in preparing accounting statements. These are acceptable methods designed to reduce subjectivity, e.g. the use of historic cost or revaluation as a method used to value assets.

A change in accounting estimates is an adjustment to the *carrying amount* (i.e. the amount shown in the balance sheet) of an *asset* or *liability* following a reassessment of the future benefits and obligations relating to the asset or liability. Such adjustments require disclosure if the change affects current or future financial statements.

The standard deals with the effect of errors on *financial statements*. It states that material errors that occurred in previous accounting periods must be corrected by comparing the incorrect with the correct information.

**accounting principles:** the name given to the fundamental accounting concepts used to prepare the *financial statements of limited companies* in the *Companies Act 1985*.

**accounting rate-of-return method of capital investment appraisal (ARR)** measures the profit earned on investment expressed as a percentage of the average investment. The formula for its calculation is:

$$FORMULA: \quad \frac{\text{average annual profit}}{\text{average investment}} \times \frac{100}{1}$$

Note: the average annual profit is used, not cash flows. This may mean that a calculation of profit may need to be undertaken if the cash-flow figures are given.

## Worked example

James & Co. Ltd requires a new piece of machinery. Two new machines are under consideration. They both require an initial investment of £200 000 and have an anticipated useful life of 4 years. The annual cash flow that each is expected to generate is given below:

|  | Machine LCJ | Machine HER |
|---|---|---|
|  | £ | £ |
| Year 1 | 80 000 | 70 000 |
| Year 2 | 60 000 | 60 000 |
| Year 3 | 60 000 | 50 000 |
| Year 4 | 40 000 | 50 000 |

### Required:

Calculate the accounting rate of return for each machine.

### Solution:

#### Average profits

|  | Machine LCJ Cash flow – depreciation | £ | Machine HER Cash flow – depreciation | £ |
|---|---|---|---|---|
| Year 1 | 80 000 – 50 000 | 30 000 | 70 000 – 50 000 | 20 000 |
| Year 2 | 60 000 – 50 000 | 10 000 | 60 000 – 50 000 | 10 000 |
| Year 3 | 60 000 – 50 000 | 10 000 | 50 000 – 50 000 | – |
| Year 4 | 40 000 – 50 000 | (10 000) | 50 000 – 50 000 | – |
|  |  | 40 000 |  | 30 000 |
| Average profits (£40 000/4) |  | 10 000 | (£30 000/4) | 7 500 |

#### Average investment (same for both machines)

|  | Start of year | End of year | Average investment over year |
|---|---|---|---|
|  | £ | £ | £ |
| Year 1 | 200 000 | 150 000 | 175 000 |
| Year 2 | 150 000 | 100 000 | 125 000 |
| Year 3 | 100 000 | 50 000 | 75 000 |
| Year 4 | 50 000 | – | 25 000 |
|  |  | Total | 400 000 |

Average investment = £400 000/4 = £100 000

#### Accounting rate of return

Machine LCJ

$$\frac{£10\,000}{£100\,000} \times 100 = 10\%$$

Machine HER

$$\frac{£7\,500}{£100\,000} \times 100 = 7.5\%$$

The average investment can be calculated more simply

$$\frac{\text{Initial investment} + \text{scrap value}}{2}$$

so $\dfrac{£200\,000}{2}$ + £0 (in this example) = £100 000

5

This method can be used to decide between alternative capital projects when other factors are very similar. It is not particularly valuable as the only determinant, since it ignores the time value of money and the timing of the returns – average profits will remain the same whether profits are anticipated to be higher in the early years of the project or in the late years. For example, the average profits on the following three projects are the same over a three-year time period:

| | Project A £ | Project B £ | Project C £ |
|---|---|---|---|
| Year 1 profits | 70 000 | 1 000 | 30 000 |
| Year 2 profits | 10 000 | 1 000 | 30 000 |
| Year 3 profits | 10 000 | 88 000 | 30 000 |
| Average profits | 30 000 | 30 000 | 30 000 |

**Worked example**

Douglas Ltd presently earns a return on capital employed of 15%. The managers are considering the purchase of a new machine costing £80 000. The machine is expected to yield additional profits of £18 000 per annum.

*Required:*

Calculate the accounting rate of return expected from the purchase of the new machine and advise the managers of Douglas Ltd whether or not they should purchase the new machine.

*Solution:*

$$ARR = \frac{18\ 000}{40\ 000} = 45\%$$

(the average capital employed in the new machine is half of £80 000)

On financial grounds the managers should purchase the machine, since the accounting rate of return (45%) is greater than the return they presently enjoy on capital employed (15%).

**accounting ratios** is the generic name applied to many different types of financial calculation that may be used to measure the performance of a business. To be meaningful the results must be used either in *trend analysis* or in comparing the results of two or more businesses. See *ratio analysis*.

**accounting records** is the generic term applied to the books of account kept by a business.

**accounting standards:** the rules applied in accounting practice that have been recommended by the *International Accounting Standards Board (IASB)*. These standards are 'concerned with principles rather than fine details'. The standards should be applied in the spirit of the standard rather than by strict observance of the actual wording; the emphasis is on 'substance over form'.

New standards are referred to as *IFRS*s and *IAS*s.

**accounting technician:** a person who assists a fully qualified accountant to prepare financial statements. (See also *Association of Accounting Technicians*.)

**accruals:** amounts owed for services used by a business during its normal *accounting period*. (See *accrued expenses*.)

For example, a manufacturing business might pay the wages of its factory workers in the week following that in which the work was done. These wages must be included in the end-of-year *manufacturing account*, even though they may be paid in the next financial year.

**accruals concept:** also sometimes referred to as the matching concept. Costs and revenues are matched so that the financial records refer to the same goods and services in the same time period.

Accountants are interested in accounting for the resources that a business has used during the financial year to generate the *revenue receipts* for that same year, rather than accounting for the money paid to acquire those resources.

The concept recognises the difference between the actual payment of cash and the legal obligation to pay cash. For example, the annual rent of Sybil's shop is £4800 per annum, payable quarterly in advance. At the end of her financial year she has only paid her landlord £3600. The amount shown on her *income statement* is £4800 since she has had the use of £4800 worth of resource to help generate her revenues for that year.

The accruals concept also recognises the distinction between the receipt of cash and the right to receive that cash. For example, Sybil sublets the garage at the rear of her shop for a rental of £10 per week to Jack. At Sybil's financial year end Jack owes Sybil two weeks' rent. Sybil's profit and loss account would show 'Rent received £520' even though she has received only £500 from Jack.

### Worked example

Yvonne rents business premises at a rental of £600 per calendar month, her financial year end is 31 December. Yvonne makes the following payments:

| | £ |
|---|---|
| 7 January | 1800 |
| 22 April | 1800 |
| 13 July | 1800 |
| 4 October | 1800 |
| 6 December | 1800 |

Yvonne sublets part of her premises to Tony at a rental of £300 per quarter, payable in advance on 1 January, 1 April, 1 July, 1 October. Tony makes the following payments to Yvonne:

| | |
|---|---|
| 23 February | 300 |
| 8 June | 300 |
| 6 December | 300 |

*Required:*

The rent payable and rent receivable accounts as they would appear in Yvonne's general ledger.

| Rent payable | | | | | Rent receivable | | | |
|---|---|---|---|---|---|---|---|---|
| 7 Jan Cash | 1800 | | | | | | 23 Feb Cash | 300 |
| 22 Apl Cash | 1800 | 31 Dec Inc St | 7200 | 31 Dec Inc St | 1200 | 8 Jun Cash | 300 |
| 13 Jul Cash | 1800 | | | | | 6 Dec Cash | 300 |
| 4 Oct Cash | 1800 | | | | | 31 Dec Bal c/d | 300 |
| 6 Dec Cash | 1800 | 31 Dec Bal c/d | 1800 | | 1200 | | 1200 |
| | 9000 | | 9000 | | | | |
| 1 Jan Bal b/d | 1800 | | | 1 Jan Bal b/d | 300 | | |

Both balances will appear as current assets on Yvonne's year-end balance sheet.

**accrued expenses:** those revenue expenses that remain unpaid at the financial year end. (See *accruals*.)

**accrued income:** that revenue income that remains unpaid at the end of the financial year. (See *accruals concept*.)

**accumulated depreciation:** the total amount of *depreciation* deducted from a *non-current asset* since its *acquisition*.

**accumulated fund:** the '*capital account*' of a non-trading organisation.

**accumulated profits:** the total profits earned by a business that have not been taken out of the business either as *drawings* (in the case of a *sole trader*) or as *dividends* (in the case of a *limited company*). They are the profits retained in the business; the 'ploughed back' profits from this and all previous years. In the case of a limited company they are known as *retained earnings*.

**accumulated reserves:** the total *reserves* set aside out of profits by a *limited company*.

**acid test ratio** measures the immediate *liquidity* position of a business. It is sometimes called the quick ratio. The model (formula) is:

$$FORMULA: \quad \frac{\text{current assets} - \text{inventory}}{\text{current liabilities}}$$

It should be expressed as 'something : 1'.

The immediate liquidity position excludes inventory, since it can be quite difficult to dispose of inventory quickly. Even if inventory could be disposed of immediately, the business could not continue to trade because it would have no goods to trade with.

If a business has a slow *rate of inventory turnover*, the acid test ratio should ideally be greater than 1. With a fast rate of inventory turnover, the ratio can be less than 1 without causing alarm.

When making an assessment, trends over a number of years should be observed rather than considering absolute figures. However, one should not be too pedantic about the ratio without referring to the nature of the business being observed. For example, many supermarkets will operate with an acid test ratio considerably lower than 1.

**Worked example**

Raymond Yong has the following current assets and current liabilities:

Inventory £12 509, trade receivables £3881, cash and cash equivalents £578, trade payables £3877.

*Required:*

Raymond's acid test ratio.

*Solution:*

Quick Ratio

$$\text{Raymond's acid test ratio} = \frac{\text{current assets} - \text{inventories}}{\text{current liabilities}}$$

$$= 1.15{:}1 \ (3881 + 578 : 3877)$$

**ACMA:** an Associate (member) of the Chartered Institute of Management Accountants.

**acquisition:** the taking over of one business by another business, i.e. it acquires control or ownership. The acquisition may take the form of an aggressive *takeover* or be by consent of the managers or owners of the business being acquired.

**ACT:** see *advance corporation tax*

**activity-based costing (ABC):** analyses an organisation's activities into groups of functions which lead to a particular output. Activity costing then seeks to identify factors that influence indirect cost levels for those activities. Output is then costed according to the activities undertaken.

**activity levels:** a measurement of outcomes; the amount of work produced by a business in a set time period. Activity levels are usually used as a comparison when budgeting.

**activity ratios** measure a business's ability to meet its *current liabilities*. This depends on the rate at which *trade receivables* and *inventories* can be converted into cash. (See *rate of inventory turnover* and *trade receivables* payment period.)

**actuary:** a person employed, generally, by an insurance company to calculate the statistical likelihood of how often an occurrence will take place. The insurance company can then calculate the premiums necessary to cover such eventualities.

**added value:** see *value added*

**adjustment accounts:** see *club accounts* and *incomplete records*

**adjustments** are made in *ledger* accounts (or to the figures on the *trial balance*), usually at the end of the financial year, to give the correct figure to be posted to the *income statement*. The adjustments may be necessary to correct any errors discovered in the *double-entry bookkeeping* system or to take into account any *accruals* or *prepayments*.

**administration expenses:** expenses incurred in providing management of the affairs of the business.

**administration overheads:** expenses incurred in providing management and administration for the business. All overheads need to be absorbed if a business is to cover its costs. It is very difficult to find a satisfactory way of absorbing administration overheads, as overheads in general are difficult to relate to levels of productive activity.

Administration overheads may be absorbed by using:

FORMULA: $\dfrac{\text{total administration overhead}}{\text{total production cost}} \times 100$

the result is then applied to the total factory cost of each unit produced; or:

FORMULA: $\dfrac{\text{total administration overhead}}{\text{total sales revenue}} \times 100$

the result is then applied to the selling price of each unit produced.

### Worked example

The following information relates to Watton plc:

| | |
|---|---|
| Total production cost | £720 000 |
| Total sales revenue | £1 500 000 |
| Total administration overhead | £120 000 |
| Total number of units produced | 1 000 000 |

*Required:*

Calculate the administrative overhead absorption rate for Watton plc using:

i) total production cost as the basis for absorption, and

ii) total sales revenue as the basis for absorption

*Solution:*

i) administration overhead rate $= \dfrac{\text{total administration overhead}}{\text{total production cost}} \times 100$

$= \dfrac{£120\ 000}{£720\ 000} \times 100$

$= 16.67\%$

ii) administration overhead rate $= \dfrac{\text{total administration overhead}}{\text{total sales revenue}} \times 100$

$= \dfrac{£120\ 000}{£1\ 500\ 000} \times 100$

$= 8\%$

Using total production cost as the basis for absorbing the administration overhead, each unit would absorb:

72 pence* × 16.67% = 12 pence        *(£720 000/1 000 000)

Using total sales revenue as the basis for absorbing the administration overhead, each unit would absorb:

£1.50* × 8% = 12 pence        *(£1 500 000/1 000 000)

**administrator:** a person appointed to try to rescue a company or to protect certain types of creditors when a company is in serious financial difficulties. If the rescue attempt fails it may have to be wound up (go out of business). Companies do not necessarily go into *liquidation* immediately.

**admission of a new partner:** a structural change to a business involving the addition of one or more new partners. This requires that the business be revalued immediately prior to the admission of the new partner(s), and that the 'old' partner(s) is credited with any increase in the value of the net assets shown on the *balance sheet* (or debited with any decrease) before the new partner(s) takes up office.

## Worked example

George and Mildred have been in partnership for over 25 years sharing profits and losses in the ratio 2:1 respectively. They decide to admit Veronica as a partner with effect from 1 July 20*9. The new partners will share profits and losses equally.

The partnership balance sheet at 30 June 20*9 was as follows:

|  | £ |  |  | £ |
|---|---|---|---|---|
| Premises at cost | 46 000 | Capital accounts | George | 45 000 |
| Fixtures and fittings at cost | 14 000 |  | Mildred | 30 000 |
| Vehicles at cost | 9 000 |  |  |  |
| Inventory | 4 000 |  |  |  |
| Trade receivables | 5 000 | Trade payables |  | 6 000 |
| Cash and cash equivalents | 3 000 |  |  |  |
|  | 81 000 |  |  | 81 000 |

The following asset values have been agreed between George, Mildred and Veronica:

| Premises | £100 000 |
|---|---|
| Fixtures and fittings | £10 000 |
| Vehicles | £7 000 |
| Goodwill | £12 000 |

All other asset and liability values are agreed at book value.

Veronica is to introduce £20 000 cash.

*Required:*

The accounts in the partnership books of account to record the admission of Veronica as a partner and the partnership balance sheet as it would appear immediately after her admission as a partner.

*Solution:*

### Revaluation account

| Fixtures and fittings |  | 4 000 | Premises | 54 000 |
|---|---|---|---|---|
| Vehicles |  | 2 000 | Goodwill | 12 000 |
| Capital | George | 40 000 |  |  |
|  | Mildred | 20 000 |  |  |
|  |  | 66 000 |  | 66 000 |

## Capital accounts

|  | George | Mildred | Veronica |  | George | Mildred | Veronica |
|---|---|---|---|---|---|---|---|
| Goodwill | 4 000 | 4 000 | 4 000 | Bal. b/d | 45 000 | 30 000 | |
|  |  |  |  | Reval. a/c | 40 000 | 20 000 | |
| Bal. c/d | 81 000 | 46 000 | 16 000 | Cash |  |  | 20 000 |
|  | 85 000 | 50 000 | 20 000 |  | 85 000 | 50 000 | 20 000 |
|  |  |  |  | Bal. b/d | 81 000 | 46 000 | 16 000 |

## Goodwill

| Revaluation |  | 12 000 | Capitals | George | 4 000 |
|---|---|---|---|---|---|
|  |  |  |  | Mildred | 4 000 |
|  |  |  |  | Veronica | 4 000 |
|  |  | 12 000 |  |  | 12 000 |

George, Mildred and Veronica balance sheet at 1 July 20*9 immediately after the introduction of Veronica as a partner.

| Premises at valuation | 100 000 | Capital | George | 81 000 |
|---|---|---|---|---|
| Fixtures and fittings at valuation | 10 000 |  | Mildred | 46 000 |
| Vehicles at valuation | 7 000 |  | Veronica | 16 000 |
| Inventory | 4 000 |  |  |  |
| Trade receivables | 5 000 |  | Trade payables | 6 000 |
| Cash and cash equivalents | 23 000 |  |  |  |
|  | 149 000 |  |  | 149 000 |

*Note:* The goodwill has been written off immediately.

**advance corporation tax (ACT):** company taxation that might be paid by a *limited company* that has paid out *dividends* during an *accounting period*. ACT is paid on a quarterly basis by reference to the date of payment to which the dividend relates.

The four quarterly return periods established by Her Majesty's Revenue and Customs end on 31 March, 30 June, 30 September and 31 December. If a limited company's accounting period does not coincide with any of the quarterly dates, its return period will end on the *balance sheet* date. ACT is payable 14 days after the end of the return period. The balance of the company's *tax liability* will be paid nine months after the end of the relevant accounting period as *mainstream corporation tax*.

**adverse variances** arise when actual results do not correspond to the results predicted. If the actual results reduce the profit that has been predicted in the budget, the variance is said to be an adverse variance. If, however, the variance increases the profit that was predicted in the budget then the variance will be a *favourable variance*. (See *standard costing, variance analysis*.)

Adverse variances arise when:

- actual revenue is less than budgeted revenue, or
- actual expenditure is greater than budgeted expenditure

**advice note:** used by the person in charge of receiving goods into stores to check that the goods received are the same as those described on the invoice.

**ageing schedule of trade receivables:** a list of all debts categorised by age. The longer a debt is outstanding, the more likely it is that the debt will need to be written off as bad. An estimated percentage of doubtful debts in each age category is made and the total provision is calculated.

An ageing schedule for doubtful debts might look like this:

| Period outstanding (months) | Amount £ | Estimated percentage of potential bad debts | Provision for doubtful debts |
|---|---|---|---|
| 0–1 | 20 000 | 1 | 200 |
| 1–2 | 16 000 | 2 | 320 |
| 2–3 | 7 000 | 3 | 210 |
| 3–6 | 4 000 | 4 | 160 |
| 6–12 | 3 000 | 5 | 150 |
| over 12 months | 500 | 50 | 250 |
| | 50 500 | | 1 290 |

£1290 would be credited to the provision for doubtful debts account in the *general ledger*.

**agent:** a person who acts on behalf of another with his or her full authority and consent.

**age profile of trade receivables:** see *ageing schedule of trade receivables*

**aggregate depreciation:** the total depreciation deducted from the value of a *non-current asset*. The *published accounts* of a *limited company* must show this figure for each non-current asset.

**AGM:** see *annual general meeting*

**AIM:** see *alternative investment market*

**allocation of overheads:** the process of charging whole items of overhead to *cost centres* or *cost units*. The costs allocated are easily identified as deriving from the cost centre.

**allotment of shares:** when a new issue of shares is oversubscribed the issuing company can give each potential shareholder a proportion of the shares applied for. Applicants receive an allotment letter detailing how many shares they have been allocated.

**allottee:** a prospective shareholder who has been allotted shares in a *limited company*.

**allowable expenses:** those expenses that can legitimately be included in the *income statement* of a business and so are *tax deductible*.

**alpha stocks** are shares of, in the main, highly successful companies listed on the London stock exchange.

**alternative investment market (AIM)** is the market for buying and selling shares in young or small businesses that are not quoted on the full London *stock exchange*.

**amalgamation** takes place when two or more businesses join together to form a new business.

**amortise:** the writing off of intangible assets such as goodwill and leases. According to IAS 38 *intangible assets* should be amortised systematically to the *income statement*. The process is similar to *depreciation* of a *tangible non-current asset*. The bookkeeping entries are:

**Debit:** Income statement          **Credit:** Goodwill account

**analyse:** to examine a subject in detail.

**analysis** involves detailed study of a subject and a report based on the findings of that study.

**analyst:** a person who studies a subject in fine detail and can then draw conclusions from their examination.

**ancillary activities:** activities that are not the *core activity* of an organisation. In clubs and societies the ancillary activities may include discos, raffles, and the provision of bar facilities. These activities serve two purposes: they raise more funds, thus keeping down annual subscriptions, and they act as a way of maintaining members' interest.

**annual general meeting (AGM)** of a *limited company* is the yearly meeting to which all *shareholders* are invited. The *directors* present the financial statements for the *financial year* which has just finished. The company's results can then be discussed with the *board of directors*.

The financial statements are approved at this meeting. The *dividends* are approved and *auditors* are appointed, and any vacancies on the board of directors are filled.

**annual percentage rate (APR):** the annual rate of *compound interest* charged on a *bank loan* or *hire-purchase* transaction which includes fees and management charges.

**annual report and accounts:** a summary of a company's activities which must be sent to *shareholders* in both *private* and *public limited companies* each year. The report must contain at least the minimum of information required by the *Companies Act 1985*. A copy must also be filed with the *Registrar of Companies* at Companies House. This document will contain:

- the *directors' report* on the previous year's financial results
- the *balance sheet* at the end of the trading year
- the *income statement*
- a *statement of cash flows IAS 7*

The company's *auditors* will also report on whether the financial statements show a true and fair view of the company's financial position.

**annual return:** documents sent to the *Registrar of Companies* each year. The return gives particulars of *directors* and members plus a copy of the last *balance sheet* and *income statement*.

**annuity:** the payment made to someone (usually a retired person) on an annual basis in return for a lump-sum investment. The annual payment made will depend on the amount invested and also the age of the person when the investment was initially made.

**application and allotment account:** the account to which monies are credited when prospective *shareholders* apply for shares (on application) and when shares have been allocated to them (on allotment).

When all monies are received on allotment, the account is closed by a transfer to the *ordinary share capital* account in the *general ledger.*

## Worked example

Redorf plc offers 200 000 ordinary shares of £1 each for sale at par on the following terms:

| | |
|---|---|
| on application | 50 pence |
| on allotment | 50 pence |

Applications were received for 275 000 shares. The directors of Redorf plc rejected applications for 25 000 shares and the money was returned to the applicants. The remaining shares were allotted to the remaining applicants on a pro rata basis. The excess monies held by the company on application were used to reduce the amount due on allotment.

*Required:*

Journal entries (including those for cash transactions) to record the entries in the books of Redorf plc.

*Solution:*

### Journal

| | Dr | Cr |
|---|---|---|
| Cash | 137 500 | |
| Application and allotment | | 137 500 |
| Monies received for 275 000 ordinary shares; 50 pence on application | | |
| Application and allotment account | 12 500 | |
| Cash | | 12 500 |
| Monies returned to unsuccessful applicants; 50 pence on 25 000 shares | | |
| Cash | 75 000 | |
| Application and allotment | | 75 000 |

Balance of money paid by successful applicants who received 4 shares for every 5 they applied for. £100 000 should have been paid but the company is holding £25 000 that was overpaid when the applications were made.

| | | |
|---|---|---|
| Application and allotment | 200 000 | |
| Ordinary share capital | | 200 000 |
| Called-up capital being transferred to the ordinary share capital account | | |

(See also *calls on share issue*.)

**application of funds:** outlines the way that the managers of a business have spent the funds available to them during an *accounting period*.

**apportion:** to share. (See *apportionment of overheads*.)

**apportionment of overheads:** the process whereby some overhead costs are charged to *cost centres* on some rational basis chosen by the cost accountant (see *cost accounting*). The total rent of a factory, for example, will generally be apportioned according to the percentage of floor area occupied by each cost centre within the factory;

15

the maintenance crew's wages might be apportioned according to the number of machines working within each cost centre; canteen facilities might be apportioned according to the numbers of personnel working in each cost centre.

**apportionment of reciprocal service overhead costs:** an internal transfer of costs between service departments that provide support services for each other. For example, the maintenance department workers may use the canteen for their breaks, and service and repair any kitchen machinery used in the canteen. The overhead costs incurred by each service department are **apportioned** in one of three ways:
- the elimination method, sometimes called the simplified method
- the continuous allotment method, sometimes called the repeated distribution method
- the algebraic method, sometimes called the simultaneous equation method (not examined at A-level)

---

**Worked example**

Spellers Manufacturing plc has three production departments (A, B and C) and two service departments (W and X).

Estimated overhead costs have been allocated and apportioned to each department as follows:

|  | Production departments | | | Service departments | |
|  | A | B | C | W | X |
|  | £ | £ | £ | £ | £ |
| Estimated overheads | 42 000 | 16 000 | 20 000 | 10 000 | 18 000 |

The service departments' overheads are to be apportioned as follows:

|  |  |  |  |  |  |
|---|---|---|---|---|---|
| Department W | 50% | 30% | 15% |  | 5% |
| Department X | 25% | 40% | 15% | 20% |  |

*Required:*

Show how the overheads of the service departments W and X could be apportioned by using:

a) the simplified (elimination) method
b) the continuous allotment method

*Solution:*

a) the simplified method

|  | Production departments | | | Service departments | |
|  | A | B | C | W | X |
|  | £ | £ | £ | £ | £ |
| Overheads | 42 000 | 16 000 | 20 000 | 10 000 | 18 000 |
| Apportionment of dept X costs | 4 500 | 7 200 | 2 700 | 3 600 | (18 000) |
|  | 46 500 | 23 200 | 22 700 | 13 600 | – |
| Apportionment of dept W costs | 4 250 | 6 800 | 2 550 | (13 600) | – |
|  | 50 750 | 30 000 | 25 250 | – | – |

Always start with the service department with the largest overhead costs.

This simplified method is slightly inaccurate, but the estimated overheads themselves may be inaccurate since they are estimates; the accurate figures will only become available after the financial year end.

b) the continuous allotment method

|  | A | B | C | W | X |
|---|---|---|---|---|---|
|  | £ | £ | £ | £ | £ |
| Overheads | 42 000 | 16 000 | 20 000 | 10 000 | 18 000 |
| Apportionment of dept X's costs: 18 000 split 25:40:15:20 | 4 500 | 7 200 | 2 700 | 3 600 | (18 000) |
|  | 46 500 | 23 200 | 22 700 | 13 600 | – |
| Apportionment of dept W's costs: 13 600 split 50:30:15:5 | 6 800 | 4 080 | 2 040 | (13 600) | 680 |
|  | 53 300 | 27 280 | 24 740 | – | 680 |
| Apportionment of dept X's costs: 680 split 25:40:15:20 | 170 | 272 | 102 | 136 | (680) |
|  | 53 470 | 27 552 | 24 842 | 136 | – |
| Apportionment of dept W's costs: 136 split 50:30:15:5 | 68 | 41 | 20 | (136) | 7 |
|  | 53 538 | 27 593 | 24 862 | – | 7 |
| Apportionment of dept X's costs: 7 split 25:40:15:20 | 1 | 3 | 1 | 1 | (6) |
|  | 53 539 | 27 596 | 24 863 | 1 | 1 |
|  |  |  |  | (ignore) | (ignore) |

This is close enough without using pence.

The overheads of both service departments have been apportioned to the production departments repeatedly until (almost) all the service costs have been transferred in full to the production departments.

**apportionment of service cost centre overheads:** each service department's overheads are charged to production departments according to how much each production department uses the service. Service departments (maintenance, canteen, stores, etc.) are not directly involved in the production process. For example, the cost of providing canteen facilities will be **apportioned** to each department according to the numbers of workers employed in each production department. (See **apportionment of reciprocal services**.)

**appraisal:** the process of determining the value of something. (See **capital investment appraisal** and **staff appraisal**.)

**appreciation:** an increase in the value of an asset. Under normal accounting procedures any appreciation in the value of non-current assets is ignored, since to use appreciated figures would contravene the concept of prudence. (See also **asset revaluation**.)

**appropriation account:** part of the **income statement** showing the **users of financial reports** what has happened to the profits of a partnership. See **partnership appropriation accounts**.

**APR:** see **annual percentage rate**

**area:** the basis used to **apportion** certain **overheads** to various **cost centres** within a business: for example, rent, rates, heating costs, lighting costs, etc. are generally apportioned according to the floor area occupied by the particular cost centre.

**ARR:** see **accounting rate-of-return method of capital investment appraisal**

**arrangement fee:** the amount charged by a bank or other financial institution to a client for arranging a loan or other type of credit facility.

**Articles of Association:** the document containing the rules which will govern the internal organisation of a **limited company**. This must be filed with the **Registrar of Companies** together with the **Memorandum of Association**.

The Articles of Association shows the company's rules regarding:
- organisation and control
- voting rights
- conduct of **directors'** meeting
- conduct of **shareholders' annual general meeting**
- directors' powers
- rights attached to the different classes of shares

**A shares** are ordinary shares with limited voting rights or, in some cases, no voting rights at all.

**asset:** see **current assets, intangible assets, liquidity, non-current assets, tangible non-current assets**

**asset backed:** a term generally applied to shares indicating that they are backed by the security of the company's assets.

**asset disposal account** is used when a **non-current asset** is sold or scrapped. The asset must be removed from the **ledger** of the business. Any **depreciation** relating to the asset must also be removed from the ledger. An asset disposal account is used to calculate whether the asset was disposed of at a profit or a loss.

## Worked example

Bluemore Ltd depreciates its machinery at 10% per annum and vehicles at 25% per annum, both using the straight-line method. The following is an extract from the balance sheet of Bluemore Ltd at the end of the last financial year:

| Non-current assets | Cost | Depreciation | Net |
|---|---|---|---|
| | £ | £ | £ |
| Property, plant and equipment | | | |
| Machinery | 135 000 | 64 000 | 71 000 |
| Vehicles | 98 000 | 48 000 | 50 000 |

Recently a machine which cost £38 000 was sold for £8000. The aggregate depreciation relating to the machine was £22 800. Last week a vehicle which cost £20 000 was exchanged for a new vehicle costing £26 000. The aggregate depreciation on the vehicle traded in amounted to £10 000. Bluemore Ltd paid £15 000 in full settlement for the new vehicle.

### Required:

The journal entries to record the disposal of the machine and the vehicle (show cash entries).

### Solution:

Narratives have not been included.

**Journal**

| | Dr | Cr |
|---|---|---|
| | £ | £ |
| Disposal of machinery | 38 000 | |
|    Machinery | | 38 000 |
| Provision for depreciation of machinery | 22 800 | |
|    Disposal of machinery | | 22 800 |
| Cash | 8 000 | |
|    Disposal of machinery | | 8 000 |
| Income statement | 7 200 | |
|    Disposal of machinery | | 7 200 |
| Disposal of vehicles | 20 000 | |
|    Vehicles | | 20 000 |
| Provision for depreciation of vehicles | 10 000 | |
|    Disposal of vehicles | | 10 000 |
| New vehicle | 11 000 | |
|    Disposal of vehicles | | 11 000 |
| Disposal of vehicles | 1 000 | |
|    Income Statement | | 1 000 |
| New vehicle | 15 000 | |
|    Cash | | 15 000 |

The vehicle account in the general ledger:

**Vehicles**

| | | | | |
|---|---|---|---|---|
| Balance b/d | 98 000 | Disposal | 20 000 | |
| Disposal* | 11 000 | | | *£26 000 |
| Cash* | 15 000 | Balance c/d | 104 000 | for new vehicle |
| | 124 000 | | 124 000 | |
| Balance b/d | 104 000 | | | |

**asset replacement reserve:** a *revenue reserve* which is represented by a liquid asset (see *liquidity*) that can be converted into cash when it is necessary to replace a *non-current asset.*

**asset revaluation** will take place immediately before any structural change to the partnership (see *structural changes in partnerships*). Any overall increase in the value of the partnership assets will be credited to the partners' *capital accounts*; any overall decrease in the partnership assets will be debited to the partners' capital accounts.

## Worked example

Norman, Olive and Peter are in partnership, sharing profits and losses in the ratios 3:2:1 respectively. The partnership has net assets that have a book value of £320 000. Norman has decided to retire from the partnership with effect from today. The partners have agreed that the net assets should be valued at £380 000.

### Required:

The entries in the partnership books of account to record the increase in the value of the net assets.

### Solution:

**Net assets**

| | |
|---|---|
| Balance b/d | 320 000 |
| Revaluation | 60 000 |

**Revaluation**

| | | | |
|---|---|---|---|
| Capital Norman | 30 000 | Net assets | 60 000 |
| Capital Olive | 20 000 | | |
| Capital Peter | 10 000 | | |
| | 60 000 | | 60 000 |

**Capitals**

| | Norman | Olive | Peter |
|---|---|---|---|
| Balances b/d | *** | *** | *** |
| Revaluation | 30 000 | 20 000 | 10 000 |

The managers of a *limited company* may have the assets of the company revalued by a professional valuer to reflect the current *market values* of the assets. The unrealised profit is recorded as a capital reserve.

### Worked example

Four years ago Irthing plc purchased land and buildings at a cost of £100 000. The directors of the company have recently had the asset valued. The land and buildings are currently valued at £170 000.

#### Required:

i) Entries in the books of Irthing plc to record the increase in the value of the land and buildings.
ii) Balance sheet extracts as they would appear after the revaluation of the land and buildings.

#### Solution:

i)

| Land and buildings | Revaluation reserve |
| --- | --- |
| Balance b/d 100 000 | Land & buildings 70 000 |
| Reval. reserve 70 000 | |

ii) Irthing plc balance sheet extract at*****

| Non-current assets | £ |
| --- | --- |
| Property, plant and equipment: | |
| Land and buildings at valuation | 170 000 |
| Equity | |
| Revaluation reserve | 70 000 |

**assets employed:** the book value of all assets, less current liabilities.

**asset stripper:** a person who buys a company or a controlling interest in a company with the intention of selling off its assets.

**asset stripping** takes place when a company is bought at a price that is lower than its *net asset value*. The assets of the company are then sold for a profit.

**asset structure:** the relationship between *non-current assets* and *current assets*.

**asset turnover** is one of the methods of measuring the efficiency with which the resources of a business have been used. This ratio seeks to calculate the amount of sales generated by every £100 of non-current assets held by the business. The calculation is:

FORMULA:
$$\frac{\text{revenue}(\text{sales})}{\text{net book value of non-current assets}}$$

The result should be as high as possible, showing an efficient use of non-current assets. A very low result could mean a lack of efficiency and could indicate that the resources tied up in the non-current assets could be better used in another way.

**asset utilisation ratios** are used to measure the efficiency with which assets are used. The term covers three separate ratios:

### Utilisation of total assets

FORMULA:
$$\frac{\text{sales}}{\text{total non-current assets} + \text{total current assets}}$$

## Utilisation of non-current assets

FORMULA: $\dfrac{\text{sales}}{\text{total non-current assets}}$

## Utilisation of current assets

FORMULA: $\dfrac{\text{sales}}{\text{total current assets}}$

### Worked example

The following information relates to the business of Becky Boo:

|  | £ |
|---|---|
| Sales | 4 500 000 |
| Non-current assets | 1 350 000 |
| Current assets | 520 000 |

*Required:*

Calculate the following ratios:

i)  utilisation of total assets
ii) utilisation of non-current assets
iii) utilisation of current assets

*Solution:*

i) utilisation of total assets

$$= \frac{\text{sales}}{\text{total non-current assets} + \text{total current assets}}$$

$$= \frac{4\ 500\ 000}{1\ 870\ 000}$$

$$= 2.41 \text{ times}$$

ii) utilisation of non-current assets $= \dfrac{\text{sales}}{\text{total non-current assets}}$

$$= \frac{4\ 500\ 000}{1\ 350\ 000}$$

$$= 3.33 \text{ times}$$

iii) utilisation of current assets $= \dfrac{\text{sales}}{\text{total current assets}}$

$$= \frac{4\ 500\ 000}{520\ 000}$$

$$= 8.65 \text{ times}$$

**associated company:** a company that is partly owned by another and where the share-owning company can exert a significant influence over the associated company. Associated companies are referred to in the **Companies Acts** as **associated undertakings**.

**associated undertakings:** another term used to describe **associated companies**.

**Association of Accounting Technicians** was set up in 1980 by the four chartered bodies of accountants (the Institute of Chartered Accountants in England and Wales, the Chartered Institute of Management Accountants (*CIMA*), the Chartered Association of Certified Accountants and the Chartered Institute of Public Finance and Accountancy). It is a professional body for accounting-support staff such as clerks and accounting assistants. Membership of the Association is gained by proving competence in the field of accountancy and by passing central assessments set by the Association at three levels, foundation, intermediate and technician levels, and by completing one year's approved experience.

**at arm's length** is to treat a transaction as if there was no connection between the parties involved. For example, when a company purchases supplies or services from one of its own subsidiary companies the transaction is treated as if the purchase had been made from a totally unrelated other business.

**at par:** when shares are issued by a *limited company* at their *nominal* (face) *value* they are said to be 'issued at par'.

**at sight:** when a financial instrument is payable on presentation, it is said to be 'payable at sight'.

**attainable standard** is, according to the *CIMA* definition, 'a standard which can be attained if a standard unit of work is carried out efficiently, a machine properly operated or a material properly used. Allowances are made for normal losses, waste and machine downtime'.

Since these standards are achievable they can act as a powerful motivational factor. If staff are encouraged to beat the standard, this will benefit the business by increasing productivity.

**attributable profit** is the proportion of the total profit on a long term contract that fairly reflects the profit earned on the part of the work already completed by the contractor.

**audit** is the process of checking the financial records of a business by an independent person, the *auditor,* in order to ensure that the records show a *true and fair view*. Internal audits are regular checks conducted by employees of the business to ensure that systems operating within the business are being adhered to. Internal auditors report to the management of the business.

**auditors:** people, usually trained accountants, who specialise in checking financial accounts that have been prepared by someone else. External auditors are appointed from outside the organisation to ensure objectivity. The auditors of a *limited company* are appointed by the *shareholders*.

**auditors' remuneration:** the amount paid to the *auditors* for the work done in checking the business's *financial statements*.

**auditors' report:** the auditors' report will indicate that the financial statements have been *audited* and it will also give the *auditors*' opinion about the financial statements. The report is usually quite brief and would normally contain very little information. (See *Companies Act 1985*.)

The auditors' report is attached to the main financial statements published by a *limited company* as a statutory requirement.

**audit trail** is used to verify information presented in the *financial statements* by tracing the passage of the information from its inception as a source document; through the *books of prime entry*; through the *ledger(s)* to the figure on the financial statements.

**authorised share capital** gives the details of the number, classes (i.e. *ordinary shares*, *preferred shares*) and *nominal value* of the shares that a *limited company* may issue. The authorised share capital sets the upper limit to the number of shares the company can issue. This figure can only be exceeded with the approval of the existing *shareholders*. The authorised capital must be shown in the *published accounts* of a limited company. It is usually shown as a note.

**authorised signatories** are the people who have the authority to sign cheques on behalf of an organisation. In clubs and societies it is usual to require two of the officials to sign every cheque. This is an attempt to reduce the incidence of fraud.

**AVCO:** see *methods of inventory valuation*

**average cost** also known as unit cost.

$$FORMULA: \quad \text{average cost} = \frac{\text{total production cost}}{\text{number of units producted}}$$

It is equal to:

average fixed cost + average variable cost

**average cost of inventory:** see *weighted average cost method of inventory valuation (AVCO)*

**average fixed cost:** this figure shows how the total fixed costs are spread over the number of units produced. In the short run the average fixed costs fall as the number of units produced increases.

**average rate of return** is a term used to describe the *accounting rate of return*.

**average variable cost** is the total variable cost divided by the number of units produced.

**avoidable costs:** costs which would disappear if the *cost centre* ceased to carry out its function. The classification is useful when calculating the *contribution* made by an activity. *CIMA* defines avoidable costs as 'the specific costs of an activity or sector of a business which would be avoided if that activity or sector did not exist'.

**A–Z Online**

Log on to A–Z Online to search the database of terms, print revision lists and much more. Go to **www.philipallan.co.uk/a-zonline** to get started.

**backer:** a person(s) who provides financial support for someone else in business.

**back office:** where the paperwork involved in a broking firm is done.

**bad debt relief:** if a debt is more than two years old and has been written off in the accounts of the business, it is eligible for *VAT* relief.

**bad debts:** debtors who are unable to settle their debt. If it is impossible to collect the amount owed, it is necessary to write off that debt. If a debt cannot be collected it is no longer a *current asset*. The entries to write off a debt that has proved to be bad are:

    **Debit:** Bad debts account    **Credit:** The individual debtor

(See also *provision for doubtful debts*, *bad debts recovered account*.)

**bad debts account:** found in the *general ledger*, it is used when individual *bad debts* are written off. The bad debts account is itself written off to the *income statement* at the end of the financial period.

### Worked example

Arthur Benson owes £72. Charlotte Dixon owes £47. Ellis Fylde and Co. owes £93. These debts are now irrecoverable and need to be written off.

*Required*:

The bad debts account as it would appear in the general ledger at the financial year end. Transfer the appropriate amount to the income statement.

*Solution*:

### Sales ledger

| Arthur Benson | | | Charlotte Dixon | | | Ellis Fylde & Co. | | |
|---|---|---|---|---|---|---|---|---|
| Balance b/d | 72 | Bad debts | 72 | Balance b/d | 47 | Bad debts | 47 | Balance b/d | 93 | Bad debts | 93 |

### General ledger

| Bad debts accounts | | | |
|---|---|---|---|
| A Benson | 72 | Income statement | 212 |
| C Dixon | 47 | | |
| Ellis Fylde & Co. | 93 | | 212 |
| | 212 | | |

### Income statement

| | |
|---|---|
| Bad debts | 212 |

**bad debts recovered account** is used when a debt that has previously been written off will now be paid by the customer. This event must be treated in a special way using the customer's account in order to indicate that the debt has been recovered and that the customer can once again be considered for credit facilities in the future.

### Worked example

Graham Harris owed £49 in 1999 and the debt was written off to the bad debts account when it was thought to be irrecoverable. Harris repaid the £49 yesterday.

*Required:*

Write up the appropriate ledger accounts to show the entries relating to the recovered debt.

*Solution:*

| Graham Harris | | | | | Bad debts recovered | | | | |
|---|---|---|---|---|---|---|---|---|---|
| 1 Bad debt recovered | 49 | 2 Bank | 49 | | 3 Income statement | 49 | 1 Graham Harris | 49 |

| Bank | | | Income statement | | |
|---|---|---|---|---|---|
| 2 Graham Harris | 49 | | | 3 Bad debt recovered | 49 |

*Note:*

It is important to record the fact that Graham has now paid his debt by reinstating the fact in his personal account in the sales ledger. The £49 entered in the income statement could be deducted from any debit entry for bad debts written off.

**balance:** the amount put in either the debit or credit column of an account to make the totals of the two columns equal to each other.

**balance brought down (balance b/d):** the balance used to open an account in the present *accounting period*. It is the closing balance on the account from the previous accounting period.

**balance brought forward (balance b/fwd):** another version of *balance b/d*.

**balance carried down (balance c/d):** the balance used to close an account at the end of an *accounting period*. It is used as the balance brought down at the start of the next time period.

**balance carried forward (balance c/fwd):** another version of *balance c/d*.

**balanced budget:** a budget where costs and revenues are equal.

**balance sheet** is a statement which shows the assets and liabilities of an organisation. It is generally prepared at the end of an *accounting period*. It is a 'sheet' showing all the balances remaining in the organisation's *ledgers* after the preparation of the *income statement.*

A balance sheet can be prepared using a vertical format, for example:

## Ken Sharpe plc balance sheet at 31 December 20*9

| Non-current assets | Cost | Depreciation | Net |
|---|---|---|---|
| | £ | £ | £ |
| Property, plant and equipment | | | |
| Land and buildings | 150 000 | 40 000 | 110 000 |
| Machinery | 180 000 | 30 000 | 150 000 |
| Vehicles | 90 000 | 45 000 | 45 000 |
| | 420 000 | 115 000 | 305 000 |
| Current assets | | | |
| Inventory | | 34 000 | |
| Trade receivable | | 26 000 | |
| Cash and cash equivalents | | 12 000 | |
| | | 72 000 | |
| Current liabilities | | | |
| Trade payables | | (18 000) | |
| Tax liabilities | | (32 000) | |
| | | (50 000) | |
| Net current assets | | | 22 000 |
| | | | 327 000 |
| Non-current liabilities | | | (75 000) |
| Net assets | | | 252 000 |
| | | | |
| Equity | | | |
| Ordinary shares of 50p each | | | 80 000 |
| 8% preferred (preference) shares of £1 each | | | 50 000 |
| Share premium account | | | 40 000 |
| Retained earnings | | | 82 000 |
| | | | 252 000 |

Balance sheets for **sole traders** and **partnerships** can be prepared using a horizontal layout, for example:

## Jeff Bellis balance sheet at 31 December 20*9

| Non-current assets | Cost | Dep | Net | Capital | |
|---|---|---|---|---|---|
| Premises | 150 000 | 20 000 | 130 000 | Balance at 1 January 20*9 | 105 000 |
| Machinery | 70 000 | 40 000 | 30 000 | Add profit | 67 500 |
| Vehicles | 47 000 | 28 000 | 19 000 | | 172 500 |
| | 267 000 | 88 000 | 179 000 | Less drawings | 38 500 |
| | | | | | 134 000 |

27

| Current assets | | | Non-current liability | | 80 000 |
|---|---|---|---|---|---|
| Inventory | 27 000 | | | | |
| Trade receivables | 13 000 | | Current liabilities | | |
| Cash and cash | | | Trade payables | 10 000 | |
| equivalents | 7 000 | 47 000 | Other payables | 2 000 | 12 000 |
| | | 226 000 | | | 226 000 |

**balance sheet date:** the date on which a *balance sheet* is drawn up. Although a balance sheet can be drawn up by extracting outstanding balances from the *ledgers* at any time, balance sheets are generally drawn up at the end of an *accounting period*.

**balance sheets of limited companies** show the financial position of the company at one moment in time (generally on the last day of the financial year).The balance sheet is prepared in great detail for management purposes and in a less detailed form for publication. An example of a balance sheet is shown:

### Sihon plc balance sheet at 31 December 20*9

| | £000 |
|---|---|
| *Non-current assets* | |
| Goodwill | 1 000 |
| Property, plant and equipment | 6 430 |
| | 7 430 |
| *Current assets* | |
| Inventories | 877 |
| Trade and other receivables | 1 436 |
| Cash and cash equivalents | 219 |
| | 2 532 |
| Total assets | 9 962 |
| *Current liabilities* | |
| Trade and other payables | (971) |
| Tax liabilities | (150) |
| Bank loans and overdraft | (30) |
| | (1 151) |
| *Non-current liabilities* | |
| 4% debentures (2049) | (2 000) |
| Total liabilities | (3 151) |
| | 6 811 |
| *Equity* | |
| Share capital | 3 600 |
| Share premium account | 900 |
| Revaluation reserve | 450 |
| Retained earnings | 1 861 |
| Total equity | 6 811 |

Note that the amounts shown for total assets (£9 962 000) and total liabilities (£3 151 000) are provided for information purposes only.

**balancing figure:** the amount that needs to be inserted in the debit or credit column of an account to make the two totals equal. For example:

| An account | |
| --- | --- |
| 58 | 42 |
| 63 | |
| 97 | |

176 is the balancing figure to be inserted into the credit side of the account. When this is done the account balances – both sides equal 218.

**balancing item:** see *balancing figure*

**balancing the accounts** makes the totals of the debit and credit sides of an account equal, usually at the end of an *accounting period*. This is achieved by entering a *balancing figure* on the debit side of the account and carrying it down to the credit side of the account to start the next accounting period, or by entering a balancing figure on the credit side of the account and carrying it down onto the debit side of the account to start the next accounting period.

**bank:** a business that holds money for its clients and lends money to clients.

**bank account:** an account that a customer has with a bank. The customer uses the bank account to deposit and to withdraw money.

**bank balance:** the amount of money that a bank owes a business. The balance in the *cash book* will be shown on the debit side. This is the balance that is shown on the debit of the *trial balance* and it will be shown as a *current asset* in the business's *balance sheet*. (See also *bank overdraft*.)

**bank cash book:** a *cash book* recording a business's payments made into and out of its bank account. In many businesses all receipts of cash and cheques will be banked on a daily basis. All cash transactions will be recorded in a *petty cash book*.

The bank cash book can be written in the traditional way with a debit side and a credit side. In a large business, the bank cash book might be divided into a bank receipts book and a bank payment book; each may be the responsibility of separate members of staff. The receipts book will have columns for *discounts allowed*, *VAT*, amounts received and totals banked. The payments side will have columns for *discount received*, *VAT* and cheques paid.

**bank columns** in a traditional *cash book* record *lodgements* made by a business into the bank account held for the business by its bankers, and *cheques* drawn by the business on the business bank account. Lodgements are recorded in the debit column while cheques drawn are recorded in the credit column of the cash book.

**bank current account:** an account at a clearing bank on which cheques can be drawn.

**bank deposits:** monies placed in a bank by its customers.

**bank giro transfer:** the method used by clearing banks to transfer money rapidly from one bank account to another.

**bank identification number (BIN):** a six-digit number which identifies a bank for *charge card* purposes.

**bank loan:** capital borrowed from a bank. The borrower must pay interest on the loan. This type of borrowing is generally used by a business to fund a specific project, for example the purchase of *non-current assets*. A bank loan will, generally, be shown on the *balance sheet* as a *non-current liability*.

The total interest charged annually by the bank is shown as an expense on the *income statement*. Any *capital repayments* will reduce the *non-current liability* on the balance sheet.

Short-term borrowing to help fund a temporary shortage of funds is more likely to involve negotiation of a *bank overdraft*.

**bank mandate:** a written order from a potential customer addressed to a bank used to open a new account. It contains the customer's(s') specimen signature(s) and allows the customer(s) to sign cheques on behalf of the account holder.

**bank overdraft:** an amount that is owed to a bank on a current account. An overdraft arises when cheques are drawn on an account that has insufficient funds to cover that cheque. If there are insufficient funds to cover any cheque drawn, it cannot be assumed that the bank will honour (pay) the amount. The bank may well dishonour the cheque by referring it to *drawer*.

If a person or business believes that the current account will move into overdraft in the future, they should arrange overdraft facilities. This will ensure that the bank will honour cheques (up to the agreed limit), even though there are insufficient funds in the account to cover the value of cheques drawn. When a cheque is dishonoured and referred to drawer it is sometimes said to have '*bounced*'.

The balance in the *cash book* will be shown on the credit side. The balance is shown on the credit of the *trial balance* and as a *current liability* in the *balance sheet*.

**bank paying-in slip:** normally used when money and/or cheques are paid into a bank account.

**bank reconciliation statement** makes sure that an organisation's record of bank transactions agrees with the record of the organisation's bank transactions recorded in the bank's *ledger*. This rarely happens because of the difference in the time cheques are written and sent to a creditor and the time the creditor receives and pays the cheque into his/her bank account.

A copy of the bank's records are sent regularly to the organisation as a bank statement. Businesses will prepare a bank reconciliation statement on a regular basis, whenever a bank statement is received. The process is generally undertaken in two stages:

1 Making sure that the business bank *cash book* is written up to date. This is necessary since items may appear on the business bank statement which have not yet been

entered in the business bank cash book, e.g. direct debit transfers, standing orders, bank charges, credit transfers, etc.

2 The actual reconciliation statement.

## Worked example

The following details relate to Brian Tsen's business at 31 December 20*9:

| | £ |
|---|---|
| Cash at bank as per the bank columns in Brian's cash book at 31 December 20*9 | 196 |
| Cheques drawn by Brian but not presented for payment | 692 |
| Direct debits, standing orders and bank charges entered on Brian's bank statement but not yet entered in the bank columns of his cash book | 312 |
| Credit transfers entered on Brian's bank statement but not yet entered in the bank columns of his cash book | 87 |
| Cheques received by Brian and paid into the bank but not yet entered on the bank statement | 401 |
| Cash at bank as per Brian's bank statement at 31 December 20*9 | 262 |

## Required:

Brian Tsen's business bank reconciliation statement at 31 December 20*9.

## Solution:

### Cash book (bank columns only)

| | £ | | £ |
|---|---|---|---|
| Balance b/d | 196 | Direct debits etc. | 312 |
| Credit transfers | 87 | | |
| Balance c/d | 29 | | |
| | 312 | | 312 |
| | | Balance b/d | 29 |

**Bank reconciliation statement at 31 December 20*9**

| | £ |
|---|---|
| Balance at bank as per Brian's cash book | (29) |
| Add unpresented cheques | 692 |
| | 663 |
| Less cheques not yet presented | 401 |
| Balance at bank as per bank statement | 262 |

Alternatively:

**Bank reconciliation statement at 31 December 20*9**

| | £ |
|---|---|
| Balance at bank as per bank statement | 262 |
| Less unpresented cheques | 692 |
| | (430) |
| Add cheques not yet presented | 401 |
| Balance at bank as per Brian's cash book | (29) |

Bank reconciliations check:

- the accuracy of the entries in the bank cash book
- the accuracy of entries on the bank statement
- that unpresented cheques from previous reconciliation statements have been presented for payment

**bankruptcy:** a legal procedure applied to an individual giving him/her protection from his/her creditors. It occurs when the person is unable to pay his/her debts. The person's assets may be sold to pay off as many debts as possible.

Note that a *limited company* will go into *liquidation* if it is unable to discharge its liabilities.

**bank statement:** a copy of a bank account as it appears in the bank's *ledger*. When a deposit (*lodgement*) is made on behalf of a person, the bank owes that amount to the depositor. These deposits are shown on the bank statement as credits. When a cheque is drawn on the account, the amount is debited to the account and the balance is reduced by that amount.

---

**Any Bank plc**

UPPER DOWNING BRANCH
01999 123456

**Statement of Account**

CURRENT ACCOUNT –
INTEREST OPTION

REQUEST
13 JAN
POST NO.  52

| Details | | Payments | Receipts | Date | Balance |
|---|---|---|---|---|---|
| | | | | 2009 | |
| BALANCE FORWARD | | | | 14DEC | 330.14DR |
| | 100220 | 25.00 | | 15DEC | |
| CALOR LTD | | | | | |
| | DDR | 60.00 | | 15DEC | 415.14DR |
| | 100222 | 28.74 | | 18DEC | |
| COUNTER CREDIT | | | 1312.80 | 18DEC | 868.92 |
| | 100224 | 18.00 | | 23DEC | 850.92 |
| | 100223 | 70.00 | | 24DEC | 780.92 |
| | 100225 | 49.35 | | 30DEC | |
| COL MUT LIFE ASSCE | | | | | |
| | DDR | 83.32 | | 30DEC | |
| SUN ALLIANCE LONDON | | | | | |
| | DDR | 50.00 | | 30DEC | 598.25 |
| N.A.T.F.H.E. | | | | | |
| | DDR | 8.00 | | 31DEC | 590.25 |
| | | | | 2010 | |
| | 100227 | 50.25 | | 4JAN | |
| | 100228 | 17.99 | | 4JAN | |
| | 100229 | 5.48 | | 4JAN | |
| | 100230 | 17.48 | | 4JAN | |
| | 100231 | 41.50 | | 4JAN | |
| FRASERCARD SRV | | | | | |
| | STO | 100.00 | | 4JAN | |
| NORWEB | | | | | |
| | STO | 5.00 | | 4JAN | |
| XXXXXXXXXXXXXXXXXXXXXX | | | | | |
| UNAUTH O/D FEE £25.00 | | | | | |
| | 7DEC/3JAN | 25.00 | | 4JAN | 327.55 |
| XXXXXXXXXXXXXXXXXXXXXX | | | | | |
| | 100232 | 988.60 | | 5JAN | |
| HOMEOWNERS | | | | | |
| | DDR | 27.00 | | 5JAN | 688.05DR |
| | 100234 | 110.00 | | 6JAN | 798.05DR |
| COUNTER CREDIT | | | 30.62 | 7JAN | 767.43DR |
| | 100233 | 54.40 | | 8JAN | 821.83DR |

**ABBREVIATIONS**   DIV Dividend  STO Standing Order  BGC Bank Giro Credit  DDR Direct Debit
DR Overdrawn Balance  ATM Cash Dispenser Transaction

---

The bank will send a copy of the account, as a bank statement, as often as a person or business requires. The statement is used to check the entries in the **bank columns** of a business **cash book** prior to the preparation of a **bank reconciliation statement**.

**bank statement balance** shows the amount of cash a business has in its current account. This balance is used in a **bank reconciliation statement**, but it is not the balance used in the **trial balance** or the **current assets** section of the **balance sheet** of the business.

**barter:** the system whereby goods are given in exchange for other goods rather than in exchange for money.

**base rate** is the interest rate set by the Bank of England. This rate of interest applies to the UK high street banks, and through them to all individuals and businesses in the country. The base rate therefore influences financial activity throughout the economy.

**basic pay:** a person's normal gross wage before the addition of **overtime** or other additional payments.

**basic standards:** standards which once set are not changed. They are used as base figures in order to indicate trends in price levels and production methods. Managers may use basic standards as a means of extrapolating future movements in prices and production.

**basis of assessment:** the method of deciding into which year financial transactions should be included for the purposes of calculating tax liability.

**batch costing:** a method of costing used when a large number of identical products are to be produced either for a customer or as a component for another product being manufactured.

**batch processing:** the method of processing similar data at one time. For example, all sales invoices for a week may be processed on one particular day each week.

**bear:** a **stock exchange** speculator who believes that the price of shares that he/she has sold will fall and that he/she will be able to purchase them back at a lower price, thus making a profit.

**bearer bond:** indicates a debt to an unnamed party. When the bond matures the person holding the bond at that time will receive payment of the sum originally borrowed. (See **bond**.)

**bear market:** a period when share prices in general are falling because **shareholders** are selling their shares in the belief that they will be able to purchase the shares later at a lower price.

**below the line** refers to extraordinary financial transactions which are shown in the **income statement**, but after the net profit after taxation figure has been calculated.

**bill of exchange:** a document drawn up by a business stating the amount owed by a debtor. It is sent to the debtor who will 'accept it' by signing it. The debtor then returns the signed bill. It is a commitment to pay a stated amount on a particular date.

There are three ways the business may treat the bill:

1 To settle a debt with an agreeable third party.

2 To deposit it with a bank. The bank will pay the business the value of the bill less an agreed discount rate. When the bill matures the bank will present it to the debtor for payment.

3 To hold the bill until it matures, when the business will present it to the debtor for payment.

33

**bills payable:** *bills of exchange* which a business will have to pay to its creditors when the bills mature. They are shown as a *current liability* in the *balance sheet*.

**bills receivable:** *bills of exchange* which are due to be paid to a business by a business's debtors when the bills mature. They are shown as a *current asset* on the *balance sheet*.

**bin card:** a name given to an *inventory record card*.

**black economy:** trade in cash or by barter between suppliers and customers which is not recorded in the *books of account* and so will not be included in the business's *financial statements*. The profits on such transactions are therefore not declared for taxation purposes.

**black list:** a list of potential customers or businesses that an organisation will not deal with.

**black market:** the buying and selling of goods illegally. This type of market flourishes in times of war when certain types of goods are hard to come by or when certain types of goods are not legally available.

**blank cheque:** a cheque which the *drawer* has signed but has not indicated the amount to be paid.

**blanket absorption of overheads:** rather than calculate an absorption rate for individual *cost centres*, some manufacturing businesses calculate an overhead absorption rate for the factory as a whole.

> **Worked example**
>
> Total factory overheads for the Bodbred Manufacturing Company plc for the year are £1 000 000. Direct labour hours worked in the factory during the year are 250 000 hours.
>
> *Required:*
>
> Calculate the blanket overhead absorption rate per direct labour hour for the factory.
>
> *Solution:*
>
> $$\text{blanket overhead absorption rate} = \frac{£1\ 000\ 000}{250\ 000} = £4 \text{ per direct labour hour}$$
>
> so all units produced will be charged £4 per direct labour hour no matter how much time was spent in each individual section or department of the factory.

**blue chip stocks:** very low risk stocks or shares issued by a sound company with a record of paying good *dividends*.

**board meeting:** a meeting of the *board of directors* of a *limited company*.

**board of directors:** the group of people who run a *limited company*. They are elected by the *shareholders* of the company. (See *directors*.)

**bond:** a legally binding contract made by a company (or a government in the case of treasury bonds) promising to repay borrowed money at some date in the future. The holders of bonds receive interest from the issuer. The interest is generally paid half yearly.

**bonded warehouse:** a place where goods are stored until any duty due is paid.

**bonus:** a payment made to employees in addition to their normal wage or salary.

**bonus issue:** see *bonus shares*

**bonus schemes** allow individuals to earn extra payments when their levels of efficiency exceed the norm. The schemes are usually closely monitored in order to ensure that quality of the finished product does not suffer as employees try to increase output to earn bonuses.

**bonus shares:** shares issued to existing *shareholders* without payment. The shares are given in proportion to the shareholder's holding by using the company's *reserves*. For this reason the issue is also referred to as a capitalisation issue.

The company's reserves provide permanent finance for a company. The transfer from reserves to share capital by a book entry has no effect on the capital structure of the company.

A bonus issue is also known as a scrip issue.

The *directors* may propose a bonus issue if:
- the company has large reserves
- the bulk of the reserves are *capital reserves*
- the payment of a cash *dividend* could cause *liquidity* problems

**Worked example**

The following is an extract from the balance sheet of Pocklinton plc.

| Equity | £ |
|---|---|
| Ordinary shares of £1 each | 4 000 000 |
| Share premium | 500 000 |
| Revaluation reserve | 200 000 |
| Retained earnings | 653 000 |

The directors propose a scrip issue on the basis of one bonus share for every four shares already held. It is company policy to maintain reserves in the most flexible form.

*Required:*

Journal entries to record the scrip issue.

*Solution:*

Journal

| | Dr £ | Cr £ |
|---|---|---|
| Share premium | 500 000 | |
| Revaluation reserve | 200 000 | |
| Retained earnings | 300 000 | |
| Bonus account | | 1 000 000 |
| Bonus account | 1 000 000 | |
| Ordinary share capital account | | 1 000 000 |

*Note:*

The two *capital reserves* are used first. The remainder of the required sum is transferred from the retained earnings account; this reserve is used last because it is the most flexible of the company's reserves.

**bookkeeper:** a person employed to record the financial transactions undertaken by his/her employer.

**bookkeeping:** the recording of all financial transactions undertaken by a business (or an individual). (See *single-entry bookkeeping*, *double-entry bookkeeping*.)

**books of account:** the generic name given to the *ledgers* and *books of prime entry* in which all business transactions are recorded.

**books of original entry:** see *books of prime entry*

**books of prime entry:** see *purchases day book*, *purchases returns day book*, *sales day book*, *sales returns day book*, *journal*, *cash book*

**book value:** see *carrying amount*

**borrowing costs:** interest and other costs incurred in connection with borrowed funds.

**bottom line:** literally, the last line in the *income statements* of a business. It will indicate whether the business has made a profit or a loss in the financial year under review.

**bottom-up budgets** are functional budgets prepared by lower levels of management. These budgets are incorporated into the *master budget* after approval at senior management level. The danger is that some managers may set low targets in order to reduce the likelihood of not meeting their budget.

**bought day book:** also known as the *purchases day book* or purchase journal.

**bought ledger:** see *purchases ledger*

**bounced:** a colloquial expression indicating that a bank has dishonoured a cheque. The cheque will be referred to *drawer*, i.e. it will be returned to the person who tried to cash it or deposit it in their bank account.

**brackets** are used in some financial statements to indicate a negative figure.

**branch:** an outlet in an area away from head office or the main part of a business.

**brand name:** the name of a particular make of product, e.g. 'Coke' and 'Pepsi' are brand names of two makes of cola.

**break-even analysis:** the calculation of the level of output and/or sales revenue at which a business makes neither a profit nor a loss.

**break-even chart:** a graphical representation showing the point at which a business breaks even. The limitations of a break-even chart include:
- the assumption that all data used behave in a linear manner
- the assumption that all production is sold
- charts, generally, only relate to a single product
- the chart does not show clearly the amount of profit or loss made by the product

(For a worked example, see *break-even point*.)

**break-even point:** the lowest level of sales or units sold at which total revenue received by a business is equal to the business's total costs. It can be ascertained by:

1   The unit contribution method

$$\textit{FORMULA:}\quad \text{break-even} = \frac{\text{total fixed costs}}{\text{contribution per unit}} = \text{number of units required to be sold}$$

## Worked example

The following information relates to the production and sales of 40 000 puttles.

|  | £ per unit |
|---|---|
| Selling price | 40 |
| Raw material costs | 8 |
| Direct labour costs | 14 |
| Fixed costs | 11 |

### Required:

i) the break-even point in units for sales of puttles

ii) the margin of safety in units for puttles

### Solution:

|  | £ |  |
|---|---|---|
| Contribution per puttle | 18 | [SP – VC, 40 – (8 + 14)] |
| Total fixed costs | 440 000 | [11 × 40 000] |

i) $\text{break-even} = \dfrac{\text{total fixed costs}}{\text{contribution per unit}} = \dfrac{440\,000}{18}$

$= 24\,445 \text{ puttles } \left(\text{always round-up}\right)$

ii) margin of safety = forecast sales – break-even sales = 40 000 – 24 445

$= 15\,555 \text{ puttles}$

## 2 The contribution/sales method

Some textbooks refer to this as the profit/volume method.

*FORMULA:* $\quad \text{break-even} = \dfrac{\text{total fixed costs}}{\dfrac{\text{total contribution}}{\text{sales}}} = \text{total sales revenue required}$

## Worked example

Use the information above relating to the production and sales of puttles.

### Required:

i) Calculate the total revenue required from the sales of puttles in order to break even.

ii) Calculate the margin of safety for puttles (answer required in sales revenue).

### Solution:

i) $\dfrac{\text{contribution}}{\text{sales revenue}} = \dfrac{1\,600\,000 - 888\,000}{1\,600\,000} = \dfrac{720\,000}{1\,600\,000} = 0.45$

$\text{break-even} = \dfrac{\text{total fixed costs}}{\dfrac{\text{total contribution}}{\text{sales}}} = \text{total sales revenue required}$

$$\text{break-even} = \frac{440\ 000}{0.45} = £977\ 777.78$$

ii) margin of safety = forecast sales revenue – break-even level of sales revenue

$$= £1\ 600\ 000 - £977\ 777.78 = £622\ 222.22$$

This method is more useful if some form of income statement is available. It is also useful to determine the break-even sales revenue if a number of products are being sold by a business.

### 3 The algebraic method

*FORMULA:*   break-even occurs when total costs = total revenue

**Worked example**

Use the information given above relating to the production and sales of puttles.

*Required:*

Calculate the break-even point in units for sales of puttles.

*Solution:*

Let Q = the number of puttles to be sold in order to break even.

break-even =                                   total costs = total revenue

fixed costs + variable costs = total revenue

$$440\ 000 + 22Q = 40Q$$

$$440\ 000 = 40Q - 22Q$$

$$440\ 000 = 18Q$$

$$Q = 440\ 000/18$$

number of puttles to be sold
in order to break even = 24 445

### 4 The graphical method

**Worked example**

Use the information given above relating to the production and sales of puttles.

*Required:*

A break-even chart showing the break-even point and the margin of safety for sales of puttles.

*Solution:*

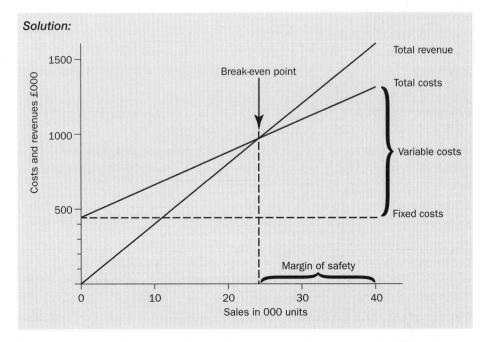

broker: a person who acts as an intermediary between a buyer and a seller. Examples include stockbrokers who buy and sell shares or *bonds* on behalf of their clients, and insurance brokers who sell insurances to clients.

brokerage: the *commission* charged by a *broker*.

B shares: ordinary shares with special voting rights. They are often owned by the original owner(s) of a business and his/her family.

budget: a short-term financial plan. *CIMA* defines a budget as 'a plan expressed in money.' It is prepared in advance of a defined period of time, generally a year (although monthly and quarterly budgets are often prepared). Budgets are based on the objectives of the business and they show how policies are to be pursued during that time period in order that business objectives can be achieved. (See *business objectives*, *capital expenditure budget*, *cash budget*, *trade receivables budget*, *trade payables budget*, *flexible budget*, *production budget*, *sales budget*.)

budgetary control delegates financial planning to managers. It evaluates the performance of managers by continuous comparison of actual results achieved by their department against those set in the budget. This process allows remedial action to be taken. It also ensures that all departmental decision making is related to the corporate plan (see *strategic planning*).

budgeting: the preparation of *budgets*.

budget period: the time covered by a particular budget. The budget period can be broken down into smaller time periods called *control periods* in order that managers may exercise greater control over their departments.

buffer stocks: *inventory* held to ensure that there will always be goods available for production purposes no matter what eventualities are encountered. (See *inventory reorder level*.)

39

**building society:** a mutual organisation, owned by its members, not by shareholders. Building societies specialise in providing mortgages, although in recent years they have widened the scope of the products that they offer in order to compete with banks.

**bulk buying** is the purchasing of goods in large quantities. This enables the purchaser to negotiate a lower price per unit.

**bull:** a *stock market* speculator who purchases shares in the belief that their market price will rise and that the shares can be sold in the future at a higher price.

**bull market:** a period when share prices in general are rising on the *stock market*. The increase in prices reflects general optimism in the economy, causing people to purchase shares.

**business cycle:** the rise and fall in trade within the economy that tends to be repeated on a regular basis. Boom times are followed by *recession*, then slump, which later gives way to recovery and another boom.

**business entity concept** states that only transactions affecting the financial position of a business are recorded in the business *books of account*. The owner's(s') private financial affairs are not recorded.

If, for example, the owner of a business wins £9 000 000 on the national lottery, this will not be recorded in the business books of account. Only if he decided to inject part of his winnings into the business as capital introduced would the business accounts be affected.

**business objectives** set out what the managers of a business hope to achieve. The objectives may be short term (e.g. to introduce a new product line in the next few months) or they may be long term (e.g. the strategic plan for the next ten years).

Whatever the business objectives are, managers must plan for their implementation. These plans take the form of budgets.

**business plan:** a document that is drawn up to show interested parties how a business is to progress in the future. It usually comprises:
- a *marketing* strategy in the short and long run
- a *cash budget*
- a projected *income statement* and *balance sheet*
- details of financial needs of the business
- details of staffing needs
- details of capital equipment needs

An *entrepreneur* will generally be asked to prepare a business plan when seeking funding from a bank or other financial institution, either when first starting in business or when seeking extra finance to expand.

**business rates:** a form of local taxation levied on business premises.

**business review:** a section of the *directors' report* presented to the *shareholders* at the *annual general meeting* of a *limited company*, outlining in general terms the business carried out by the company over the last financial year.

**bust:** a colloquial expression indicating that a business has gone into *liquidation* or that a person has been declared *bankrupt*.

**buyer:** the person responsible for purchasing materials or products for a business.

**buyers' market** occurs when there are few buyers but many sellers. This usually results in goods or services being sold more cheaply than on previous occasions.

**buying department:** the department responsible for the purchase of raw materials or components to be used by a business.

**by-product** is defined by CIMA as the 'output of some value produced incidentally in manufacturing something else'. If the sales value of the by-product is low, the processing costs may be reduced by the revenue generated from the sale. Revenue derived from by-products is deducted from total process cost.

**Do you need revision help and advice?**

Go to pages 259–72 for a range of revision appendices that include plenty of exam advice and tips.

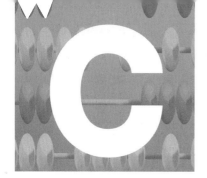

**called-up capital:** the part of the total amount to be paid on a share issue that has been requested by a *limited company.* Further calls are to be made at a later date. The amount asked for is known as the called-up capital.

For example, a company has received £562 500 on application and allotment from an issue of 750 000 ordinary shares of £1. This is shown on the balance sheet thus:

| Equity | £ |
|---|---|
| 750 000 ordinary shares of £1 each | 750 000 |
| Called-up capital: | |
| 750 000 ordinary shares of 75 pence each | 562 500 |
| Paid-up capital: | |
| 750 000 ordinary shares of £1 each 75 pence paid | 562 500 |

  (so the uncalled capital is £187 500.)

**calls in advance:** monies received from *shareholders* before a company has actually made the call. (See *calls on share issue*.)

**calls in arrears:** calls on share capital for which the money has not yet been received from the *shareholders*. (See *calls on share issue*.)

**calls on share issue:** any instalments due to be paid after application and allotment monies have been paid. Many share issues now require the prospective *shareholder* to pay for the shares by instalments.

The instalments are monies paid on:
- application
- allotment
- call(s)

(See *issue of shares*.)

**capacity** is the maximum production that an organisation can achieve in a given time period without increasing the resources it has.

**capacity ratio** expresses the actual hours worked by the labour force as a percentage of the budgeted labour hours.

$$FORMULA: \quad \text{capacity ratio} = \frac{\text{actual labour hours worked}}{\text{budgeted labour hours}} \times 100$$

**capacity utilisation** measures how effectively an organisation is using the resources at its disposal.

$$FORMULA: \quad capacity\ utilisation = \frac{actual\ output\ achieved\ in\ a\ given\ period}{possible\ maximum\ output\ in\ same\ period} \times 100$$

**capital** represents the investment made by the owner(s) of a business. It is the excess of assets over liabilities. It comprises the initial investment made by the owner(s) plus any **retained profits**, less any profits withdrawn from the business as **drawings** in the case of a **sole trader** or a **partnership**. (See also **loan capital**.)

**capital account** records the dealings that the proprietor(s) of a business has with the business. It records what the proprietor(s) has initially contributed to the business out of his/her private resources; it also records the profits that have been left in the business.

---

### Worked example

Yoon Ling has invested £35 000 in a business. During the first year of trading:

i)  the business made a profit of £9307

ii) Yoon Ling withdrew £6411 in cash and £456 in goods from the business

*Required:*

Yoon Ling's capital account as it would appear at the end of her first year's trading.

*Solution:*

| Yoon Ling capital account | | | |
|---|---|---|---|
| Drawings | 6 411 | Cash | 35 000 |
| Drawings | 456 | Income statement | 9 307 |
| Balance c/d | 37 440 | | |
| | 44 307 | | 44 307 |
| | | Balance b/d | 37 440 |

---

Partners' capital accounts are prepared in a similar way, although, obviously, there will be a capital account for each partner. (See **fluctuating capital accounts**, **fixed capital accounts**.)

Generally, the only entries shown in partners' capital accounts are injections of capital. Entries regarding the division of profits and partners' drawings are usually entered in **partnership current accounts**.

**capital allowances:** statutory tax allowances based on **capital expenditure** which can be set off against business profits, thus reducing the business's **tax liability**. The allowances are based on the **depreciation** that has arisen from wear and tear or diminution in the value of **non-current assets**.

**capital budgeting:** the process of appraising proposed **capital expenditure**. The major evaluation techniques used by UK businesses are **payback**, **accounting rate of return**, **internal rate of return** and **net present value**.

**capital employed:** the total of **non-current assets** and **current assets** used in a business, less **current liabilities**. The accuracy of this figure depends on the accuracy of the valuation of the non-current assets shown in the **balance sheet**.

There are a number of different measures of capital employed, so when making **inter-firm comparisons** it is essential to compare like with like. It may be necessary to adjust the data to take into account any differences in **accounting policies**.

**capital expenditure:** money spent on **non-current assets** or their improvement. It includes any costs that are necessary in preparing the non-current assets for use within a business. For example, if land and buildings were purchased, the amount of capital expenditure would include estate agents' fees, legal costs, etc. If a new machine were purchased, the capital cost would include transport costs associated with delivery and any installation costs.

**capital expenditure appraisal:** see *capital investment appraisal*

**capital expenditure budgeting** involves the planned investment in **non-current assets**.

**capital gain** is the profit made when a **non-current asset** is sold for more than its historic cost

**capital gearing:** see *gearing*

**capital goods** is a term sometimes used for **non-current assets**.

**capital intensive** businesses produce their goods using a greater proportion of capital goods (**non-current assets**) than labour. An example of a capital intensive business is the pharmaceutical industry.

**capital investment appraisal:** the process of determining the future **net cash flows** or **profitability** of a capital project. (See **accounting rate of return**, **payback method of capital investment appraisal**, **net present value method of capital investment appraisal** and **internal rate-of-return method of capital investment appraisal**.)

**capital investment budget:** the plans for future **capital expenditure**. The items included in the budget will normally have been subjected to various methods of **capital investment appraisal**. The capital investment budget is a vital part of the **strategic plan** because:
- it often involves large sums of money
- once undertaken, the business could be committed to particular business strategies for many years

**capitalisation issue:** see *bonus shares*

**capital/labour ratio** compares the proportion of the two factors of production used in an organisation. Organisations with a high capital/labour ratio are said to be capital intensive. Organisations with a low ratio are said to be labour intensive.

**capital market:** source of long-term finance for businesses. The capital market is dominated by the London **stock exchange**. The **alternative investment market** is also an important capital market.

**capital receipts** are derived either from the sale of **non-current assets** or by injecting cash (or more assets) into the business by the owners or lenders. These receipts are not entered in the **income statement** like **revenue receipts**; they appear directly on the balance sheet. See also **capital expenditure** and **revenue expenditure**.

**capital reconstruction:** see *capital reduction* and *bonus shares*

**capital redemption reserve:** created when a **limited company** redeems shares or buys back some of its own shares without issuing new shares to fund the redemption.

The company must protect its creditors by replacing the redeemed shares, which have not been funded by a new issue of shares, with a **capital reserve** transferred out of profits that would otherwise have been available for distribution as **dividends**.

The capital redemption reserve is available to issue **bonus shares**.

## Worked example

The following is an extract from the balance sheet of Dibson plc:

|  | £ |
|---|---|
| Cash | 140 000 |
| Ordinary share capital | 400 000 |
| 8% redeemable (preferred) preference shares | 80 000 |
| Share premium | 100 000 |
| Retained earnings | 370 000 |

Dibson plc redeems all the redeemable (preferred) preference shares at a premium of 20%. There is an issue of £45 000 ordinary shares at par for the purpose. The preferred (preference) shares had originally been issued at a premium of 15%.

*Required:*

Show the journal entries to record the above transactions in the books of Dibson plc.

*Solution:*

Narratives have not been used. Explanations of some entries are included in brackets.

### Dibson plc: Journal

|  | Dr £ | Cr £ |
|---|---|---|
| 8% redeemable preferred (preference) shares | 80 000 | |
| Redemption account | | 80 000 |

(The redemption account is used to 'collect' the shares and the premium.)

|  | Dr £ | Cr £ |
|---|---|---|
| Share premium account | 12 000 | |
| Redemption account | | 12 000 |

(Only £12 000 of the £16 000 premium to be paid to the preferred (preference) shareholders can be taken from the share premium account since this is the amount that was raised when the shares were originally issued. The remainder of the £16 000 premium must be transferred out of the company's retained profits.)

|  | Dr £ | Cr £ |
|---|---|---|
| Retained earnings | 4 000 | |
| Redemption account | | 4 000 |

|  | Dr £ | Cr £ |
|---|---|---|
| Redemption account | 96 000 | |
| Cash | | 96 000 |

|  | Dr £ | Cr £ |
|---|---|---|
| Cash | 45 000 | |
| Ordinary share capital | | 45 000 |

|  | Dr £ | Cr £ |
|---|---|---|
| Retained earnings | 35 000 | |
| Capital redemption reserve | | 35 000 |

(Only £45 000 was raised by a new issue of shares, so £35 000 has to be transferred out of distributable reserves into a capital reserve.)

**capital reduction:** a revaluation of both assets and liabilities at a lower level than previously recorded. It might be necessary when the share capital of a *limited company* is not represented by the assets of the company. This generally happens when a company has suffered poor results over a number of years, leading to a debit balance on the *retained earnings* account.

A capital reduction scheme needs the support of *shareholders* and other interested parties and must receive the consent of the Court. This support will only be forthcoming if the *directors* of the company can give assurances that the same situation will not occur again in the future.

## Worked example

Seok Chin plc has the following balance sheet at 31 December 20*9:

|  | £ |
|---|---|
| Net assets | 270 000 |
| Equity |  |
| 500 000 ordinary shares of £1 each | 500 000 |
| Less debit balance – retained earnings | (230 000) |
|  | 270 000 |

The following scheme of capital reduction has been agreed by the shareholders and sanctioned by the Court:
The ordinary shares are to be reduced to 50 pence per share.
The net assets are to be written down to £250 000.
The retained earnings balance is to be written off.

*Required:*

i) journal entries to record the above transactions in the company's books
ii) the balance sheet of Seok Chin plc after the scheme has been completed

*Solution:*

i) **Seok Chin plc journal**

|  | Dr | Cr |
|---|---|---|
|  | £ | £ |
| Ordinary share capital | 250 000 |  |
| Capital reduction account |  | 250 000 |
| Capital reduction account | 250 000 |  |
| Net assets |  | 20 000 |
| Retained earnings |  | 230 000 |

The principles involved in a reconstruction can be seen very clearly if we construct our balance sheet using a horizontal layout:

|  | £ |  | £ |
|---|---|---|---|
| Net assets | 270 000 | Equity | 500 000 |
| Retained earnings | 230 000 |  |  |
|  | 500 000 |  | 500 000 |

46

The left-hand side of the balance sheet has to be reduced by £250 000, so the right-hand side must also be reduced by £250 000.

ii) Seok Chin plc balance sheet after the capital reduction scheme has been implemented

|  | £ |
|---|---|
| Net assets | 250 000 |
| Equity |  |
| 500 000 ordinary shares of 50 pence each | 250 000 |

**capital repayments** are deducted from the outstanding balance owed on a long-term loan. They reduce the amount shown as owing in the *balance sheet*. Interest payments are *revenue expenditure* and as such they are shown as an expense on the *income statement*.

**capital reserves:** amounts set aside out of profits that are not *provisions*. They are not created by setting aside amounts out of operating profits. They are not available for cash dividend purposes. They may be distributed in the form of *bonus shares*.

Examples of capital reserves are:
- *share premium account*
- *revaluation reserve*
- *capital redemption reserve*

**carriage, insurance and freight (CIF):** the estimate of a price inclusive of the charge for insurance cover and any transport costs incurred.

**carriage inward:** *revenue expenditure* incurred in the transporting of raw materials or products for resale into a business. Sometimes delivery charges are included in the total purchase price, at other times a separate charge is made. This separate charge is termed carriage inwards. Any such carriage charges should be debited to the carriage inwards account in the *general ledger*. At the end of the *accounting period* the carriage inward account will be written off to the *prime cost* section of the *manufacturing account* (if the carriage charge was incurred in transporting raw materials to the factory) or to *cost of sales* (if the carriage charge was incurred in transporting goods for resale in a retail outlet).

**carriage on sales:** see *carriage outward*

**carriage outward:** *revenue expenditure* incurred in delivering goods or raw materials to a customer. These costs are debited to the carriage outward account in the *general ledger*. Since this cost is incurred after the goods have been made ready for sale, the account is written off to the *income statement* at the end of the *accounting period*. Carriage outwards is sometimes referred to as carriage on sales.

**carrying amount:** the net value of a *non-current asset* as it appears in the *general ledger* of a business. It is calculated by taking the *aggregate depreciation* and any *impairment losses* of the *non-current asset* from the value in the asset account. The carrying amount is also known as the net book value or the written-down value.

## Worked example

The ledger of Westby Industries Ltd shows the following accounts at 31 December 2009:

| | | | | |
|---|---|---|---|---|
| Land and buildings | Balance b/d | 500 000 | Balance b/d | 40 000 |
| Vehicles | Balance b/d | 127 000 | Balance b/d | 67 000 |
| Machinery | Balance b/d | 430 000 | Balance b/d | 120 000 |

### Required:

Calculate the carrying amount of land and buildings, vehicles and machinery for Westby Industries Ltd.

### Solution:

Carrying amounts:

| | |
|---|---|
| Land and buildings | £460 000 (£500 000 – £40 000) |
| Vehicles | £60 000 (£127 000 – £67 000) |
| Machinery | £310 000 (£430 000 – £120 000) |

Remember: the carrying amount does not represent how much the assets would fetch if they were sold.

**cash:** money in notes and coins. The most liquid of all business assets.

**cash and cash equivalents:** comprise the cash in hand and bank balances of the business.

**cash balance:** the amount of money and notes held in the business. The amount should agree with the balance of the cash columns in the *cash book*. The balance should be checked every day.

**cash book:** a *book of prime entry* in which all cash and bank transactions are recorded. It contains two *general ledger* accounts:
- the business cash account
- the business bank account

Since it is part of the general ledger it follows that it is part of the double-entry system. The *cash book* for a *VAT*-registered business will have four columns on the debit side and four columns on the credit side:

| Debit | Credit |
|---|---|
| Discount (1) VAT (2) Cash (3) Bank (4) | Discount (1) VAT (2) Cash (3) Bank (4) |
| 1  Discount allowed to customers for prompt payment | 1  Discount received for prompt payment to suppliers |
| 2  VAT collected from customers on behalf of HMRC | 2  VAT paid to suppliers on goods and services received |
| 3  Cash receipts | 3  Cash payments |
| 4  Cheque receipts | 4  Cheque payments |

**cash budget** shows estimates of future cash incomes and cash expenditure for revenue and capital transactions. It is drawn up to help make the management aware of any potential shortages or surpluses of cash resources that could occur, thus allowing management to make necessary financial arrangements.

A cash budget deals only with transactions involving the movement of cash; it does not include non-cash expenses such as *depreciation*.

Banks often request the preparation of a cash budget when a business person seeks financial support in the form of a business loan or an *overdraft* facility.

A cash budget layout is shown below:

### Cash budget for the three months ending 30 September 20*9

|  | July | August | September |
|---|---|---|---|
|  | £ | £ | £ |
| Receipts: |  |  |  |
| Cash sales | 4 000 | 5 000 | 5 000 |
| Receipts from credit customers | 23 000 | 37 000 | 35 000 |
|  | 27 000 | 42 000 | 40 000 |
| Payments: |  |  |  |
| Payments to credit suppliers | 16 000 | 18 000 | 17 000 |
| Cash purchases | 2 300 | 2 700 | 2 400 |
| Rent |  | 16 000 |  |
| Wages | 8 000 | 8 000 | 8 800 |
| Other expenses | 1 750 | 3 560 | 3 100 |
|  | 28 050 | 48 260 | 31 300 |
| Balance b/fwd | 1 450 | 400 | (5 860) |
| Receipts | 27 000 | 42 000 | 40 000 |
|  | 28 450 | 42 400 | 34 140 |
| Payments | (28 050) | (48 260) | (31 300) |
| Balance c/fwd | 400 | (5 860) | 2 840 |

This cash budget shows that the business requires an overdraft facility during August and September.

**cash columns** in a traditional *cash book* record cash received on the debit side, and cash payments on the credit side.

**cash discount:** an allowance that can be deducted from the total amount shown on an *invoice* if the debt is settled within a time specified by the supplier of the goods. (See *discount allowed* and *discount received*.)

**cash equivalents** are highly liquid short-term investments that are easily converted into cash.

**cash flows:** cash movements in and out of a business. Since *liquidity* is vitally important for the short-term survival of a business, it is important that cash inflows (receipts of cash and cheques) are greater than cash outflows (expenditure in cash and cheques).

Cash flows need to be calculated for use in:
- *cash budgets*
- *statements of cash flows IAS 7*
- *capital investment appraisal*

**cash in hand:** money and notes not banked but kept within a business to make necessary cash payments. The balance at the year end is shown in the *balance sheet* as a *current asset*.

**cash inflows:** monies received by a business, e.g. money received from customers, money received from the sale of a *non-current asset*.

**cash in transit:** cash sent by a branch to head office or vice versa. The cash is an asset of the business and so must be included as part of the business's *cash in hand*.

**cash on delivery (COD):** cash that must be paid for goods when they are delivered.

**cash operating cycle** measures the continuous movement of cash being received by a business and cash going out of the business. A business needs a continuous source of money to pay for the resources it requires.

The cash operating cycle is calculated as follows:

$$\left(\frac{\text{rate of inventory}}{\text{turnover}} + \frac{\text{average period of credit}}{\text{taken by customers}}\right) - \frac{\text{average period of credit taken}}{\text{from suppliers}}$$

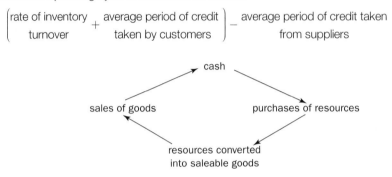

**Worked example**

The following extract from the income statement for Christell Polydor has been prepared for the year ended 31 December 20*9:

|  | £ | £ |
|---|---|---|
| Sales (all on credit) |  | 220 000 |
| Less cost of sales |  |  |
| Inventory 1 January 20*9 | 2 500 |  |
| Purchases | 106 800 |  |
|  | 109 300 |  |
| Inventory 31 December 20*9 | 2 700 | 106 600 |
| Gross profit |  | 113 400 |

*Additional information*

|  | at 31 December 20*9 |
|---|---|
| Trade receivables | £30 136 |
| Trade payables | £10 780 |

*Required:*

Calculate the cash operating cycle for Christell Polydor.

*Solution:*

|  | Days |
|---|---|
| Inventory turnover | 9 |
| Trade receivables collection period | 50 |
|  | 59 |
| Trade payables payment period | 37 |
| Cash operating cycle | 22 |

*Workings*

Inventory turnover $\dfrac{106\ 600}{2600}$ = 9 days

Trade receivables collection period $\dfrac{30\ 136 \times 365}{220\ 000}$ = 50 days

Trade payables payment period $\dfrac{10\ 780 \times 365}{106\ 800}$ = 37 days

**cash outflows:** monies paid out by a business to acquire resources.

**casting** is the term sometimes used by accountants for adding.

**certificate of incorporation:** a document issued by the *Registrar of Companies*. The certificate is needed before a company can start to trade.

**certification of work done:** an interim valuation of work completed by a professional quantity surveyor or architect. The valuation will include an element of profit and forms the basis of the contractor's interim *invoices*.

When a long-term *contract* takes many years to complete it would be unreasonable to expect the contractor to wait until the contract is complete before the client pays. It would also be unreasonable to expect the client to pay for the whole contract before the contract is started. *Progress payments* are made by the client, based on interim valuations of work completed.

**chairman of the board of directors:** the person who presides over the *board meetings* of a *limited company*.

**chairman's statement:** a general comment on the performance of the company made by the *chairman of the board of directors*.

*Limited companies* usually include a statement written by the chairman in the *annual report*. The statement is not a statutory requirement, but it can be used as a vehicle for comments on outside influences which might have affected the company over the time covered by the annual report.

**change in profit sharing ratios of partners** affects the structure of the partnership. One partnership ceases to exist and another 'new' partnership takes its place, when partners decide to alter their *profit sharing ratios*. This means that a revaluation of the partnership assets must take place so that the 'old' partners are credited with what are their dues, before the 'new' partnership takes over.

**changes in financial position:** information derived from a *statement of cash flows IAS 7*.

**charge card:** a credit card whose balance must be paid off at the end of each month.

**chartered accountant:** a person who has passed the professional examinations and has become a member of the Institute of Chartered Accountants. They may use the designation ACA (Associate of the Institute of Chartered Accountants in England and Wales).

**checking cash:** checking the balance of cash shown in the *cash columns* of the *cash book* and *petty cash book* against the cash in the till. Checks should be conducted regularly, at least once per day.

**cheque:** an instruction to a bank to pay or transfer a sum of money to a named person. The instructions are written on a preprinted form (the cheque) supplied by the bank.
- The person filling in the cheque and who signs it is the *drawer*.
- The *drawee* is the bank on which the cheque is drawn.
- The person to whom the cheque is payable is the *payee*.

Cheques are out of date six months after the date specified.

**cheque book:** a booklet issued by a bank to its customers which contains blank cheques.

**cheque crossings** are made in order to restrict the use of a cheque. If a cheque is uncrossed, the *payee* can cash the cheque at the bank. An uncrossed cheque is also known as an open cheque.

The main crossings in use are:
1 general crossing – the cheque must be paid into another bank account
2 not negotiable – the holder of the cheque cannot have a better claim to it than the previous holder
3 a/c payee only – the cheque must be paid into the payee's account
4 special – the cheque can only be paid into the payee's account at the bank named on the crossing

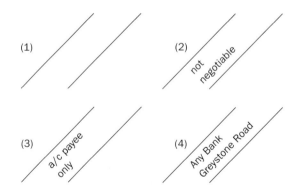

**cheque guarantee card:** this guarantees that a bank will honour a cheque up to a pre-agreed amount (e.g. £50, £100 or £250). When a cheque is offered by a cash customer in settlement of a debt, it is usual to accept the cheque only when it is supported by a cheque guarantee card. The card has a specimen of the holder's signature.

**cheque signatories:** the people who are authorised to sign cheques on behalf of a business. Their signatures will appear on the *bank mandate*.

**CIF:** see *carriage, insurance and freight*

**CIMA:** Chartered Institute of Management Accountants.

**circulating assets:** another name for *current assets*.

**circulating capital** is another name for *current assets*. It comprises *cash and cash equivalents*, *trade receivables* and *inventories*. Circulating capital is necessary to enable an organisation to carry on its day-to-day business.

**clearing banks** are the major 'high street' banks that provide normal banking business for individuals and businesses.

**clock cards:** a record of the time of arrival and departure of employees to and from their place of work. They are often issued to production staff in order to record the time they spend on the business premises.

Each worker is given a clock card. When the card is inserted into a time recorder the card is stamped with the time. The clock card provides the wages department with a record of:

- how long the employee has spent on the business premises
- whether the employee has been late
- whether the employee has been absent from work

(See *time sheet*.)

**closing inventory:** this value is obtained by a physical check on inventory held at the end of the financial year of a business when the other accounts relating to goods have been closed. The bookkeeping entries to record the introduction of inventories into the final accounts are:

|  | Debit | Credit |
|---|---|---|
| Purchases account is closed by | Income statement | Purchases account |
| Sales account is closed by | Sales account | Income statement |
| An inventory account is opened |  |  |
| Since inventory is an asset |  |  |
| it should be recorded as such |  |  |
| Inventory account is opened by | Inventory account | Income statement |

## Worked example

Mary McDougal completed her first year of trading on 30 November 20*9.

The entries on the debit side of her purchases account total £26 000.
The entries on the credit side of her sales account total £48 000.
Mary values her inventory on 30 November 20*9 at £4500.

### Required:

The income statement and the inventory account as they would appear in the general ledger of Mary McDougal at the end of her first year of trading.

### Solution:

Mary's inventory is an asset.

An inventory account is opened and the amount debited.

The double-entry system requires a credit entry – so the income statement is credited. Mary's general ledger would show the following:

**Inventory**

| | £ |
|---|---|
| Income Statement | 4 500 |

An extract from the income statement for the year ended 30 November 20*9 shows:

| | £ | | £ |
|---|---|---|---|
| Purchases | 26 000 | Sales | 48 000 |
| Gross profit c/d | 26 500 | Inventory | 4 500 |
| | 52 500 | | 52 500 |
| | | Gross profit b/d | 26 500 |

Income statements are generally presented using a vertical format. In this case the closing inventory is deducted from the purchases to give a cost of sales figure.

**Income statement extract for the year ended 30 November 20*9**

| | £ | £ |
|---|---|---|
| Sales | | 48 000 |
| Less cost of sales: | | |
| Purchases | 26 000 | |
| Less inventory | 4 500 | 21 500 |
| Gross profit | | 26 500 |

**club accounts** are the *financial statements* of clubs and societies. They differ from those of business organisations in a number of respects:

| Club and society accounts | Business accounts |
|---|---|
| Income and expenditure account | Income statement |
| Surplus of income over expenditure | Profit |
| Excess of expenditure over income | Loss |
| Accumulated fund | Capital account |

There are four key stages in preparing the final accounts of clubs and societies:
- prepare an opening **statement of affairs** (similar to an opening **balance sheet**)
- prepare a **receipts and payments account** (summary of the **cash book**); this is often given as part of the information in an examination question)
- prepare **adjustment accounts** (to take into account the **accruals concept**)
- prepare the **financial statements**

## Worked example

The following is the receipts and payments account of the Stanegate Badminton Club for the year ended 31 October 20*9:

| | £ | | £ |
|---|---|---|---|
| Cash and bank balances b/fwd | 211 | Secretarial expenses | 141 |
| Subscriptions | 824 | Rent of village hall | 700 |
| Competition entry fees | 72 | Dinner dance expenses | 210 |
| Dinner dance receipts | 248 | Stationery and printing | 38 |
| Balance c/fwd | 78 | Other expenses | 224 |
| | | Competition prizes | 120 |
| | 1433 | | 1433 |

The following additional information has been given:

| | 20*8 £ | 20*9 £ |
|---|---|---|
| Equipment at valuation | 210 | 180 |
| Subscriptions paid in advance | 48 | 64 |
| Subscriptions in arrears | 32 | 16 |
| Amount owing to Matthews & Co. for stationery | 29 | 37 |

### Required:

Prepare an income and expenditure account for the Stanegate Badminton Club for the year ended 31 October 20*9 and a balance sheet at that date.

### Solution:

**Stage 1:** prepare an opening statement of affairs.

Statement of affairs at 1 November 20*8

| | £ |
|---|---|
| Equipment at valuation | 210 |
| Subscriptions in arrears (members owe club = receivables) | 32 |
| Cash and bank balances in hand | 211 |
| | 453 |
| Subscription in advance (club owes members = payables) | 48 |
| Payable for printing – Matthews and Co. | 29 |
| Accumulated fund (missing figure) | 376 |
| | 453 |

**Stage 2:** prepare receipts and payment account. Already done – given in the question.

**Stage 3:** important stage. Prepare adjustment accounts. One for each item on statement of affairs.

| Equipment | | | | | |
|---|---|---|---|---|---|
| Balance b/fwd | 210 | Missing figure (1) | 30 | | |
| | | Balance c/fwd | 180 | | |
| | 210 | | 210 | | |
| Balance b/fwd | 180 | | | | |

| Matthews and Co. | | | |
|---|---|---|---|
| Cash | 38 | Balance b/fwd | 29 |
| Balance c/fwd | 37 | Missing figure (2) | 46 |
| | 75 | | 75 |
| | | Balance c/fwd | 37 |

| Cash and bank |
|---|
| Already done – stage 2! |

| Accumulated fund |
|---|
| Will be adjusted on closing balance sheet. |

The most testing account when preparing club accounts is the subscriptions account:

| Subscriptions | | | |
|---|---|---|---|
| Balance b/fwd | | Balance b/fwd | |
| (subscriptions in arrears) | 32 | (subscriptions in advance) | 48 |
| Missing figure (3) | 792 | Cash | 824 |
| Balance c/fwd | 64 | Balance c/fwd | 16 |
| | 888 | | 888 |
| Balance b/fwd | | Balance b/fwd | |
| (subscriptions in arrears) | 16 | (subscriptions in advance) | 64 |

Missing figure (1) is the annual depreciation charge on the club's equipment.
Missing figure (2) is the actual printing done during the year by Matthews & Co.
Missing figure (3) is the subscriptions figure for the year.

**Stage 4:** preparation of the final accounts.

**Stanegate Badminton Club income and expenditure account for the year ended 31 October 20\*9**

| | £ | £ |
|---|---|---|
| Incomes: | | |
| Subscriptions | | 792 |
| Profit on dinner dance (it is usual to show activities that are not central to the purpose of the club as 'net' figures) | | 38 |
| | | 830 |
| Less expenditure: | | |
| Secretarial expenses | 141 | |
| Rent | 700 | |
| Loss on competitions | 48 | |
| Stationery and printing | 46 | |
| Other expenses | 224 | |
| Depreciation: equipment | 30 | 1189 |
| Excess of expenditure over income | | 359 |

## Balance sheet at 31 October 20*9

| | | |
|---|---:|---:|
| Equipment at valuation | 210 | |
| Less depreciation | 30 | 180 |
| Subscriptions in arrears | | 16 |
| | | 196 |
| Accumulated fund | 376 | |
| Less excess of expenditure over income | 359 | 17 |
| Bank overdraft | | 78 |
| Stationery creditor | | 37 |
| Subscriptions in advance | | 64 |
| | | 196 |

**COD:** see *cash on delivery*

**collateral** is used to guarantee a loan. Often the collateral will be the title deeds to land or buildings.

**collective bargaining:** the process of negotiation between employers and employee representatives covering wage rises and working conditions for a whole group of workers.

**columnar day books** allow a business to analyse its purchases and sales into different categories.

### Worked example

Robert Caffrey is a sole trader who sells kitchen and bedroom furniture. The following invoices in respect of goods for resale have been received:

| | | |
|---|---|---|
| 6 May Kwality Kitchens | £963 + VAT | |
| 13 May Snoozabed Ltd | £1673 + VAT | |
| 26 May Kitchen Fans plc | £450 + VAT | £50 + VAT |
| | (kitchens) | (bedroom fittings) |
| 27 May Headboards Ltd | £875 + VAT | |

The following sales invoices in respect of credit sales have been sent to customers:

| | |
|---|---|
| 14 May Howard Sellers for fitted kitchen | £1698 + VAT |
| 23 May Bill Blakemore for bedroom furniture | £765 +VAT |
| 30 May Louise Harrison for fitted kitchen | £4300 + VAT |
| VAT = 17.5% | |

### Required:

The purchases day book and the sales day book for Robert Caffrey.

### Solution:

### Purchases day book

| Date | Details | Kitchens | Bedrooms | Total | VAT | Gross |
|---|---|---:|---:|---:|---:|---:|
| | | £ | £ | £ | £ | £ |
| 6 May | Kwality Kitchens | 963 | | 963 | 168.52 | 1131.52 |
| 13 May | Snoozabed Ltd | | 1673 | 1673 | 292.77 | 1965.77 |

| Date | Details | Kitchens £ | Bedrooms £ | Total £ | VAT £ | Gross £ |
|---|---|---|---|---|---|---|
| 26 May | Kitchen Fans plc | 450 | 50 | 500 | 87.50 | 587.50 |
| 27 May | Headboards Ltd | | 875 | 875 | 153.12 | 1028.12 |
| | | 1413 | 2598 | 4011 | 701.91 | 4712.91 |

The ledger accounts for the entry on 26 May would be:

| Debit (in general ledger) | Kitchen purchases | £450 |
|---|---|---|
| | Bedroom purchases | £50 |
| | VAT | £87.50 |

(These amounts would not be posted individually but would be included in the totals posted at the month end.)

| Credit (in purchases ledger) | Kitchen Fans plc | £587.50 |
|---|---|---|

**Sales day book**

| Date | Details | Kitchens £ | Bedrooms £ | Total £ | VAT £ | Gross £ |
|---|---|---|---|---|---|---|
| 14 May | Howard Sellers | 1698 | | 1698 | 297.15 | 1995.15 |
| 23 May | Bill Blakemore | | 765 | 765 | 133.87 | 898.87 |
| 30 May | Louise Harrison | 4300 | | 4300 | 752.50 | 5052.50 |
| | | 5998 | 765 | 6763 | 1183.52 | 7946.52 |

The ledger accounts for the entry on 14 May would be:

| Credit (in general ledger) | Kitchen sales | £1698 |
|---|---|---|
| VAT | | £297.15 |

(These amounts would not be posted individually but would be included in the totals posted at the month end.)

| Debit (in sales ledger) | Howard Sellers | £1995.15 |
|---|---|---|

Many businesses use columnar day books to record all non-cash transactions. The following is an example of how this type of analysis book may be written up:

**Purchases day book**

| | | Net £ | VAT £ | Gross £ | Purchases £ | Stationery £ | Motor exp. £ | Rates etc. £ |
|---|---|---|---|---|---|---|---|---|
| 7 April | Gladstone Ltd | 38 | 6.65 | 44.65 | 38 | | | |
| 12 April | Easton CBC | 78 | | 78.00 | | | | 78 |
| 15 April | Todd plc | 125 | 21.87 | 146.87 | | 125 | | |
| 23 April | Jeff's garage | 651 | 113.92 | 764.92 | | | 651 | |
| | | 892 | 142.44 | 1034.44 | 38 | 125 | 651 | 78 |

At a convenient time the following postings will be made to the general ledger:

Totals of the: purchases column to the debit of the purchases account
stationery column to the debit of the stationery account
motor expenses column to the debit of the motor expenses account
rates column to the debit of the rates account and any other
analysis columns to the debit of the respective accounts
VAT column to the debit of the VAT account

The following postings will be made to the purchases ledger:

| | |
|---|---|
| Credit Gladstone Ltd | £44.65 |
| Credit Easton CBC | £78.00 |
| Credit Todd plc | £146.87 |
| Credit Jeff's garage | £764.92 |

**columnar presentation of income statements** is a useful source of financial information with regard to the profitability of different departments or sections of a business. An analysis of purchases and sales must be made (see **columnar day books**). A departmental check of inventory must be undertaken in order to prepare an **income statement** for each department. An extract from the departmental income statement might look like this:

### Robert Caffrey departmental income statement for the year ended 30 June 20*9

| | | Kitchen department | | Bedroom department | | Total |
|---|---|---|---|---|---|---|
| | | £ | | £ | | £ |
| Sales | | 126 000 | | 93 000 | | 219 000 |
| Inventory 1 July 20*8 | 8 000 | | 4 500 | | 12 500 | |
| Purchases | 74 000 | | 28 000 | | 102 000 | |
| | 82 000 | | 32 500 | | 114 500 | |
| Less | | | | | | |
| Inventory 30 June 20*9 | 7 500 | | 5 200 | | 12 700 | |
| Cost of goods sold | | 74 500 | | 27 300 | | 101 800 |
| Gross profit | | 51 500 | | 65 700 | | 117 200 |

Each department must be charged with its share of the business's expenses. This can present problems. Expenses that can easily be identified with a department should be allocated accordingly, e.g. bedroom fitters' wages are easy to identify and can therefore be charged to the bedroom department. Other expenses should be **apportioned** using some rational basis, e.g. rent, business rates, heating costs, electricity charges, etc. can be apportioned according to the floor area occupied by each department. Administration expenses, sales assistants' salaries, advertising, etc. can be apportioned according to the proportion of total sales generated by each department.

| | Kitchen department | | Bedroom department | | Total |
|---|---|---|---|---|---|
| | | £ | | £ | £ |
| Gross profit | | 51 500 | | 65 700 | 117 200 |
| Less expenses | | | | | |
| Wages and salaries | 21 800 | | 27 400 | | 49 200 |
| Rent and rates | 7 000 | | 14 000 | | 21 000 |
| Admin. expenses | 13 808 | | 10 192 | | 24 000 |
| Electricity charges | 3 333 | | 6 667 | | 10 000 |
| Depreciation | 3 500 | | 3 500 | | 7 000 |
| | | 49 441 | | 61 759 | 111 200 |
| Net profit | | 2 059 | | 3 941 | 6 000 |

**commercial banks** offer banking services to the general public. (See **merchant bank**.)

**commission:** a payment made to another party for business done or for sales revenue achieved. The amount is generally a percentage based on the **agent's** or salesperson's performance. Commission payable is an expense and appears on the **income statement**. Commission receivable is income earned by a business and is shown as part of **revenue** on the income statement.

**commission error:** see *errors not affecting the balancing of the trial balance*

**common costs:** costs incurred in the production of more than one product. They must therefore be **apportioned** between joint products. The following are the usual methods used:
- Sales value at the stage when joint products are recognisable as individual products (the split-off point or point of separation) in their own right. For example, product P and product Q incur joint costs of £35 000. At the split-off point, product P has a saleable value of £36 000 and product Q has a saleable value of £24 000. The joint costs will be apportioned:

$$\text{product P} = \frac{36\,000}{60\,000} \times 35\,000 = £21\,000$$
$$\text{product Q} = \frac{24\,000}{60\,000} \times 35\,000 = £14\,000$$

- Sales value after further processing has taken place. For example, using the data above:

After the split-off point, product P incurs additional expenses of £8000, the saleable value rises to £45 000; product Q incurs additional expenses of £1000, the saleable value rises to £27 000.

| | Product P | Product Q |
|---|---|---|
| Sales value after further processing | £45 000 | £27 000 |
| Additional processing costs incurred | £8 000 | £1 000 |
| Contribution value (sales – additional costs) | £37 000 | £26 000 |

The total contribution value = £63 000

The joint costs are apportioned according to the contribution value of each product expressed as a proportion of the total contribution value.

product P is apportioned with $\dfrac{37\ 000}{63\ 000} \times 35\ 000 = £20\ 556$ of the joint costs

product Q is apportioned with $\dfrac{26\ 000}{63\ 000} \times 35\ 000 = £14\ 444$ of the joint costs

- Units produced method. For example, using the data given above:

At the point of separation, 5400 units of product P were produced and 3200 units of product Q were produced. The joint costs are apportioned according to the number of units of each product produced, expressed as a proportion of total production.

Product P is apportioned with $\dfrac{5400}{8600} \times 35\ 000 = £21\ 977$ of the joint costs

Product Q is apportioned with $\dfrac{3200}{8600} \times 35\ 000 = £13\ 023$ of the joint costs

**Companies Act 1985:** the main piece of legislation governing the activities of *limited companies* in England, Scotland and Wales.

Limited companies are required to prepare and publish accounts annually. The Act sets out the legal requirements with regard to the information that must be shown in the company's *annual report*. The annual report must contain:

1 A *directors' report* giving information:
- about the business activities
- allowing the *shareholders* to assess the asset backing of their shares
- making shareholders aware of material changes in the ownership of the *issued share capital*
- indicating the company's activities in the community
- recommending a *dividend*

2 The criteria for information appearing in the published *income statement*:
- financial statements are required to present a *true and fair view* of the profits, assets and liabilities of the company
- statements are required to comply with fundamental *accounting concepts*
- presentational format is prescribed
- sensitive information is required to be disclosed by way of a note to the accounts

3 The criteria for information appearing in the published *balance sheet*:
- presentation of the format is prescribed
- rules for asset valuation
- disclosure of accounting policies (see *accounting principles*, *accounting bases* and *accounting policies*)

4 The **auditors' report**, which explains the work that the **auditors** have completed. In most cases the report will state that the **audit** has been carried out according to auditing standards and that in the auditors' opinion the accounts show a true and fair view and have been properly prepared in accordance with the Act. The auditors may qualify their report if they disagree with the **directors** of the company on a matter of principle or if they are not satisfied that the accounts do show a true and fair view.

**Companies Act 1989:** this Act made a number of amendments to company law, mainly in the areas of **group accounts** and **auditing**. The **Companies Act 1985** remains the principal Act. The 1989 Act includes some sections which are expressed to be sections of the 1985 Act in replacement for the original sections. The main objective of the 1989 Act is to implement EEC directives into English company law.

**Companies Acts** rule how companies should conduct their financial affairs.

**company accounts** are the **financial statements** of a **limited company**. They are drawn up by the **directors** of the company in the way that best suits their own purposes as managers of the business.

However, when the directors publish the company's accounts to send to the **shareholders** and to the **Registrar of Companies**, schedule 4 of the **Companies Act 1985** lays down the information that must be shown in the accounts and how it should be shown.

**Company Securities (insider dealing) Act 1985** has made it a criminal offence to profit from using financial information that has been gained from working within an organisation, e.g. selling a shareholding in an employer company for £3.00 per share, knowing that poor results are to be announced and so cause the share price to fall dramatically.

**comparability of financial statements:** it is important that the users of accounting information can make valid **inter-firm comparisons** and **trend analysis** over a number of years. In order to make such comparisons meaningful, accounts are prepared in accordance with guidelines laid down by the **Companies Acts**, **International Accounting Standards (IASs)** and **International Financial Reporting Standards (IFRSs)**.

**compensating errors** occur when a number of different errors cancel each other out.

**compensation** is a payment made to a worker who has lost his/her job or a director who has lost his/her office. A compensation package of a high salary, pension rights and other benefits may be used to entice someone to leave their current position to take up a new post elsewhere.

**competing courses of action:** when faced with having to choose between competing courses of action, managers need to consider only the **marginal costs** incurred for each option.

**Competition Commission:** this body replaced the Monopolies and Mergers Commission in 1999. It reports on anti-competition practices that it believes are 'against the public interest',

## Worked example

Mandy Carruthers has started a small furniture manufacturing business. She specialises in producing only one product. She will produce either kitchen tables, armchairs or sideboards. She provides the following information:

|  | Table | Armchairs | Sideboards |
|---|---|---|---|
|  | £ | £ | £ |
| Selling price per unit | 460 | 180 | 290 |
| Direct material costs per unit | 110 | 65 | 90 |
| Direct labour costs per unit | 85 | 70 | 105 |
| Total fixed costs £35 000 |  |  |  |

### Required:

Advise Mandy which product she should produce.

### Solution:

Since the fixed costs will be incurred whichever product is produced, it can be disregarded in your decision making.

> Tables make a positive contribution of £265.
> Armchairs make a positive contribution of £45.
> Sideboards make a positive contribution of £95.

Mandy should produce tables since they will earn her the greatest net profit. Once this decision has been made, all costs must be included in any revenue statement.

so these matters can then be passed to government to take the necessary action. The appeals side hears appeals against prohibition rulings enforced under the Competition Act 1998.

**competitive pricing** means taking the price of competitors' products into account when setting the price of one's own.

**competitive tendering** encourages businesses in the private sector to tender for services that had previously been undertaken by council employees. Examples include road maintenance and refuse collection.

**complete reversal of entries:** see *errors not affecting the balancing of the trial balance*

**compound interest** is interest calculated on the capital sum plus any interest that has accrued since the previous interest calculation was made.

## Worked example

Sean O'Hare deposited £1000 in a bank deposit account three years ago today. Interest rate payable on the account is 10% per annum.

### Required:

Calculate the value of Sean's deposit today.

### Solution:

Value of Sean O'Hare's bank deposit account

| | | £ | |
|---|---|---|---|
| Year 0 | (time of original deposit) | 1000 | |
| Year 1 | | 1010 | (£1000 + 10% interest) |
| Year 2 | | 1111 | (£1010 + 10% interest on £1010) |
| Year 3 | | 1222.10 | (£1111 + 10% interest on £1111) |

Today Sean's bank deposit account will have a balance of £1222.10.

For examination purposes, assume that interest will be calculated on a compound basis unless the question indicates otherwise.

**computerised accounts:** many businesses now use computers to process substantial amounts of their accounting information.

Computers are extremely useful where large quantities of data need to be processed. They are used extensively in *financial accounting* in:

- the preparation of *sales invoices* and the posting of these to the *sales ledger*
- posting *invoices* received to the *purchase ledger*
- maintaining the *general ledger* (*nominal ledger*)
- maintaining *inventory* records
- maintaining payroll records and preparing wages slips
- maintaining a record of receipts and payments
- the preparation of reports to managers
- the preparation of *financial statements*
- maintaining *credit control*

Computers are equally useful in the fields of *cost* and *management accounting*, for example:

- the preparation of budgets
- the preparation of other forecast statements, e.g. forecast *financial statements*, estimates for clients
- the construction of *capital investment appraisals*
- keeping costing records

Advantages of using computers in accounting:

- data are processed extremely quickly
- one entry of data will update all relevant parts of the system
- large quantities of data can be processed simultaneously
- very complex information using different data banks can be produced and analysed easily (previously, preparation of such information was time consuming and therefore expensive)
- *software* packages allow information to be presented in a wide variety of forms, e.g. graphics, tables, drawings, graphs, etc., thus making complex information more user friendly
- they are very accurate (the vast majority of errors are operative errors)

- grouping of similar data can be achieved quickly
- dissimilar data can be identified easily
- exception reports can be compiled easily; this aids *management by exception*
- reduction in staff, therefore saving on wage costs

Disadvantages of using computers in accounting:
- sophisticated equipment is expensive
- staff need training and regular skill updating when new packages are introduced
- some staff may feel threatened if they lack confidence in using computers
- if there has been a reduction in staffing, there may be a lowering of morale in the remaining workforce
- it may be expensive to adapt a system to an individual manager's needs

**concepts and conventions of accounting** are the assumptions, or basic rules, that are applied to accounting procedures. Since 1971 the accountancy profession has issued a series of guidelines to encourage uniformity in the preparation of financial statements.

Until 1990 the guidelines were known as Statements of Standard Accounting Practice (SSAPs). Currently the standards are issued as *International Accounting Standards (IASs)* and *International Financial Reporting Standards (IFRSs)*.

(See *accruals concept, business entity concept, consistency, dual aspect concept, going-concern concept, materiality, money measurement concept, prudence, realisation concept*.)

**conservatism:** see *prudence*

**consignor** is the owner of goods that are sent to an overseas agent to be sold.

**consistency:** once a business adopts a policy for use in recording financial transactions, it should continue to use the same methods in subsequent years. This means that year-on-year figures can be compared, safe in the knowledge that any changes that occur in the results are due to the performance of the business and not to a change in the *accounting policies*.

Changes can be made in policy if the circumstances of the business change. When changes of this nature are made and profits are affected by a material amount, then the effect of the change should be stated clearly in the accounts so that any comparative figures can be adjusted accordingly by the users of the accounts.

**consumer credit** is the means by which customers purchase goods and pay for them later, over a period of time, thus spreading the cost. This is an important method of expanding the customer base of a business. However, it is not without risk, and there is a greater chance of the business incurring bad debts through use of consumer credit.

**Consumer Credit Act 1974:** this regulates the purchase of goods on credit.

**consolidated accounts:** the combination of the *financial statements* of a group of companies.

**consolidated balance sheet:** all resources of a holding company and its *subsidiary companies* are included in a group balance sheet.

**consolidated income statement** shows the profit or loss of a group of companies as if it were a single entity. If the subsidiary company(ies) is wholly owned then the *income* *statement* is added to that of the holding company to form a consolidated income statement.

**consumables:** goods that are used up during the everyday administration of a business, e.g. stationery.

**contingent asset** is a possible asset that arises from a previous event that may or may not be confirmed by a future event not necessarily within the business's control.

**contingent liabilities:** a potential liability which exists when a *balance sheet* is drawn up, the full extent of which is uncertain. The *Companies Act 1985* requires that the following details be given in respect of any contingent liability:
- the amount (or estimated amount) of the liability
- its legal nature
- whether any valuable security has been provided by the company in connection with the liability and if so, what

(See *provisions, contingent liabilities and contingent assets IAS 37.*)

**continuous allotment method:** see *apportionment of reciprocal services*

**continuous operation costing** is used when a number of repetitive processes are needed to produce an end product. An example would be the refining of oil. See *process costing*.

**contra** items occur in a *cash book* when money is paid out of cash takings into a bank or when money is drawn out of a bank and put into the till. Both the debit entry and the credit entry appear in the same book.

The business is neither better nor worse off because of the transaction; it is rather like a person taking a £10 note from their wallet and putting the money in a pocket.

Contra entries are identified by placing a 'C' alongside each entry.

---

**Worked example**

George has cash sales for the day amounting to £834. He pays £750 into the business bank account.

*Required:*

Show how the entries would be entered in the two-column cash book.

*Solution:*

**Cash book**

|            | Cash | Bank |          | Cash | Bank |
|------------|------|------|----------|------|------|
|            | £    | £    |          | £    | £    |
| Cash sales | 834  |      | Bank C   | 750  |      |
| Cash C     |      | 750  |          |      |      |

---

### Worked example

Carol withdraws £4352 from the business bank account in order to have sufficient cash to pay her staff wages the next day.

*Required:*

Show how the entries would be entered in the two-column cash book.

*Solution:*

#### Cash book

|  | Cash £ | Bank £ |  | Cash £ | Bank £ |
|---|---|---|---|---|---|
| Bank C | 4352 |  | Cash C |  | 4352 |
| The following day … |  |  |  |  |  |
|  |  |  | Wages | 4352 |  |

**contract:** a legally binding agreement between two parties.

**contract account:** similar to an *income statement* for a *contract*.

**contracting out:** the use of an external supplier to supply services that were previously provided 'in house'. Many businesses now use agencies to provide administration and pay of wages.

**contribution:** the difference between selling price and *variable costs*. Contribution should correctly be named 'contribution towards *fixed costs* and profit'. It is available to pay the fixed costs of a business; once they are covered, contribution becomes profit.

Contribution can be calculated in total or per unit.

Contribution is a key element in using *marginal costing* as a management tool.

**contribution accounting** focuses on identifying *fixed* and *variable costs* and calculating the total *contribution* generated by a business. The total fixed costs are then deducted to arrive at the net profit.

### Worked example

Gronk Ltd is a small manufacturing business. The following information relates to the year ended 31 May 20*9:

|  | £ |
|---|---|
| Direct wages | 210 000 |
| Direct materials | 100 000 |
| Factory overheads | 80 000 |
| Administration overheads | 60 000 |
| Total sales revenue | 503 000 |

Assume direct wages are a variable cost and that all overheads are fixed costs.

*Required:*

An income statement showing clearly contribution and profit for the year ended 31 May 20*9 for Gronk Ltd.

*Solution:*

**Gronk Ltd income statement for the year ended 31 May 20*9**

|  |  | £ | £ |
|---|---|---:|---:|
| Sales |  |  | 503 000 |
| Less variable costs | – direct wages | 210 000 |  |
|  | – direct materials | 100 000 | 310 000 |
| Contribution |  |  | 193 000 |
| Less fixed costs | – factory overheads | 80 000 |  |
|  | – administrative overheads | 60 000 | 140 000 |
| Profit for the year |  |  | 53 000 |

**contribution costing** values a product by only considering the *variable costs* incurred in its production. It is often used when a business produces a wide variety of products; in such a case the *allocation* and *apportionment of overheads (fixed costs)* and other *overheads* is very difficult.

**contribution graph:** the name given to an alternative presentation of a *break-even chart*. Sales revenue is graphed from the origin as in a traditional break-even chart. *Variable costs* are also graphed from the origin, and then *fixed costs* are built onto the variable costs.

### Worked example

André Baget produces and sells one product – a nont. The following information relates to the production and sales of 25 000 nonts.

|  | £ per unit |
|---|---|
| Selling price | 13 |
| Fixed costs | 6 |
| Variable costs | 3 |

*Required:*

i) a traditional break-even chart for sales of nonts
ii) a contribution break-even chart for sales of nonts

*Solution:*

i)

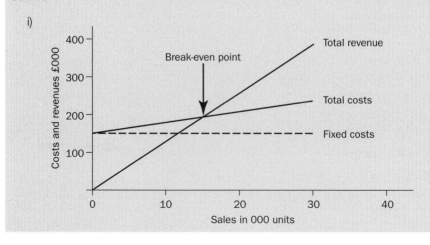

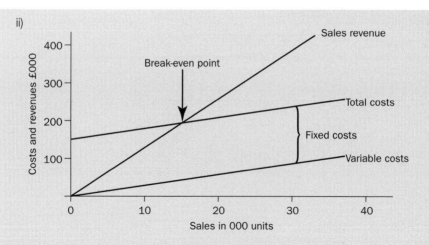

ii)

This graph emphasises the total contribution earned by the product at every level of sales.

**contribution pricing** sets the selling price of a product at a value below total *unit cost* but at one that will cover *variable costs*. As long as the selling price of the product is set at a level that gives a positive *contribution*, short-term profits will increase (or short-term losses will be reduced).

### Worked example

Mitzon & Co. produces gugs which sell at a price of £14 each. Total fixed costs amount to £37 500 per annum. The variable costs of producing a gug are £6.50. The factory currently has spare capacity.

A Korean retailer wishes to purchase 4000 gugs but is only prepared to pay £10 per unit.

#### Required:

Advise the management of Mitzon & Co. whether they should accept or reject the Korean order.

#### Solution:

The order should be accepted; it makes a positive contribution per unit of £3.50.

contribution per unit = selling price per unit   variable costs per unit
$$= £10.00 \quad £6.50$$
$$= £3.50$$

£14 000 (4000 × £3.50) will go towards covering fixed costs. If fixed costs are already covered, then £14 000 extra profit will be earned.

(See *marginal costing*.)

**contribution/sales ratio** expresses *contribution* as a fraction or a percentage of the sales figure. It can be used to find:

- profit at various levels of business activity
- the break-even level of sales

The contribution/sales ratio is calculated using the formula:

FORMULA: $\dfrac{\text{sales} - \text{variable costs (total contribution)}}{\text{sales}}$

### Worked example

Griffiths Ltd produces pilts. The following data refer to the production of 20 000 pilts:

|  | £ |
|---|---|
| Budgeted sales | 720 000 |
| Variable costs | 324 000 |
| Fixed costs | 134 000 |

*Required:*

Calculate:

i) the profit if sales reach £400 000

ii) the break-even point for sales of pilts

*Solution:*

i)  contribution/sales ratio $= \dfrac{\text{sales} - \text{variable costs}}{\text{sales}} = \dfrac{396\ 000}{720\ 000}$

$= 0.55 \text{ or } 55\%$

so contribution is $0.55 \times £400\ 000 = £220\ 000$

profit = contribution − fixed costs

$= £220\ 000 - £134\ 000$

$= £86\ 000$

ii)  break-even sales revenue $= \dfrac{\text{fixed costs}}{\text{c/s ratio}} = \dfrac{£134\ 000}{0.55} = £243\ 637$

**control accounts** are used as a method of checking the accuracy of the entries in the **purchases ledgers** and the **sales ledgers**.

Control accounts are prepared by using totals from the **books of prime entry**. Individual **personal accounts** in the ledgers are prepared from the individual entries in the books of prime entry. Because control accounts and the individual accounts are prepared from the same source, they should agree in every respect.

A control account should be prepared for each sales ledger and each purchases ledger each month. In this way it can be ascertained precisely which ledger(s) contains the error(s) and in which month it(they) occurred.

The balances brought down when the sales ledger control accounts have been prepared should be the same as the totals of the schedule of debtors extracted from all the accounts in the sales ledgers. Similarly, the balances brought down when the purchases ledger control accounts have been prepared should be the same as the totals of the schedule of creditors extracted from all the accounts in the purchases ledgers. If either of these conditions is not satisfied, the matter should be investigated.

## Worked example

The following information has been extracted from the books of Rashid Ltd for the month of August:

| | | £ |
|---|---|---:|
| 1 August | Sales ledger balances | 6 184 |
| | Purchases ledger balances | 4 197 |
| Totals for August: | | |
| | Sales day book | 62 491 |
| | Purchases day book | 51 773 |
| | Returns inwards | 1 067 |
| | Returns outward | 450 |
| | Cheques and cash received from credit customers | 56 415 |
| | Cheques paid to suppliers | 46 004 |
| | Discounts allowed | 764 |
| | Discounts received | 1 570 |
| | Bad debts written off | 143 |
| | Dishonoured cheque | 549 |
| | Balance in sales ledger set off against balance in purchases ledger | 720 |

### Required:

Prepare a sales ledger control account and a purchases ledger control account for the month of August for Rashid Ltd.

### Solution:

**Sales ledger control account for August**

| | | £ | | | £ |
|---|---|---:|---|---|---:|
| 1 August | balances b/d | 6 184 | 31 August | cash and cheques | 56 415 |
| 31 August | credit sales | 62 491 | 31 August | discount allowed | 764 |
| 31 August | dishonoured cheque | 549 | 31 August | returns inward | 1 067 |
| | | | 31 August | bad debts written off | 143 |
| | | | 31 August | transfer to purch. led. | 720 |
| | | | 31 August | balance c/d | 10 115 |
| | | 69 224 | | | 69 224 |
| 1 September | balance b/d | 10 115 | | | |

**Purchases ledger control account for August**

| | | £ | | | £ |
|---|---|---:|---|---|---:|
| 31 August | cheques paid to suppliers | 46 004 | 1 August | balances b/d | 4 197 |
| 31 August | discount received | 1 570 | 31 August | credit purchases | 51 773 |
| 31 August | returns outward | 450 | | | |
| 31 August | transfer from sales ledger | 720 | | | |

|  | | £ | | £ |
|---|---|---|---|---|
| 31 August | balances c/d | 7 226 | | |
| | | 55 970 | | 55 970 |
| | | | 1 September   balances b/d | 7 226 |

Control accounts can be part of the double-entry system (integrated) or they might be used merely as proof of arithmetic accuracy of the ledger. In both cases the control account is prepared in the same way.

The uses of control accounts are as follows:
- location of errors
- help to make fraud more difficult – generally the person preparing the control accounts will not be the same person writing up the ledger
- can give management quick, up-to-date information on total debtors and creditors

**controllable costs:** costs that can be regulated by the manager of a *cost centre*, and for which he/she is responsible. Control of such costs may well form part of a manager's performance criteria. It would be wrong to assess performance on costs that are outside a manager's control – these are known as *non-controllable costs*.

**controlling interest:** this is achieved when more than 50% of the shares in a company are owned by one individual or one organisation. This means that the *shareholder* can always outvote all other shareholders. In reality, powerful influence can be exerted with a much smaller shareholding than 50% of the voting shares.

**control period:** see *budget period*

**convertible loan stock** gives the holder the opportunity to exchange the loan into ordinary shares of a company at some specified time in the future.

**convertible shares:** see *convertible loan stock*

**core activity** is the main activity of the organisation. For example, the core activity of Tesco plc is general retailing, but Tesco now provides many financial services such as insurance, loans etc. The core activity of Ousby Rugby Club is the provision of facilities for rugby players. It might also provide a couple of squash courts, but its core activity is still rugby.

**corporate name:** the name of a large company.

**corporate planning:** see *strategic planning*

**corporation tax:** the tax paid by *limited companies*. All individuals are liable to pay tax on their incomes, after the deduction of certain tax allowances. Since, in the eyes of the law, limited companies are *legal entities*, they too must pay tax on their earnings. A company's taxable profits are its profit for the year before *dividends* and certain costs that attract special tax treatment.

Corporation tax is charged at different rates according to the level of each individual company's profits. Corporation tax rates are set annually in the *Finance Act*.

Companies must pay their *tax liability* nine months after the relevant *accounting period*. If a company pays dividends during the accounting period, then it may be required to pay *advance corporation tax (ACT)*. The balance of the tax due would then normally be paid nine months after the relevant accounting period.

**correction of errors:** when errors in a bookkeeping system are found they must be corrected. Errors in a *double-entry bookkeeping* system should be discovered fairly quickly if the accountant has checked the system on a regular basis. The checks that should be used are as follows:

- the *cash columns* in the *cash book* and *petty cash book* should be checked frequently by comparing *cash in hand* with the actual cash in the till and petty cash float
- the *bank columns* in the cash book should be checked against the bank statements when they are received
- each individual *ledger* should be checked by preparing a *control account* for each ledger each month
- the arithmetic accuracy of the whole double-entry system should be checked by extracting a *trial balance*. Some errors in the system will not be revealed by extracting a trial balance (see *errors not affecting the balancing of a trial balance*).

The *book of prime entry* used when correcting errors is the *journal*.

**cost** is used to value *inventories IAS 2* when this amount is less than net realisable value. Cost is defined as the normal business expenses incurred in bringing the goods (or services) to their present location and condition. It also includes conversion costs.

**cost accounting** is an essential element in the decision-making process of a business. It is a branch of management accounting which records all costs (past costs, present costs and estimated future costs) and uses these as a basis to determine prices, prepare budgets and provide the information necessary to calculate profitability.

**cost-based pricing** does not take into account market conditions when setting the price to charge for a product. Prices are set according to the costs incurred in production.

**cost–benefit analysis** compares the financial and non-financial costs involved, with the financial and non-financial benefits in arriving at a decision as to whether a certain course of action should be taken. See *social accounting*.

**cost centre:** the *CIMA* definition is 'a production or service location, function, activity or item of equipment whose costs may be attributed to *cost units*'.

**cost classification** may be:
- into elements of cost – materials, direct labour, other direct expenses, overheads
- according to function – manufacturing, distribution, selling, administration, financing
- according to whether they are *product costs* (materials, direct labour) or *period costs* (*fixed costs*)
- by behaviour – fixed costs, *variable costs*
- by the amount of control over the costs
- according to whether they are *avoidable* or *unavoidable costs*

For decision-making purposes costs can be classified as:
- *future differential costs*
- *relevant costs*
- *sunk costs*
- *opportunity costs*

**cost coding** uses letters and numbers to describe the cost, and to indicate the cost centre to which the cost relates. It is used when inputting data into a computer program. The cost coding might look like this:

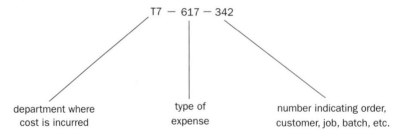

| department where cost is incurred | type of expense | number indicating order, customer, job, batch, etc. |

**cost concept:** assets are normally shown in a *balance sheet* at cost. This is an objective valuation, therefore it removes subjectivity. (But see *asset revaluation*.)

**cost drivers** are activities that cause costs to be incurred.

**cost model** is cost less *accumulated depreciation* and *impairment losses*.

**cost of borrowing:** the interest rate charged by a lender of money.

**cost of capital:** the discounting factor to be used in *net present value* calculations. It is generally based on a weighted average cost of capital available to a business.

In order to make a meaningful comparison between the original investment in a project (or in capital equipment) and the future returns of cash from the investment, there is a need to discount the *cash flows* so that they are equivalent in value to a cash flow now. A comparison of 'like with like' is then possible.

**Worked example**

Victor Abutu Ltd has the following capital structure:

|  | £ |
|---|---|
| Ordinary shares (currently paying a dividend of 10%) | 700 000 |
| 8% preferred (preference) shares | 300 000 |
| 9% debenture stock | 200 000 |
| Bank loan (current rate of interest payable 11%) | 50 000 |

*Required:*

Calculate the weighted average cost of capital for Victor Abutu Ltd

*Solution:*

|  | Nominal value | Rate of return paid per annum | Cost of capital |
|---|---|---|---|
| Ordinary share | 700 000 | 10% | 70 000 |
| Preferred (preference) shares | 300 000 | 8% | 24 000 |
| Debenture stock | 200 000 | 9% | 18 000 |
| Bank loan | 50 000 | 11% | 5 500 |
|  | 1 250 000 |  | 117 500 |

$$\text{average cost of capital} = \frac{\text{cost of capital per annum}}{\text{nominal value of capital}} = \frac{£117\,500}{£1\,250\,000} = 9.4\%$$

This shows that it would cost Victor Abutu Ltd an average of 9.4% to raise the required amount of capital to fund the new project.

*Note:*

This example is correct in principle, but taxation has been ignored in considering interest on debenture stock and bank loan interest. In reality, the £18 000 and £5500 would be reduced by the current rate of corporation tax being paid by Victor Abutu Ltd. Both are tax deductible as income statement expenses.

**cost of goods sold:** also known as *cost of sales.*

**cost of living allowance:** an additional payment given with wages to cover increased living costs due to inflation.

**cost of sales** is deducted from revenue to calculate the gross profit of a business. The cost of sales calculation is:

*FORMULA:*   opening inventory + net purchases – closing inventory = cost of sales

This calculation is necessary because the *income statement* is prepared on the *accruals* basis. The sales generated in the financial period need to be matched with the cost of those same sales. Consider this example:

**Income statement extract for the year ended 30 April 20*9**

| | £ | |
|---|---|---|
| Inventory 1 May 20*8 | 10 740 | These are the goods left in the shop at the end of last year. |
| Purchases | 99 640 | These are the goods purchased to be sold during the year. |
| | 110 380 | These are the goods that we could have sold during the year, but they were not all sold because we have some left … |
| Inventory 30 April 20*9 | 8 450 | … at the end of the year. If we deduct this closing inventory it will tell us the value of our sales … |
| Cost of sales | 101 930 | …but at cost price! |

If the total revenue figure for the year ended 30 April was £200 000 then the business's gross profit was £98 070 (200 000 – 101 930).

**cost pools** group together an organisation's indirect costs and then apportion them to cost centres according to the level of activity within each cost centre.

**cost-plus pricing** takes total *unit cost* of production and adds a percentage on as profit. If the set price makes the product uncompetitive, too few units may be sold to recover total costs out of sales revenue.

**cost-push inflation** is caused when rising costs of production force industries to increase their prices in order to maintain profits.

**cost unit:** a unit of production (or a unit of a service provided) which absorbs the *cost centre's* overhead costs. It could be, for example, a DVD player, a CD or a passenger-mile.

Cost units are often used for comparative purposes. The cost of one unit of production is calculated and can then be compared with alternative production methods or even the purchase of the same unit from a third party.

**cost-volume-profit analysis (CVP):** see *break-even analysis*

**'creative accounting'** is the practice of manipulating figures in the accounts to present a better picture than the correct one. This might be done in order to make a business more attractive to a potential purchaser. It could be done by reducing or cutting out certain expenditure like building maintenance or some advertising expenditure.

**credit** is the right-hand side of an account. An entry on the credit side indicates:

- a decrease in *assets*
- a decrease in *expenses*
- an increase in *liabilities*
- an increase in *revenue*, or
- an increase in *capital*

**credit balance** on an account indicates that the credit side of the account is greater than the debit side. For example:

| An Account | | | |
|---|---|---|---|
| | 31 | 216 | |

The balancing figure is 185. This figure is inserted on the debit side of the account as the balance carried down (c/d)

| An Account | | | |
|---|---|---|---|
| | 31 | 216 | |
| Balance c/d | 185 | | |
| | 216 | 216 | |

At the start of the next accounting period it is shown on the credit side of the account as the balance brought down (b/d)

| An Account | |
|---|---|
| | Balance c/d 185 |

Credit balances in the *purchases ledger* (and sometimes in the *sales ledger*) are creditors.

**credit control:** if a business sells goods on credit, the managers should make sure that the amounts outstanding from individual debtors do not get out of control. This will mean the establishment of a system covering:

- individual credit limits
- collection of outstanding balances
- sending statements and other reminders

Poor credit control will make the working capital position of the business worse and could make the possibility of *bad debts* more likely.

**credit entries** are the entries found on the right-hand side of any ledger account.

**credit limit:** the maximum that a customer can owe at any one time.

**credit management** is an important area of managing *working capital*. Prospective customers' creditworthiness must always be investigated. This type of investigation will, hopefully, minimise problems of debts being outstanding for long periods or even debts having to be written off.

**credit note:** a document that details the amount of the allowance to be made when a purchaser returns faulty goods to the supplier. The credit note is often printed in red and is sent to the customer, who will set it off against the next purchase made. The supplier records the credit note(s) in the *sales returns day book*.

**creditor:** a person or business that is owed money for goods or services supplied on credit. (See *credit sales*.)

**creditors: amounts falling due after one year** is the term used by the *Companies Act 1985* for *non-current liabilities*.

**creditors: amounts falling due within one year** is the term used by the *Companies Act 1985* for *current liabilities*.

**creditors' budget:** see *trade payables budget*

**creditors' ledger:** another name for the *purchases ledger*.

**creditors' payment period:** see *trade payables payment period*

**credit rating:** the amount that a credit rating agency feels that a customer should be allowed to borrow. The agency will research information and keep a history of a person's or business's record of settling debts. This record enables a business to determine whether a new client should be given credit facilities.

**credit sales:** sales made without an immediate payment in cash being made by the purchaser. The entries in the *ledger* are:

| General ledger | | Sales ledger | |
|---|---|---|---|
| **Sales** | | **A Customer** | |
| A Customer | 613 | Sales | 613 |

(See *sales day book*.)

**credit terms:** the time allowed by a supplier before the customer is required to pay for the goods or service received. It is indicated on the invoice and may be related to any *cash discounts* that may be available. An invoice may, for instance, stipulate that an account must be settled within 30 days from issue of the invoice.

**criterion level** sets the minimum and maximum levels of performance that are acceptable to senior managers for any potential investment decision.

### Example

| Management expect | Maximum payback period of | 2 years |
|---|---|---|
| | Minimum accounting rate of return of | 14% |
| | Minimum net present value of | 10% on outlay |
| | Internal rate of return | 18% |

**cum dividend:** the price of a share quoted 'cum dividend' entitles the buyer to the next dividend to be paid.

**cum interest:** the price of a security quoted 'cum interest' entitles the buyer to the next interest payment to be made.

**cumulative preferred (preference) shares:** if a company fails to pay the preferred (preference) *dividend* in any year, the dividend deficiency is carried forward until profits are sufficiently large to pay off the arrears. These arrears are payable before the ordinary shareholders receive a dividend. (See *preference shares*.)

**current account (bank):** a bank account on which a customer of the bank can withdraw money by writing a cheque. The other current account services include:
- transfer of monies by standing order or direct debit
- transfer of monies by credit transfer
- overdraft facilities
- bank loan facilities
- night safe facilities
- banker's draft facilities

**current account (partnership):** see *partnership current accounts*

**current assets** are cash or assets that will be turned into cash in the near future. The term 'current' means within the next twelve months. They are used for the day-to-day expenses of running a business.

Current assets are listed in reverse order of *liquidity*, i.e. with the most difficult to change into cash heading the list, and ending with cash itself. They include:
- *closing inventory* at the end of the *accounting period*
- *trade receivables*
- other receivables on expense accounts (see *prepayments of expenses*), e.g. *business rates* paid in advance
- *cash and cash equivalents* (if cash in hand plus bank balances are positive)

They are sometimes known as trading assets or circulating assets.

**current asset utilisation ratio** measures the efficiency with which the current assets have been used.

$$FORMULA: \quad \text{current asset utilisation ratio} = \frac{\text{sales}}{\text{current account}}$$

**current liabilities** are short-term debts that a business has to pay within the following *accounting period*. They include:
- *trade payables*, for debts incurred in the normal course of trade
- other payables (*accrued expenses*), e.g. wages due but unpaid, rent due but unpaid
- *cash and cash equivalents* (if cash in hand minus bank overdrafts are negative)

In the case of a limited company, current liabilities also include:
- *tax liabilities* – corporation tax for the current year less *ACT*

The term 'current' means within the next twelve months.

**current ratio** compares assets that will become liquid in less than twelve months with liabilities which fall due within the same time period. The current ratio is sometimes called the working capital ratio.

The calculation is:

*FORMULA:* $\dfrac{\text{current assets}}{\text{current liabilities}}$

The ratio is expressed as 'something':1, e.g. 2.3:1. There is no ideal ratio. Generally the ratio should be greater than unity (i.e. greater than 1:1) although some businesses prosper with a ratio of less than unity.

### Worked example

Raymond Yong has the following current assets and current liabilities:

Inventory £12 509, trade receivables £3881, cash and cash equivalents £578, trade payables £3877.

### Required:

Calculate Raymond's current ratio.

### Solution:

Raymond's current ratio = 4.38:1 (12 509 + 3881 + 578 : 3877).

**current replacement price** values assets at their replacement cost to a business. This method of valuation takes into account changes in prices which are specific to the business.

**CVP:** see *break-even analysis*

### Are you studying other subjects?

The *A–Z Handbooks (digital editions)* are available in 14 different subjects. Browse the range and order other handbooks at **www.philipallan.co.uk/a-zonline**.

**data:** information.

**database:** a store of information held in a computer. Once data have been inputted (stored), they are available to be used in any process. For example, when goods are sold on credit, this information will be inputted to the database. It can then be used to:

- update inventory records
- create a **sales invoice**
- debit the customer's account in the **sales ledger**
- debit the sales ledger **control account**
- credit the **sales account** in the **general ledger**
- prepare costings
- prepare management accounts
- prepare statistical information

**data processing:** the organising and processing of information. By using a computer to process data, much detailed, selective information can be obtained quickly from the data bank.

**Data Protection Act 1984** regulates organisations in their use of the information that they hold on computer databases. The Act seeks to guarantee that the personal data stored are accurate, and it gives the individual the right to access his/her personal file.

Organisations holding personal information have to register with the Data Protection Registrar.

**day books:** see **subsidiary books**

**day rates** calculate gross pay by multiplying the hours worked by the wage rate per hour, so if an employee works 38 hours one week and the hourly rate for the job is £6.00, the gross pay for the week is 38 × £6.00 = £228.00. Also known as hourly rates or weekly rates.

**DCF:** see **discounted cash flow**

**debenture discount:** see **discount on debentures**

**debenture interest:** the annual payment made to the holders of **debentures**. This is a fixed payment and is specified in the title, e.g. '8 per cent debentures 2049' (the annual rate of interest to be paid by the **limited company** is 8 per cent). This interest must be paid whether the company makes a profit or a loss. The interest is debited to the **income statement**.

**debenture issue:** the bookkeeping entries are similar to those used for the **issue of shares**. The word 'debenture' should be substituted for the words 'share capital'.

**debentures:** *bonds* recording a long-term loan to a *limited company*. The company pays a fixed rate of interest on debentures. They may be repayable at some date in the future (e.g. '8 per cent debentures 2049' pay 8 per cent interest to the lender and are redeemable in the year 2049) or they may be irredeemable: that is, the holder will only be repaid when the company is liquidated.

Some debentures have the loan secured against specific assets or all of the company's assets; these are known as mortgage debentures. If the company was wound up or the company failed to pay the interest due, the holders of mortgage debentures could sell the assets and recoup the amount outstanding.

**debit** is the left side of an account. An entry on the debit of an account indicates:

- an increase in *assets*
- an increase in *expenses*
- a decrease in *liabilities*
- a decrease in *revenue*, or
- a decrease in *capital*

**debit balance** on an account indicates that the debit side is greater than the credit side. For example:

| An Account | | |
|---|---|---|
| 199 | | 54 |

The balancing figure is 145. This figure is inserted on the credit side of the account as the balance carried down (c/d)

| An Account | | |
|---|---|---|
| 199 | | 54 |
| | Balance c/d | 145 |
| 199 | | 199 |

At the start of the next accounting period it is shown as the balance brought down (b/d) on the debit side of the account.

| An Account | |
|---|---|
| Balance b/d | 145 |

**debit note:** a note sent to a customer when an *invoice* is undercharged. Some customers send debit notes to suppliers when they return goods.

**debt equity ratio** is the ratio of fixed interest-bearing capital to the owners' equity.

It shows the proportion of capital provided by the ordinary shareholders compared to the proportion provided by others.

The calculation is

FORMULA:  $\dfrac{\text{fixed cost capital}}{\text{equity}} \times 100$

which is  $\dfrac{\text{long-term loans} + \text{preference shares}}{\text{issued ordinary shares} + \text{all reserves}} \times 100$

| High geared company | more than 100% | high risk company |
| Neutral gearing | 100% | |
| Low geared company | less than 100% | low risk company |

**debt factoring:** see *factoring*

**debtor:** a person or organisation that owes money to a business.

**debtors' budget:** see *trade receivables budget*

**debtors' ledger:** another name for the *sales ledger.*

**debtors' payment period (collection period):** see *trade receivables payment period*

**deferred income account** is another name used by clubs to record *life membership* subscriptions or *entrance fees.*

**deferred shares:** shares usually issued to the person who started a *limited company.* They often carry a disproportionately large voting right. These shares only receive a *dividend* after all other dividends have been paid.

**del credere agent:** an agent who guarantees the debt incurred by the *consignor* of goods to an overseas customer.

**del credere commission** is the additional high level of commission paid to a *del credere agent.* The agent will also be in receipt of the normal commission paid to an agent. The possibility of the *consignor* incurring a bad debt is therefore reduced by employing a del credere agent.

**delivery note:** a note signed by a purchaser when goods are delivered as proof that the goods have been received. The delivery note is taken back to the accounts department by the carrier and an *invoice* is raised.

**departmental accounts:** see *columnar presentation of income statements*

**departmental budgets** are prepared showing projected income and expenditure for each department. Departmental budgets may form part of an overall system of *budgetary control.*

**depletion method of providing for depreciation:** a method of *depreciation* based on the purchase price of an exhaustible *non-current asset.* It can be used when the value of a physical asset, for example a gravel pit or a quarry, is being reduced in value by an extractive process.

---

**Worked example**

Digem Ltd purchases a limestone quarry for £10 000 000. It is estimated that the quarry contains 2 500 000 tonnes of limestone.

**Required:**

Calculate the annual depreciation charge in a year when 450 000 tonnes of limestone have been extracted from the quarry.

**Solution:**

Depreciation charge for year = £1 800 000 (450 000 tonnes extracted × £4)

Workings: $\dfrac{£10\ 000\ 000}{£2\ 500\ 000} = £4$ per tonne

---

**deposit account:** a bank account in which surplus cash, which is not needed immediately, is deposited. Individuals and businesses can use deposit accounts. Balances attract interest and, theoretically, notice must be given to withdraw money from a deposit account, but banks generally waive the notice required. However, they may penalise the depositor by charging interest on the sum withdrawn. Deposit accounts do not usually carry the right to use a cheque book.

**depreciable amount:** the cost of a *non-current asset* less any expected residual amount.

**depreciation:** the *apportioning* of the cost of a *non-current asset* over its useful economic life. All assets with a finite life should be depreciated (*Companies Act 1985*), so the only asset that is not subject to depreciation is land. The calculation of depreciation should conform to the *accruals* (or matching) *concept* and the *consistency* concept of accounting. (See *property, plant and equipment IAS 16*.)

**despatch note:** a note kept by a storekeeper noting the date on which goods are sent out to a customer. The note is retained in case there is a query regarding the goods.

**destroyer pricing:** see *penetration pricing*

**development costs:** see *intangible assets IAS 38*

**differential costs:** see *future differential costs*

**differential piece work:** see *piece work*

**direct costs** are defined by *CIMA* as 'expenditure which can be economically identified with a specific saleable cost unit'. Examples of direct costs include direct labour charges and direct materials.

**direct debit** is a system that allows a *creditor* to withdraw money from the debtor's bank account. The amount may vary for each withdrawal. The creditor sets an upper limit for the amount to be withdrawn.

For example, Mary Timson allows her telephone company a direct debit mandate with an upper limit of £150. Each quarter the telephone company can withdraw the amount that Mary owes (provided this does not exceed £150).

**direct labour:** workers whose work can be identified clearly with converting raw materials or components into the final product. It might include machine operatives, assembly workers and packers.

**direct labour costs:** the labour costs that are directly attributable to a unit of production. They form part of the *prime cost* in a *manufacturing account*. Direct labour costs are made up of workers' gross pay and related *on-costs*. They can be traced easily to the finished product.

**direct labour cost variance** is the difference between standard *direct labour cost* and actual direct labour cost. The variance is made up of:
- *direct labour efficiency variance*
- *direct labour rate variance*

**Worked example**

A business produces 'clords'. The standard direct labour costs involved in the production of 'clords' were set at 46 hours at a cost of £8.00 per hour. The actual direct labour costs were 50 hours at £7.50 per hour.

### Required:

Calculate:

a) direct labour efficiency variance
b) direct labour rate variance
c) total direct labour cost variance

### Solution:

One way of calculating all three variances is to use the following grid. If you are comfortable using it, you can also apply it to materials and sales.

standard quantity × standard price)
actual quantity × standard price) = quantity variance
actual quantity × actual price = price variance

total variance

So:

$$sq \times sp \quad 46 \times 8.00 = 368.00$$
$$aq \times sp \quad 50 \times 8.00 = 400.00$$
= 32.00 adverse labour efficiency variance
$$aq \times ap \quad 50 \times 7.50 = 375.00$$
= 25.00 favourable wage rate variance

total labour variance                         7.00 adverse

**direct labour efficiency variance** is favourable when the direct workforce saves time and therefore money for a business. A *favourable variance* could be due to:
- higher skilled workers being employed
- workers using good machines suited to the job
- good conditions in the workplace
- good working methods being employed
- good quality control

An *adverse variance* will occur if the opposite conditions apply.

For a worked example, see *direct labour variance*.

**direct labour hour rate method of absorbing overheads:** see *absorption*

**direct labour rate variance:** the difference between the budgeted labour rate and the actual labour rate. This will be adverse when the direct workforce wages are increased (see *adverse variances*). This could be due to:
- use of a more highly skilled workforce
- wage inflation since the standard was set
- overtime or premium rates being paid

A *favourable variance* could be due to workers with a lower level of skill being employed and being paid at a lower rate than the standard.

For a worked example, see *direct labour cost variance*.

**direct material cost variance** is the difference between the standard **direct material cost** and the actual direct material cost. The variance is made up of:
- **direct material usage variance**
- **direct material price variance**

---

### Worked example

A business produces gritos. The standard direct material costs involved in the production of gritos were set at 16 square metres at a cost of £3.00 per square metre. The actual direct material costs were 18 square metres at £2.60 per square metre.

**Required:**

Calculate:

a) the direct material usage variance
b) the direct material cost variance
c) the total direct material cost variance

**Solution:**

Using the grid shown in **direct labour cost variance**:

standard quantity × standard price)
actual quantity × standard price)  } = quantity variance
actual quantity × actual price } = price variance

$$\underline{\text{total variance}}$$

So:

| | £ | £ |
|---|---|---|
| sq × sp  16 × 3.00 = | 48.00 | = 6.00 adverse direct material usage variance |
| aq × sp  18 × 3.00 = | 54.00 | = 7.20 favouable direct material usage variance |
| aq × ap  18 × 2.60 = | 46.80 | |
| total direct material cost variance | | 1.20 favourable |

---

**direct material costs:** the costs involved in the acquisition of materials that can be identified clearly as being part of a finished product. They form part of the prime cost in a *manufacturing account*.

**direct material price variance:** the difference between the budgeted or standard cost of materials and the actual cost of materials used. The variance will be favourable if the materials cost less than was set in the standard, thus saving the business money.
A *favourable variance* could be due to:
- the supplier charging less
- increase in quantity being purchased, so gaining discount for larger orders
- use of a cheaper alternative material
- currency movement if materials were purchased abroad

An *adverse variance* could be due to the opposite conditions applying, plus general or specific inflation.

For a worked example, see *direct material cost variance*.

**direct materials:** the materials that can be identified as being used in a specific product. They might include timber in a furniture manufacturing business, or cloth in clothes manufacturing.

**direct material usage variance** will be favourable if fewer materials are used than was set in the standard, thus saving the business money. A *favourable variance* could be caused by:

- use of better materials than those budgeted for
- use of well-trained workers
- use of good machinery suited to the job

An *adverse variance* could be due to the opposite conditions applying plus:

- theft of materials
- deterioration of materials

For a worked example, see *direct material cost variance*.

**directors** are appointed by, and are accountable to, the *shareholders* of a *limited company*, and help manage the company. Executive directors are actively involved with the day-to-day running of the company. They usually head a large division or section of the company. Non-executive directors are not company employees. They attend *board meetings* but only act as independent advisors.

Although accountable to the shareholders, directors exert a great deal of influence over the affairs of the company because of the diffusion of shares among large numbers of shareholders.

The board of directors reports annually to the shareholders of the company.

**directors' emoluments, directors' fees, directors' remuneration** are all payments made to *directors* of a *limited company* for the work that they do on behalf of the company.

**directors' report:** a summary, prepared by the *directors*, of the main activities undertaken by a business during the year. It is a requirement of the *Companies Act 1985*. It should deal with:

- the principal activities of the company during the year and significant changes in those activities
- *dividend* payments recommended
- future developments in the business of the company
- *research and development* activities of the company
- significant changes in the company's *non-current assets* during the year
- names of directors who have served the company during the year, also their interests in shares or *debentures* in the company
- donations to political parties or charities
- information regarding the health, safety and welfare of the workforce
- policy regarding the employment of disabled persons if the company employs more than 250 people

**discount allowed** may be given to a customer if the outstanding debt is settled in a time specified by the creditor. It is treated as an expense on the *income statement*.

**discount columns of the cash book:** cash discounts allowed to and received by a business are listed in the discount columns of a *cash book*. They are totalled independently. The 'discount allowed' column is then posted to the debit side of the discount allowed account in the *general ledger*. The total of the 'discount received' column is posted from the credit side of the cash book to the credit side of the discount received account in the general ledger.

It may seem that the posting is debit to debit and credit to credit, but clearly this cannot be so in a *double-entry bookkeeping* system. Both discount columns in the cash book are memorandum columns: that is, they are not part of the double-entry system – they are merely there as reminders. The double entry is:

**Debit:** Discount allowed account      **Credit:** The customers' accounts

**Debit:** The suppliers' accounts      **Credit:** Discount received account

**discounted cash flow:** methods of *capital investment appraisal* recognising the *time value of money*. The various methods compare future *net cash flows* which accrue over the life of a project, at their present value, with the value of the initial investment.

(See *payback method of capital investment appraisal*, *internal rate-of-return method of capital investment appraisal*, and *net present value method of capital investment appraisal*.)

**discounted payback method of capital investment appraisal:** see *payback method of capital investment appraisal*

**discount on debentures** allows an investor to purchase *debentures* at a price lower than par. Debentures are usually issued in multiples of £100. If some 9 per cent debentures were to be issued at a 3 per cent discount, the price would be quoted as '9 per cent debentures at 97'.

The total discount on the issue is treated as a capital loss and is shown separately on the *balance sheet* until it is written off.

Interest paid on the debentures is calculated on their nominal value, not their discounted value.

**discount received** might be given by a supplier if the outstanding debt is settled in a time specified by the supplier. It is credited to the *income statement*, thus increasing the *profit for the year* of the business.

**dishonoured cheque:** if a cheque is presented for payment and the *drawer* has insufficient funds in his/her account to cover the cheque, it will be returned to the *payee* marked 'refer to drawer'.

When a supplier (payee) receives a cheque from a customer (drawer) the supplier's *cash book* is debited and the customer's account in the *sales ledger* is credited with the amount of the cheque.

A dishonoured cheque is shown in the debit column of the bank statement. It should be entered in the credit side of the supplier's cash book and the debit side of the customer's account in the sales ledger.

**distributable profits** are the profits of a *limited company* that are available for distribution to the *shareholders* as *dividends*. These are the *revenue reserves*, including the *retained earnings* and the *general reserve*.

**distribution overheads** are the costs involved in storing, packing and sending goods to a customer.

**dividend cover** measures how many times a company's total ordinary *dividend* could have been paid out of the current year's profits after tax and interest. The result gives an indication of the company's potential to maintain dividends in the future.

The calculation is:

$$FORMULA: \quad \frac{\text{profit after tax and interest}}{\text{ordinary dividend paid}}$$

---

**Worked example**

Ginalatti plc has paid an ordinary dividend of £75 000 out of total profits after tax and interest of £460 000.

**Required:**

Calculate the dividend cover for Ginalatti plc.

**Solution:**

$$\text{dividend cover} = \frac{\text{profit after tax and interest}}{\text{ordinary dividend paid}} = \frac{£460\ 000}{£75\ 000} = 6.13 \text{ times}$$

---

**dividends:** the rewards paid to *shareholders* out of the profits of a *limited company*. The dividends are paid to individual shareholders in proportion to the size of their shareholding. They are usually paid annually, but there may be an interim (half-year) dividend.

*Ordinary shares* do not entitle the shareholder to a specific dividend; this will vary according to the level of company profits. Holders of **preferred shares** will normally receive a fixed dividend. In years when profits are too low to pay a dividend, the cumulative preferred (preference) shareholders' dividends accrue until such time as company profits are large enough to pay the arrears.

All dividends are dependent on the availability of:
- profits
- cash to pay the dividends

All dividends paid appear in the *statement of changes in equity* and as a detailed note to the published accounts.

**dividends in the financial statements:** only dividends paid during the year are to be recorded in the financial statements (*events after the reporting period IAS 10*). The final dividend based on the profits reported at the financial year end has to be approved by the *shareholders* at the *AGM*, which usually takes place some weeks after the financial year end, therefore these will include financial statements for the year in which they are paid.

## Worked example

31 December 20*8: Directors propose a total final dividend amounting to £7 500

February/March 20*9: Shareholders approve final proposed dividend at AGM

April/May 20*9: Final dividend £7 500 for year ended 31 December 20*8 paid

August 20*9: Interim dividend for the year ended 31 December 20*9 £2 900 is paid based on reported profits for half year ended 30 June 20*9

31 December 20*9: Directors propose a total final dividend for the year ended 31 December 20*9 of £8 900

*Required:*

Prepare a note to the accounts detailing dividends for the year ended 31 December 20*9.

*Solution:*

Dividends

| Amounts recognised as distributions to equity holders during the year | £ |
|---|---|
| Final dividend for the year ended 31 December 20*8 | 7 500 |
| Interim dividend for year ended 31 December 20*9 | 2 900 |
| | 10 400 |
| Proposed dividend for the year ended 31 December 20*9 | 8 900 |

**dividend yield** measures the actual percentage rate of return that an investor in *ordinary shares* is receiving on the investment made. The calculation is:

FORMULA: $\dfrac{\text{dividend per share}}{\text{market price per share}}$

Investors who require an annual income should compare the yield on many different alternative investment opportunities before committing themselves to one in particular.

## Worked example

Croft plc has an issued ordinary share capital of 500 000 £1 shares.

The total dividend for the year is £140 000. The current market price per share is £4.80.

*Required:*

Calculate the dividend yield on Croft plc's ordinary shares.

*Solution:*

$$\text{dividend per share} = \frac{140\ 000}{500\ 000} = 0.28$$

$$\text{dividend yield} = \frac{\text{dividend per share}}{\text{market price per share}} = \frac{0.28}{4.80} = 5.83\%$$

**divisional reporting** measures the performance of branches, divisions or subsidiaries.

**division of the ledger:** all financial transactions of a business using a *double-entry bookkeeping* system are recorded in the *ledger*. In a small business, it may be feasible to use only one ledger. From a practical point of view, it makes more sense for a larger business to segregate parts of the ledger according to the entries:

- Since the bank and cash accounts are used more frequently than any other accounts, they are kept separate in a **cash book**.
- All credit suppliers' accounts are kept in the **purchases ledger**.
- All credit customers' accounts are kept in the **sales ledger**.
- All real and nominal accounts are kept in the **general ledger**.

In addition, some business people will keep a **private ledger** in which confidential financial information can be recorded, for example **capital accounts**, proprietor's **drawings**, loan accounts, **income statements**.

**donations made:** gifts of money or goods made by limited companies to charities or political parties. Such donations, if material (see **materiality**), must be disclosed as a note to the accounts.

**donations received:** gifts of money or goods given to a club or society. They should be treated in a similar manner to **legacies**, i.e. credit the income and expenditure account unless the donation is material (see **materiality**), in which case the donation should be capitalised and shown separately on the club's balance sheet. Examination candidates will be given instructions as to whether donations should be capitalised (entered on the balance sheet) or not.

**double-entry bookkeeping** requires that there must always be a debit entry and a credit entry when recording financial transactions which affect the business. The system works on the principle that whenever value is given, value must also be received. The system ensures that the **dual aspect concept** of accounting is adhered to.

**draft:** a first copy that will probably need amending or updating before the final copy is produced. For example, a draft income statement may have to be amended in light of some information that was not available when the draft was prepared.

**drawee:** see **cheque**

**drawer:** see **cheque**

**drawings:** the resources that are withdrawn from a business by the proprietor(s) for private use outside the business. Drawings can be cash, goods or services taken from the business. (See **drawings account**.)

**drawings account** is used to record all resources withdrawn from a business by the proprietor(s) for private use. At the end of the **accounting period** the total of the drawings account is transferred to the debit side of the proprietor's **capital account**.

### Worked example

Sahera and Bhupesh are in partnership. The following is a list of the resources they withdrew from the partnership during the year for their own private use:

| | Sahera | Bhupesh |
|---|---|---|
| | £ | £ |
| Cash | 10 463 | 14 761 |
| Goods | 869 | 301 |
| Private telephone calls | 177 | 106 |
| Private motoring expenses | 618 | 799 |
| Tax paid | 3 002 | 3 244 |

*Note:*

Sole traders and partnerships are not legal entities and therefore do not pay tax.

However, the owners of the business do pay tax on their earnings. If they use the business bank account to settle their tax liability to the Revenue and Customs then this is a withdrawal of cash and is therefore drawings.

### Required:

The partnership drawings account showing clearly the transfer to the partners' current accounts.

### Solution:

**Partnership drawings account**

|  | Sahera | Bhupesh |  | Sahera | Bhupesh |
|---|---|---|---|---|---|
|  | £ | £ |  | £ | £ |
| Cash | 10 463 | 14 761 | Current accounts | 15 129 | 19 211 |
| Purchases | 869 | 301 |  |  |  |
| Telephone | 177 | 106 |  |  |  |
| Motor expenses | 618 | 799 |  |  |  |
| Bank – tax | 3 002 | 3 244 |  |  |  |
|  | 15 129 | 19 211 |  | 15 129 | 19 211 |

Remember that the narrative in an account shows where the 'other' entry is.

There is a credit entry in the cash book every time the partners withdrew cash during the year.

There will be two credits in the purchases account (£869 and £301), telephone account (£177 and £106), motor expenses account (£618 and £799) and bank account (£3002 and £3244) in the business cash book.

The total of partners' drawings accounts are transferred to the debit side of the partners' current accounts.

**drawings of goods:** see *goods for own use*

**dual aspect concept (duality)** states that there are always two ways of looking at every accounting transaction. One considers the assets of the business, the other considers the claims against them.

The concept is clearly shown in the accounting equation:

*FORMULA:*

non-current assets + current assets = capital + non-current liabilities + current liabilities

the assets = the claims aganist the assets

The *double-entry bookkeeping* system ensures that the concept is upheld.

**E & O E** is the abbreviated form of 'errors and omissions excepted'. This is generally printed on an *invoice* to indicate that the business issuing the invoice takes no responsibility for any mistakes printed on the invoice.

**earnings per share IAS 33** measures the amount of profits earned by a company attributable to each issued share. It is widely used by investors or potential investors as a measure of a company's performance. It can be used to compare:

- the results of one particular company over a number of years
- the performance of one company's *ordinary shares* against the performance of another company's ordinary shares
- the earnings against the return obtainable from alternative investments

It is also used as part of the *price/earnings ratio* of a *limited company*.

The standard applies only to companies listed on a recognised *stock exchange*. It is calculated using the profit attributable to ordinary shareholders after tax, minority interest, extraordinary items, *preferred share* dividends, and other appropriations in respect of preferred shares. The calculation is:

$$FORMULA: \quad \text{earnings per share} = \frac{\text{earnings in pence}}{\text{number of issued ordinary shares}}$$

---

**Worked example**

Pomfret plc has an issued capital of 10 000 000 ordinary shares of 50 pence each. Profits for the year after tax amounted to £1 751 000. Preferred (preference) share dividends for the year are £600 000.

*Required:*

Calculate the earnings per share for Pomfret plc.

*Solution:*

$$\text{earnings per share} = \frac{\text{earnings in pence}}{\text{number of issued ordinary shares}}$$
$$= \frac{175\ 100\ 000 - 60\ 000\ 000}{10\ 000\ 000} = 11.51 \text{ pence}$$

---

**economic order quantity** attempts to calculate the most cost-effective quantity of goods to order from a supplier. The calculation attempts to find a compromise between the cost saving made by ordering large quantities and the extra costs incurred when holding large quantities of inventory.

It is more cost effective to order large quantities of goods from a supplier. It involves lower administration costs and lower delivery charges, but the costs of holding large inventory are obviously greater than the costs involved in holding smaller levels of goods.

The calculation is:

$$\text{FORMULA:} \quad \frac{\text{economic order}}{\text{quantity}} = \left( \frac{2 \times \text{annual consumption} \times \text{cost per order}}{\text{annual holding cost per item}} \right)$$

**efficiency variance:** see *labour efficiency variance*

**elasticity of demand:** see *price elasticity of demand*

**elasticity of supply:** see *price elasticity of supply*

**elements of cost** are the individual costs that make up the final cost of the product. They are:
- manufacturing costs
- distribution costs
- selling costs
- administration costs
- research and development costs

Each of these can be further subdivided into their component parts (elements).
The elements of cost within the manufacturing process are:
- raw materials
- direct labour costs
- other direct expenses
- manufacturing royalties
- factory overheads

**elimination method of apportioning overhead costs of reciprocal service departments:** see *apportionment of reciprocal services*

**employee buy out:** the purchase of a business by its employees.

**entertainment allowance:** additional cash given to staff to enable them to entertain prospective customers.

**entity concept:** see *business entity concept*

**entrance fees** are often charged when a member first joins a club. Since these fees are 'extraordinary' they should not be entered in the annual *income and expenditure account*. The fees should be credited to an entrance fees account which is capitalised. Each year a proportion of the account should be transferred to the annual income and expenditure account.

### Worked example

The Bunkerhill golf club charges new members an entrance fee of £500 when they join the club. The club committee transfers each member's entrance fee to the club income and expenditure account over a five-year period.

During the year ended 30 April 20*9 entrance fees paid by new members amounted to £6500. The balance on the entrance fees account at 1 May 20*8 was £23 700. The amount to be transferred to the club income and expenditure account for the year ended 30 April 20*9 is £6040.

*Required:*

The entries in the income and expenditure account and entrance fees account of the Bunkerhill golf club for the year ended 30 April 20*9.

*Solution*:

**Bunkerhill golf club income and expenditure account for the year ended 30 April 20*9**

| Income: | £ |
|---|---|
| Entrance fees | 6 040 |

**Entrance fees account**

| | £ | | £ |
|---|---|---|---|
| I & E account | 6 040 | Balance b/d | 23 700 |
| Balance c/d | 24 160 | Cash | 6 500 |
| | 30 200 | | 30 200 |
| | | Balance b/d | 24 160 |

**entrepreneur:** a person who is prepared to take the risk of starting a new project or starting up a new business when the opportunity presents itself.

**EPS:** see *earnings per share*

**equity accounting** is the term used to describe the accounting methods used to deal with an *associated undertaking*.

**equity share capital:** the name given to the *ordinary share capital* and permanent *preferred share* capital of a *limited company*. (Note: redeemable preferred shares are non-permanent shares and so are not part of equity share capital.)

**error of commission:** see *errors not affecting the balancing of the trial balance*

**error of omission:** see *errors not affecting the balancing of the trial balance*

**error of original entry:** see *errors not affecting the balancing of the trial balance*

**error of principle:** see *errors not affecting the balancing of the trial balance*

**errors:** see *errors not affecting the balancing of the trial balance*

**errors not affecting the balancing of the trial balance** are mistakes in the *double-entry bookkeeping* system which do not alter the debit and credit totals of the *trial balance*. They can be listed under the headings:
- complete reversal of entries – the account that should have had the debit entry has been credited and the account that should have had the credit entry has been debited
- error of commission – entries are debited or credited to the wrong account
- error of omission – no entry is made in any account

- error of original entry – an error is made transferring the amount from the source document to the *book of prime entry*
- error of principle – entries are debited or credited in the wrong class of account
- compensating error – error(s) on the debit side of an account(s) equals error(s) on the credit side of account(s)

### Worked example

The following errors have been discovered in the books of Josie Chan:

i) £137 goods sold to Fiona have been debited to sales account and credited to Fiona

ii) Rent paid £700 has been debited to the rates account

iii) £1270 insurance premium paid by cheque has not been entered in the books of account

iv) A purchase invoice from Tashara £963 has been entered in the purchases day book as £936

v) Service charges for the vehicle fleet £6450 have been entered in the vehicles account

vi) Rent received £600 per quarter has been totalled as £2300. The following accounts have been undercast: wages by £34; stationery by £28; drawings by £38.

*Required:*

The journal entries necessary to correct the errors in Josie's books of account.

*Solution:*

**Journal**

| Type of error | | Dr | Cr |
|---|---|---|---|
| (not part of the answer) | | £ | £ |
| i) Reversal of entries | Fiona | 274 | |
| | Sales | | 274 |
| ii) Error of commission | Rent | 700 | |
| | Rates | | 700 |
| iii) Error of omission | Insurance | 1270 | |
| | Bank | | 1270 |
| iv) Error in original entry | Purchases | 27 | |
| | Tashara | | 27 |
| v) Error of principle | Motor expenses | 6450 | |
| | Vehicles | | 6450 |
| vi) Compensating errors | Wages | 34 | |
| | Stationery | 28 | |
| | Drawings | 38 | |
| | Rent received | | 100 |

Remember the journal is a book of prime entry – the above entries should now be posted to the correct ledger accounts.

**estimates** are given to a customer who wishes to know what a job will cost. The supplier of the goods (or service) will prepare a costing based on the likely expenditure on labour, materials, other direct costs and overheads.

**even production flow** ensures that a business can keep its resources employed at the same level throughout the year. With an uneven production flow it may be necessary for a manufacturing business to put its workforce on short time or even dismiss a number of workers when fewer goods need to be produced. (See *production budget*.)

**events after the reporting period IAS 10:** the standard recognises that there may be events that take place after the annual financial statements have been prepared and the time when the statements have been authorised for issue.

Changes can be made only in the period between the balance sheet date and the date of authorisation. After authorisation for issue no alterations can be made.

Adjusting events – these provide evidence of conditions that existed at the financial year end. If the amount(s) involved is material then the amount(s) shown in the financial statements must be changed. E.g. where a credit customer has become insolvent after the balance sheet date and the large debt is included in the year end trade receivables.

Non-adjusting events – are conditions that arose after the financial year end. No adjustment is necessary. However, if an event is material then it should be disclosed by way of a note to the accounts. The note would explain the likely financial consequences of the event, e.g. significant expansion plans contracted into after the financial year end.

Note: Proposed dividends are recognised as a non-adjusting event and as such are shown as a note to the financial statements.

**exceptional items** are items that are part of a company's normal trading activities but stand out because of their size.

**exception reporting** highlights only items that deviate adversely from the budgeted norm. It means that efforts can be concentrated on the areas which cause concern.

**excess of expenditure over income** is the term used in the *income and expenditure account* of a non-profit-making organisation in place of the term 'loss'.

**excess of income over expenditure** is the term used in the *income and expenditure account* of a non-profit-making organisation in place of the term 'profit'.

**exchange of debentures** occurs when *debentures* in a *holding company* are given in exchange for the debentures in the *subsidiary company* it has taken over.

**expenditure** is the value of resources an organisation has used in the *acquisition* of goods or services during an *accounting period*. Expenditure is calculated using the *accruals concept*. It measures actual economic activity. For example, Vanessa rents a small shop for £65 per week. She has not yet paid the rent for this week, yet her expenditure on rent for this week is £65. (See *expenses*.)

**expenses** are the cash payments made to acquire goods and services during an *accounting period*. The cash paid could relate to previous, present or future accounting periods. For example, Helen rents a small office for £50 per week. She pays this week's rent and the rent she owes for last week. The expense for rent is £100; the *expenditure* is £50 per week.

**extended trial balance** incorporates into the *trial balance* format all the adjustments that are necessary before the preparation of a business's *financial statements*. The use of the extended trial balance is now common in accountancy firms. It ensures that all adjustments that take place after the trial balance has been extracted from the business's *ledger* are incorporated into the **financial statements** using double entries.

The extended trial balance is a working document on which all post-balance-sheet adjustments are made. It should be emphasised that there is no one specific layout. Users of the extended trial balance can adapt it to suit their own needs. For examination purposes, students are advised to consult past papers to familiarise themselves with the layout favoured by particular examination boards.

m

### Worked example

The following trial balance was extracted from the books of T Trout at 31 December 20*9:

|  | Dr | Cr |
|---|---|---|
|  | £ | £ |
| Non-current assets | 120 000 | |
| Capital | | 73 550 |
| Drawings | 17 000 | |
| Sales | | 172 000 |
| Purchases | 97 000 | |
| Rent | 6 300 | |
| Insurance | 1 750 | |
| Other expenses | 43 250 | |
| Provision for depreciation of non-current assets | | 50 000 |
| Provision for doubtful debts | | 850 |
| Trade receivables | 6 000 | |
| Trade payables | | 7 500 |
| Inventory 1 January 20*9 | 11 200 | |
| Cash and cash equivalents | 1 200 | |
| Suspense | 200 | |
| | 303 900 | 303 900 |

Since the trial balance was extracted, two errors have been discovered:

i)   the rent account has been undercast by £200

ii)  a £5000 non-current asset had been debited in error to 'other expenses' account

*Additional information:*

iii) inventory at 31 December 20*9 was valued at £13 400

iv) rent £1500 was owed at 31 December 20*9

v)   insurance £250 was paid in advance at 31 December 20*9

vi) non-current assets are to be depreciated at the rate of 10% per annum on cost

vii) provision for doubtful debts is to be increased to £900

### Required:

An extended trial balance at 31 December 20*9 for T Trout.

*Solution:*

## T Trout Extended Trial Balance

| | Trial balance as at 31 Dec 19*7 | | Adjustments | | Accruals prepayments | | Income statement | | Balance sheet | |
|---|---|---|---|---|---|---|---|---|---|---|
| | DR | CR | DR | CR | DR | CR | DR | CR | DR | CR |
| Non-current assets | 120 000 | | 5 000 | | | | | | 125 000 | |
| Capital | | 73 550 | | | | | | | | 73 550 |
| Drawings | 17 000 | | | | | | | | 17 000 | |
| Sales | | 172 000 | | | | | | 172 000 | | |
| Purchases | 97 000 | | | | | | 97 000 | | | |
| Rent | 6 300 | | 200 | | 1 500 | | 8 000 | | | |
| Insurance | 1 750 | | | | | 250 | 1 500 | | | |
| Other expenses | 43 250 | | | 5 000 | | | 38 250 | | | |
| Prov. for dep. of non-current assets | | 50 000 | 12 500 | 12 500 | | | 12 500 | | | 62 500 |
| Prov. for DD | | 850 | 50 | 50 | | | 50 | | | 900 |
| Trade receivables | 6 000 | | | | | | | | 6 000 | |
| Trade payables | | 7 500 | | | | | | | | 7 500 |
| Inventory 1 Jan 19*7 | 11 200 | | | | | | 11 200 | | | |
| Bank | 1 200 | | | | | | | | 1 200 | |
| Suspense | 200 | | | 200 | | | | | | |
| | 303 900 | 303 900 | | | | | | | | |
| Inventory 31 Dec 19*7 | | | 13 400 | 13 400 | | | | 13 400 | 13 400 | |
| Accruals/Prepayments | | | | | 1 500 | 250 | | | 250 | 1 500 |
| Net Profit | | | | | | | 16 900 | | | 16 900 |
| | | | 31 150 | 31 150 | 1 500 | 250 | 185 400 | 185 400 | 162 850 | 162 850 |

**Equality and Human Rights Commission:** an organisation set up by the government to prevent *discrimination* on grounds of age, disability, gender, race, religion and sexual orientation. It also deals with human rights issues.

**external sources of finance:** cash resources obtained from agencies outside a business. This may be done by:
- selling shares
- selling *debentures*
- borrowing from financial institutions, both long and short term
- *factoring*
- obtaining grants from the government or the European Community

**ex works:** price does not include delivery costs – the purchaser must bear this cost. This item would appear as *carriage inwards* and should be added to the purchases of raw materials in the purchaser's *manufacturing account* or added to the purchases figure in the *income statement* of a retail outlet.

**Do you need revision help and advice?**

Go to pages 259–72 for a range of revision appendices that include plenty of exam advice and tips.

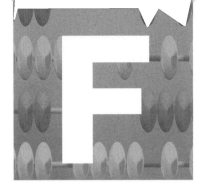

**factoring** is a service whereby a debt factor will take over the responsibility for the collection of monies owed to a business. A fee is charged for this service and is deducted from the debts recovered before payment is made to the debtor. This service is designed to improve the **cash flow** of a business. The factor might provide:

- sales accounting – including maintaining the **sales ledger**, invoicing, sending out statements and collecting the debt
- credit management facilities – including assessment of customers' creditworthiness
- finance against **sales invoices** – the factor will pay a large percentage of the total on issue of the sales invoice, with the balance being paid when the debtor settles the invoice

Factoring avoids valuable cash resources being tied up in allowing credit to customers. It guarantees a regular cash flow, and can save money that would normally have been spent on administration costs.

This service should not be confused with **invoice discounting**.

**factory overhead expenses** are costs incurred in the manufacturing process. They are also known as **indirect costs** which cannot be identified easily with the product being produced. (See also **overheads**.)

**factory profit:** see **manufacturing accounts**

**fair value:** the amount that could be obtained from the sale of a **non-current asset** in a transaction between informed and consenting parties in an **at arm's length** transaction. (See **impairment of assets IAS 36**.)

**favourable variances** occur when actual results are better than the results predicted in a budget. If the actual results increase the profit that has been predicted in the budget, the variance is said to be a favourable variance. If, however, the variance reduces the profit that was predicted in the budget, then the variance is adverse.

Favourable variances arise when:

- actual revenue is greater than budgeted revenue, or
- actual expenditure is less than budgeted expenditure

(See **variances**.)

**fictitious assets** are assets that have no resale value, but are entered on the balance sheet. An example would be prepayments.

**FIFO:** see **methods of inventory valuation**

**final accounts:** see **financial statements**

**Finance Act** is an Act of Parliament which confers, on the government of the day, the power to raise taxes. It is based on the Budget proposed each year by the Chancellor of the Exchequer.

**financial accounting** is the recording and presentation of business transactions in order to supply information to the owners of a business on the performance of their investment.

**Financial Services Act (1986)** is the Act of Parliament which regulates the financial services industry in its dealings with the general public.

**Financial statements** is the name given to the income statement and balance sheet of a business. *Manufacturing accounts* are also included in the term in the case of a business that produces its own goods for resale.

Some people also include the *balance sheet* as part of the final accounts. Technically, this is incorrect since the balance sheet is not an account, it is a compilation of the balances outstanding in the *books of account* at the business's financial year end.

**Financial statements of limited companies** are:
- an *income statement* – income statements of limited companies show the financial performance over a financial year
- a *balance sheet* – balance sheets of limited companies show the financial position at a particular date (usually the end of the financial year)
- a *statement of changes in equity* – showing the changes to share capital and reserves during the financial year
- *a statement of cash flows IAS 7* – showing changes in the financial position during the financial year
- notes explaining accounting policies and other relevant information

**financial year** is a twelve-month period for which a business prepares its *income statements*. The financial year can start at any date during the year.

**first-in-first-out method of inventory issue (FIFO):** see methods of *inventory* valuation

**fixed assets:** see *non-current assets*

**fixed budgets** remain unchanged in the short run whatever output is achieved by the organisation.

**fixed capital accounts** do not change by the introduction of profits from the *partnership income statement*. They remain fixed from year to year, unless there is a deliberate injection of new capital by a partner, or if a partner has the permission of other partners to withdraw capital.

Fixed capital accounts are almost a necessity if the partnership agreement allows the partners to be credited with interest on capital as part of their profit share.

Interest on fixed capital accounts is an appropriation of profits and should be credited to the partners' current accounts.

**fixed charge on the assets** means that *non-current liabilities* (e.g. *debentures*) have as their security certain named assets of the company. This means that if the company were to go into *liquidation* the proceeds from the sale of the specific asset(s) would first of all be used to pay off the debenture holders. Any surplus remaining would be used to help pay any other creditors of the company.

**fixed costs** are costs which do not change with levels of a business's activities. They are also called *period costs*, as they are time based. Examples include indirect wages of supervisors, rent and rates. In the long run, fixed costs can change: for example, the supervisory staff may get a pay rise, the landlord may put up the rent, the local authority may charge more for business rates.

**fixed overheads** are also known as *fixed costs.*

**fixed production overhead variance** shows the difference between the budgeted fixed production overhead and the actual fixed production overhead. Fixed production overheads are *fixed costs* incurred in a factory. These costs are absorbed into the product by using:

- a direct labour hour rate
- a direct labour cost rate, or
- a machine hour rate

(See *absorption*.)

The fixed production overhead variance has two subvariances:

- fixed production overhead expenditure variance, calculated as:

*FORMULA:*  budgeted fixed production overhead − actual fixed production overhead

- fixed production overhead volume variance, calculated as:

*FORMULA:*  standard absorbed cost − budgeted fixed production overhead

**flexible budgets** recognise that cost patterns may vary according to levels of activity. A *fixed budget* approach to *variable costs* can give very misleading results.

One of the aims of a standard costing system is that it should highlight areas of good practice and areas where problems are occurring. A standard costing system makes comparisons between standard costs and the costs actually incurred. It is always important when making comparisons of any description that like is compared with like. Standard costs need to be flexed in order to make valid comparisons.

**Worked example**

The manager of a business had budgeted to produce 480 000 pairs of trainers in a year. The standards set were:

square metres of material: 88 000          labour hours to be used: 12 000

The actual number of trainers produced was 420 000 pairs. Actual materials used were 85 000, and actual labour hours worked were 10 100.

*Required:*

A calculation to determine whether the business has been efficient in the use of materials and labour.

*Solution:*

Since the business produced only 7/8 of the trainers set in the standard (420 000/480 000), one could reasonably expect that only 7/8 of the materials set in the standard would be used and that only 7/8 of the labour hours set in the standard would be needed to complete the work.

So 7/8 × 88 000 = 77 000 m² of materials should have been used.

In fact 85 000 m² were used, so 8000 m² of materials have been wasted.

Similarly, 7/8 of the standard labour hours should have been used.
7/8 × 12 000 = 10 500 hours of labour.

In fact only 10 100 hours were used, so the labour force has been more efficient.

Standards should always be flexible to take into account variations in production levels.

**floating charge on the assets** means that *debentures* have as their security unspecified assets. If a company were to go into *liquidation*, proceeds from the sale of the assets would be used to pay the debenture holders.

**fluctuating capital accounts** show the amount of capital invested by each partner together with all residual profits and losses accrued to them. The accounts are credited with profits due to each partner, as calculated in the *income statement*.

### Worked example

Yusef and Mandy are in partnership. Their capital account balances on 1 June 20*8 are Yusef £45 000; Mandy £32 000. Their partnership agreement allows Mandy a partnership salary of £2000 per annum; it allows interest on capital of 8% per annum calculated on the balance at the start of the financial year; residual profits are to be shared in the ratio of 2:1 respectively. The profit for the year ended 31 May 20*9 was £52 400.

Partnership drawings for the year were Yusef £19 740; Mandy £ 17 891. The partnership maintains fluctuating capital accounts.

### Required:

i) an extract from the partnership income statement showing the appropriation of profit for the year ended 31 May 20*9

ii) the partnership capital accounts at 31 May 20*9

### Solution:

i) **Yusef and Mandy income statement extract for the year ended 31 May 20*9**

|  |  |  | £ |
|---|---|---|---|
| Net profit |  |  | 52 400 |
| Less salary | – Mandy |  | 2 000 |
|  |  |  | 50 400 |
| Less interest on capital | – Yusef | 3 600 |  |
|  | – Mandy | 2 560 | 6 160 |
|  |  |  | 44 240 |
| Share of residual profits | – Yusef | 29 493 |  |
|  | – Mandy | 14 747 | 44 240 |

ii)

| | Yusef | Mandy | | Yusef | Mandy |
|---|---|---|---|---|---|
| | £ | £ | | £ | £ |
| Drawings | 19 470 | 17 891 | Balances b/d | 45 000 | 32 000 |
| | | | Salary | | 2 000 |
| | | | Interest on capital | 3 600 | 2 560 |
| Balance c/d | 58 623 | 33 416 | Share of profits | 29 493 | 14 747 |
| | 78 093 | 51 307 | | 78 093 | 51 307 |
| | | | Balances b/d | 58 623 | 33 416 |

Capital accounts

**FOB (free on board)** is seen on import and export *invoices* indicating that the quoted price does not include shipping costs. All expenses are paid by the supplier only until the goods are on board.

**FOB shipping point** appears on import and export *invoices* and means that the supplier pays all costs until the goods are taken off the ship in the country of destination. The customer then pays any further transportation costs.

**folio columns** are an aid to help find the other account in the *double-entry bookkeeping* system. A ledger account is laid out like this:

| Date | Details | Folio | Amount | Date | Details | Folio | Amount |
|---|---|---|---|---|---|---|---|
| | | | £ | | | | £ |
| 3 Jan | Cash | * cb 12 | 176 | 21 Dec | Purchases | **gl 31 | 180 |
| 3 Jan | Disc Rec | ***gl 9 | 4 | | | | |

| Other entries | * | credit entry | cash column | cb 12 | cash book page 12 |
|---|---|---|---|---|---|
| | ** | debit entry | purchases account | gl 31 | general ledger page 31 |
| | *** | credit entry | discount received account | gl 9 | general ledger page 9 |

**folios** are the numbers on the pages of *books of account*.

**foreign exchange reserve:** a *revenue reserve* set aside out of profits to guard against a loss incurred through the devaluation of a foreign currency. The bookkeeping entries to record this transfer are:

**Debit:** Income statement      **Credit:** Foreign exchange reserve

**forfeiture of shares** takes place when a *shareholder* fails to pay the calls on the shares purchased when they fall due. It is now extremely rare. A shareholder who could not afford to pay the calls would normally sell the partly paid shares and the purchaser would then become liable for the calls.

When shares are forfeit, the shares are cancelled and, provided the company's *Articles of Association* do not prevent it, the company may reissue them. The original shareholder will lose any monies that have been paid. The bookkeeping entries can be followed in the worked example below.

Note: this is no longer assessed by all examination bodies, therefore you should check your syllabus to determine whether your course requires knowledge of this procedure.

## Worked example

Lemmon plc is issuing 40 000 ordinary shares of £1 each, payable 10p on application, 20p on allotment, 30p on first call and 40p on final call. Applications are received with the appropriate monies. All allotment monies are received on the due date.

Bert Hinkle, the holder of 400 shares, fails to pay the first and final calls. His shares are forfeit. Later the shares are reissued to Lesley Peacock at 90p per share. She pays in full for the shares.

### Required:

The journal entries (including cash transactions) to record the share issue, the forfeiture and the reissue of the shares in the books of Lemmon plc.

### Solution:

### Journal

| | Dr £ | Cr £ |
|---|---|---|
| Cash | 4 000 | |
| Application and allotment | | 4 000 |
| Cash | 8 000 | |
| Application and allotment | | 8 000 |
| Application and allotment | 12 000 | |
| Ordinary share capital | | 12 000 |
| Cash | 11 880 | |
| First call | | 11 880 |
| First call | 12 000 | |
| Ordinary share capital | | 12 000 |
| Forfeit shares | 120 | |
| First call | | 120 |
| Cash | 15 840 | |
| Final call | | 15 840 |
| Final call | 16 000 | |
| Ordinary share capital | | 16 000 |
| Forfeit shares | 160 | |
| Final call | | 160 |
| Ordinary share capital | 400 | |
| Forfeit shares | | 400 |
| Lesley Peacock | 400 | |
| Ordinary share capital | | 400 |
| Cash | 360 | |
| Lesley Peacock | | 360 |

| | | |
|---|---|---|
| Forfeit shares | 40 | |
| Lesley Peacock | | 40 |
| Forfeit shares | 80 | |
| Share premium | | 80 |

**formation expenses:** expenses incurred by a company when it comes into existence. They must be written off in a company's first *accounting period*.

**forward buying:** the purchase of materials, commodities or currency to be delivered at some date in the future.

**founders shares** are also known as *deferred shares*.

**free on board:** see *FOB*

**fringe benefits** are items given to employees in addition to their salary or wage. The benefits could include a company car, private medical insurance, etc. Sometimes colloquially called 'perks'.

**full-cost pricing** allocates all manufacturing costs to products. It also values unsold inventory of finished goods at their total cost of manufacture. Full-cost pricing is also known as *absorption costing*.

**functional budget:** the budget relating to a particular function. For example, the *production budget*.

**future differential costs:** costs which 'belong' to a project and would be avoided if the project were not undertaken. These should be the only costs considered when deciding between two or more alternative strategies.

**Are you studying other subjects?**

The *A–Z Handbooks (digital editions)* are available in 14 different subjects. Browse the range and order other handbooks at **www.philipallan.co.uk/a-zonline**.

**Garner v Murray (1904)** rule applies if one or more partners are unable to settle their debt to a *partnership* after dissolution. Any debit balance occurring on a *partnership capital account* after dissolution should be settled by the partner(s) introducing money from private resources outside the business. If the partner(s) is unable to do this because of his/her insolvency, the deficiency is to be shared between the other partners in the ratio of the balances in their capital accounts shown in the last *partnership balance sheet*.

### Worked example

George, Harriet and Iris were in partnership, sharing profits and losses in the ratios 3:2:1 respectively. The partnership was dissolved. After the realisation of all the partnership assets the following balances remained in the partnership books:

|  |  | Dr | Cr |
|---|---|---|---|
|  |  | £ | £ |
| Capitals | George |  | 26 432 |
|  | Harriet | 6 340 |  |
|  | Iris |  | 14 884 |
| Bank balance |  | 34 976 |  |

Harriet was unable to settle any part of her deficiency on capital account.
Before dissolution the capital account balances were:

|  |  |
|---|---|
| George | 50 000 |
| Harriet | 2 000 |
| Iris | 30 000 |

### Required:

A calculation showing how the deficiency on Harriet's capital account is cleared.

### Solution:

George will have to bear $\dfrac{£50\ 000}{£50\ 000 + 30\ 000} \times £6340 = £3962.50$

Iris will have to bear $\dfrac{£30\ 000}{£50\ 000 + 30\ 000} \times £6340 = £2377.50$

**gearing** is the ratio of fixed interest bearing capital to the company's total capital. It shows the proportions of capital provided by the owners of a business and the proportions provided by others. The calculation is:

$$FORMULA: \quad \frac{\text{fixed-cost capital}}{\text{total capital}}$$

which is:

$$\frac{\text{long-term loans} + \text{preferred shares}}{\text{issued ordinary share capital} + \text{all reserves} + \text{long-term loans} + \text{preferred shares}}$$

| More than 50 % | Less than 50% |
| --- | --- |
| High geared companies | Low geared companies |
| High debt | Low debt |
| High risk | Low risk |

### Worked example

The following balances have been extracted from the books of account of two separate businesses:

|  | Gooi plc | Tomkins plc |
| --- | --- | --- |
|  | £000 | £000 |
| Ordinary shares | 1000 | 60 |
| Reserves | 980 | 110 |
| Preferred (preference) shares | 450 | |
| 8% debentures | 300 | 50 |
| Long-term bank loan | | 250 |

*Required:*

Calculate the gearing ratio for Gooi plc and Tomkins plc.

*Solution:*

$$\text{Gooi plc} = \frac{450 + 300}{1000 + 980 + 450 + 300} = \frac{750}{2730} \times 100 = 27.47\%: \text{low geared}$$

$$\text{Tomkins plc} = \frac{50 + 250}{60 + 110 + 50 + 250} = \frac{300}{470} \times 100 = 63.8\%: \text{high geared}$$

A company with a high proportion of fixed interest, long-term capital (high geared) must service the debt whatever its profit level. In times when the company earns good profits, a highly geared company will have few problems servicing the debt, but when profits are low (or negative) the fixed return funding has still to be serviced and this may put the future of the company at risk.

**gearing ratio:** see *gearing*

**general ledger** contains all impersonal ledger accounts. Entries in *personal accounts* are recorded in the *sales* and *purchases ledgers*. In practice, some accounts that should be in the general ledger are kept separately. For example, the cash account and the bank account might be kept in the *cash book* because they are used so frequently. Also, a business person may keep his/her capital account, loan accounts and drawings accounts in a *private ledger* to which he/she alone has access.

General ledger accounts can be classified into:

- *real accounts* – the accounts where transactions dealing with **tangible non-current assets** are recorded, e.g. land and buildings, vehicles
- *nominal accounts* – where revenues and expenses are recorded, e.g. wages, rent, etc.

The general ledger is called the *nominal ledger* in computer programs.

**general reserve:** a *revenue reserve* appropriated from profits to strengthen the financial position of a company. The bookkeeping entries to record this transfer are:

**Debit:** Income statement                    **Credit:** General reserve

**going-concern concept** states that a business is assumed to be continuing in existence for the foreseeable future. *Presentation of financial statements IAS 1* names this as a fundamental accounting concept (see *accounting concepts and conventions*).

The major consequence of the going-concern concept is that assets are valued at cost (see *IAS 16*), not what they would fetch if sold (as a going concern, a business will need its assets and is therefore not going to sell them).

**going-rate pricing** means that a business may be a price taker where large numbers of producers are selling a very similar product. No one producer is large enough to dominate the market and be able to set a higher price.

In a market dominated by a price leader, the smaller producer(s) may have to accept a price for the product that is lower than that dictated by the leader.

**goods available for resale** is calculated by adding the business's *opening inventory* to the purchases made during the period under review.

---

**Worked example**

Walter Hamilton provides you with the following information.

|  | £ |
|---|---|
| Inventory 1 January 20*9 | 1 795 |
| Inventory 31 December 20*9 | 1 955 |
| Purchases for the year | 48 900 |

*Required:*

Calculate the goods available for resale for the year ended 31 December 20*9.

*Solution:*

|  | £ |
|---|---|
| Inventory 1 January 20*9 | 1 795 |
| Purchases | 48 900 |
| Goods available for resale | 50 695 |

---

**goods for own use** are goods taken from a business for private consumption by a *sole trader* (or partners in a *partnership*). The business resources withdrawn by the owner(s) of a business for private use are *drawings*.

**Worked example**

David Patel owns a clothing shop. During August he took £163 clothing from the business for his own use. He also made private telephone calls amounting to £16.

*Required:*

Journal entries to record the above transactions in David Patel's books of account.

*Solution:*

### Journal

|  | Dr £ | Cr £ |
|---|---|---|
| Drawings | 163 | |
| Purchases | | 163 |
| Drawings | 16 | |
| Telephone charges | | 16 |

**goods received note:** a document recording items that have been received into stores or a warehouse. In reality, it is often a book (goods received book) rather than a document. It provides a full list of all goods received. A copy is sent to the accounts department where it is compared to the supplier's *invoice* when it is received.

**goodwill, basis of valuation:** the accepted factors that can be taken into account when arriving at a value for the *goodwill* of a business. What is acceptable to the parties involved in the transaction will depend on the type of business in question. Methods used to value goodwill include:

- average weekly sales for the previous accounting period × an agreed figure
- gross annual fees × an agreed figure
- average annual net profit × an agreed figure
- *super profits* × an agreed figure

The agreed multiple has to be acceptable to the parties involved in the purchase of the business.

**grants** are monies given by the European Union, central government or a local authority to a business towards expenditure incurred or to be incurred. The grant may be given for *capital expenditure* or for *revenue expenditure* purposes.

**gross loss** occurs when the *cost of sales* is greater than *revenue*.

**gross profit** is calculated by deducting the *cost of sales* from revenue. The calculation takes place in the *income statement* of a business.

**gross profit margin:** also known as the *margin*.

**gross profit mark-up:** also known as the *mark-up*.

**group accounts** are prepared when two or more companies are controlled by a single management team and the businesses act as one. The *holding company* must produce a set of final accounts like any other *limited company*. In addition, to comply with statutory requirements, a set of final accounts must be prepared for the group as a whole entity.

**group undertaking** is the term used in the *Companies Act 1985* for a *subsidiary company*.

**guaranteed minimum wage** ensures by legislation that workers' pay per hour cannot fall below a set level.

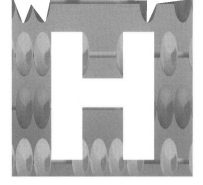

**Halsey premium bonus scheme** is used to reward *direct labour* for saving time in the production process. This method rewards the worker with a payment based on 50 per cent of the time saved.

### Worked example

Philip is paid at the rate of £6.00 per hour. The time allowed to complete a task is 20 hours. The actual time taken by Philip to complete the task is 17 hours.

*Required:*

Calculate the gross pay due to Philip using the Halsey premium bonus scheme after completing the task.

*Solution:*

$$£$$

Philip's gross pay for the task  =  111.00

(17 hours × £6.00 + 1.5 hours bonus × £6.00)

(half of the 3 hours saved)

**Halsey–Weir premium bonus scheme** is a variation on the *Halsey premium bonus scheme*, but instead of a bonus based on 50 per cent of the time saved, the bonus is based on 30 per cent of the time saved.

### Worked example

Tim is paid at the rate of £8.00 per hour. The time allowed to complete a task is 26 hours. The actual time taken by Tim to complete the task is 24 hours.

*Required:*

Calculate the gross pay due to Tim using the Halsey–Weir premium bonus scheme after completing the task.

*Solution:*

$$£$$

Tim's gross pay for the task  = 196.80

(24 hours × £8.00 + 3/5ths hour bonus × £8.00)

(30% of the 2 hours saved)

**hardware** is the generic term used to describe the machine parts of a computer. The hardware of a computer system consists of:

- microprocessor – containing the circuits and chips which are capable of storing and manipulating data
- keyboard – enables the operator to input data and to give instructions to the computer
- monitor – the television-like screen which allows the operator to see information stored in the microprocessor
- disk drive – reads the information that is stored on the hard disk and the floppy disks
- printer – produces printouts (hard copy)

**head office:** the main administrative headquarters of a business. One would normally find the more senior staff based at head office.

**high day rates** is a time-based method of paying workers. Higher hourly rates of pay are paid to workers than would normally be paid. This method of pay is designed to attract top quality workers. These workers should be able to work more effectively and more efficiently, so the firm should benefit through increased productivity.

**high-street banks** are the main British banks which accept deposits from customers and allow withdrawals by customers from their bank accounts.

**hire purchase** allows goods to pass to a 'customer' while the title (ownership) of the goods remains with the seller until the last payment, plus a small purchase fee, has been paid. The purchaser is in fact hiring the goods until the final payment has been made.

The following example shows the bookkeeping entries when an asset is purchased under a hire-purchase agreement.

### Worked example

Peters & Co. purchases a machine for a hire-purchase price of £18 090 from Duck plc on 1 January 20*7. The agreement provides that three instalments of £6030 be paid on 31 December 20*7, 20*8 and 20*9. The true rate of interest is 10% and the cash price of the machine is £15 000.

*Required:*

Prepare:  i) the supplier's account  ii) the machinery account

iii) the hire purchase interest account

*Solution:*

**Duck plc**

| 20*7 | | | 20*7 | | |
|---|---|---|---|---|---|
| 31 Dec | Cash | 6 030 | 1 Jan | Machinery | 15 000 |
| 31 Dec | Bal c/d | 10 470 | 31 Dec | HP interest | 1 500 |
| | | 16 500 | | | 16 500 |
| 20*8 | | | 20*8 | | |
| 31 Dec | Cash | 6 030 | 1 Jan | Bal b/d | 10 470 |
| 31 Dec | Bal c/d | 5 487 | 31 Dec | HP interest | 1 047 |
| | | 11 517 | | | 11 517 |

| 20*9 | | | 20*9 | | | |
|---|---|---|---|---|---|---|
| 31 Dec | Cash | 6 030 | 1 Jan | Bal b/d | 5 487 | |
| | | | 31 Dec | HP interest | 543 | This amount has been rounded down |
| | | 6 030 | | | 6 030 | |

**Machinery**

| 20*7 | | |
|---|---|---|
| 1 Jan | Duck plc | 15 000 |

**Hire purchase agreement**

| 20*7 | | | 20*7 | | |
|---|---|---|---|---|---|
| 31 Dec | Duck plc | 1 500 | 31 Dec | Income statement | 1 500 |
| 20*8 | | | 20*8 | | |
| 31 Dec | Duck plc | 1 047 | 31 Dec | Income statement | 1 047 |
| 20*9 | | | 20*9 | | |
| 31 Dec | Duck plc | 543 | 31 Dec | Income statement | 543 |

**historic cost accounting** is the traditional way of accounting whereby all financial transactions are recorded using the actual cost of purchase. The advantages of using historic cost as a basis for preparing accounts are:
- it is objective
- it is easily understood
- it is easily applied to the double-entry system
- auditors find verification fairly straightforward
- it is recognised by Her Majesty's Revenue and Customs

**HMRC:** Her Majesty's Revenue and Customs.

**holding company** owns more than 50 per cent of the *ordinary shares* in a *subsidiary company*. For example:

Masters Ltd has an issued share capital of 400 000 ordinary shares of £1 each. Driscoll plc acquires 210 000 of the shares in Masters Ltd for £437 700.

Since Driscoll plc owns more than 50% of the issued share capital of Masters Ltd, Driscoll plc is the holding company, Masters Ltd is its subsidiary company.

Extracts from each company's balance sheet would show:

**Driscoll plc balance sheet at 31 December 20*9**

|  | £ |
|---|---|
| Investment in subsidiary at cost | 437 700 |

**Masters Ltd balance sheet at 31 December 20*9**

|  | |
|---|---|
| Ordinary share capital | 400 000 |

*Note:*

It is not obvious from looking at Masters Ltd's balance sheet who are the owners of the ordinary shares.

113

**holding costs** are the costs of holding goods. They comprise storage costs, storekeepers' wages, insurance costs, interest on capital tied up in the goods being held and any other costs involved in holding goods.

**honorarium:** a payment given to a non-salaried officer of a club or society, e.g. secretary, treasurer or committee members, to cover any out of pocket expenses incurred on behalf of the club or society. Generally such payments are made to reimburse for items such as postage and other minor club/society expenses.

**horizontal financial analysis** compares each component in the financial statements of a business over a two-year period. For example:

If sales in 20*8 were £768 000 and in 20*9 they were £812 000, the percentage change is 5.73%.

Workings $\dfrac{44\ 000}{768\ 000}$

If net operating expenses in 20*8 were 134 000 and in 20*9 they rose to £141 000, the percentage change is 5.2%.

Workings $\dfrac{7\ 000}{134\ 000}$

Although the actual calculations are fairly straightforward, the skill in gaining management knowledge relies on the ability to interpret and analyse the changes shown. This enables remedial action to be taken if results indicate that this is necessary. (See also *vertical financial analysis*.)

**horizontal presentation of financial statements** means that the *income statement* is shown with a debit side and a credit side. This is how it appears in the *general ledger*, where it is used to close down the *nominal accounts*. Modern practice generally shows the *financial statements* of a business in a vertical format.

The horizontal presentation of an *income statement* could look like this:

**Theresa O'Malley income statement extract for the year ended 31 March 20*9**

| | | £ | | £ |
|---|---|---|---|---|
| Wages | | 43 876 | Gross profit | 170 419 |
| Rent and rates | | 9 451 | Discounts received | 504 |
| Discounts allowed | | 705 | Rent received | 1 500 |
| Insurances | | 2 577 | | |
| Advertising | | 650 | | |
| Bad debts | | 191 | | |
| Provision for doubtful debts | | 48 | | |
| Provision for depreciation: | | | | |
| Machinery | 350 | | | |
| Office equipment | 120 | 470 | | |
| Profit for the year | | 114 455 | | |
| | | 172 423 | | 172 423 |

(See also *vertical presentation of final statements*.)

**human resource accounting** has attempted to incorporate the value of managers and workers into traditional accounting statements. The difficulty encountered is one of objectivity. What value does one put on a good boss or a good worker? Who does the valuation?

**Aiming for a grade A\*?**

Don't forget to log on to **www.philipallan.co.uk/a-zonline** for advice.

115

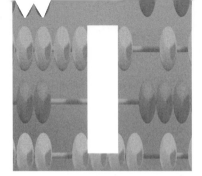

**IAS:** *international accounting standards*

**IAS 1:** see *presentation of financial statements*

**IAS 2:** see *inventories*

**IAS 7:** see *statement of cash flows*

**IAS 8:** see *accounting policies, changes in accounting estimates and errors*

**IAS 10:** see *events after the reporting period*

**IAS 11:** construction contracts (examined at professional level)

**IAS 12:** income taxes (examined at professional level)

**IAS 14:** segment reporting (examined at professional level)

**IAS 16:** see *property, plant and equipment*

**IAS 17:** leases (examined at professional level)

**IAS 18:** see *revenue*

**IAS 19:** employee benefits (examined at professional level)

**IAS 20:** accounting for government grants and disclosure of government assistance (examined at professional level)

**IAS 21:** the effects of changes in foreign exchange rates (examined at professional level)

**IAS 23:** borrowing costs (examined at professional level)

**IAS 24:** related party disclosures (examined at professional level)

**IAS 26:** accounting and reporting by retirement benefit plans (examined at professional level)

**IAS 27:** consolidated and separate financial statements (examined at professional level)

**IAS 28:** investments in associates (examined at professional level)

**IAS 29:** financial reporting in hyperinflationary economies (examined at professional level)

**IAS 30:** disclosures in the financial statements of banks and similar financial institutions (examined at professional level)

**IAS 31:** interest in joint ventures (examined at professional level)

**IAS 32:** financial instruments: disclosure and presentation (examined at professional level)

**IAS 33:** see *earnings per share*

**IAS 34:** interim financial reporting (examined at professional level)

**IAS 36:** see *impairment of assets*

**IAS 37:** see *provisions, contingent liabilities and contingent assets*

**IAS 38:** see *intangible assets*

**IAS 39:** financial instruments: recognition and measurement (examined at professional level)

**IAS 40:** investment property (examined at professional level)

**IAS 41:** agriculture (examined at professional level)

**ideal standards** are based on the assumption that production can be carried out in perfect conditions. They are also known as potential standards. The *CIMA* definition of an ideal standard is one that 'can be attained under the most favourable conditions, with no allowance for normal losses, waste and machine downtime'.

Many managers consider that the setting of ideal standards can demotivate staff.

**idle time:** see *time sheet*

**IFRS 1:** first-time adoption of international financial reporting standards (examined at professional level)

**IFRS 2:** share-based payment (examined at professional level)

**IFRS 3:** business combinations (examined at professional level)

**IFRS 4:** insurance contracts (examined at professional level)

**IFRS 5:** non-current assets held for sale and discontinued operations (examined at professional level)

**IFRS 6:** exploration for and evaluation of mineral assets (examined at professional level)

**IFRS 7:** financial instruments: disclosures (examined at professional level)

**IFRS 8:** operating segments (examined at professional level)

**impairment** occurs when the *carrying amount* of a *non-current asset* is greater than its *recoverable amount*

**impairment of assets IAS 36:** the standard seeks to ensure that assets are shown in the balance sheet at no more than their recoverable amount.

This standard seeks to ensure that:
- *non-current assets* including goodwill are shown at no more than their recoverable amount
- any *impairment loss* is measured on a consistent basis
- information regarding *impairment losses* is disclosed in such a way that the users of the accounts can understand the impact on the business

**impairment losses** occur when the *carrying amount* is greater than its *recoverable amount*. Losses should be shown in the *income statement* as an expense. The asset should be shown on the balance sheet at its *recoverable amount*.

**impersonal accounts:** accounts that do not relate to a person or business. They are found in the *general ledger*. They can be divided into:
- *real accounts* – the accounts where transactions dealing with *tangible non-current assets* are recorded, e.g. plant and machinery, office equipment, etc.
- *nominal accounts* – where revenues and expenses are recorded, e.g. insurances, advertising, etc.

**imprest system** is the system used to maintain a *petty cash book*. A set amount of money (the float) is given to the petty cashier. The petty cashier pays out small amounts of money as the need arises for postages, travelling expenses, office sundries, etc. When the float gets low the petty cashier receives money from the main cashier to restore the float to the original set amount. (See *petty cash book*.)

**incentive bonus:** extra pay given to workers to encourage them to work harder.

**incentive payment schemes** offer extra pay to workers to make them work more efficiently. (See *premium bonus pay schemes*, *Halsey premium bonus scheme*, *Halsey–Weir premium bonus scheme* and *Rowan premium bonus scheme*.)

**income and expenditure account:** the name given to the *income statement* of a non-trading organisation. The expenditure is shown on the debit side of the account and the incomes are shown on the credit side.

The income and expenditure account can be presented in a vertical format. Incomes are listed and total expenditure is deducted, giving either a surplus (excess of income over expenditure) or a deficit (excess of expenditure over income).

For the preparation of an income and expenditure account, see *club accounts*.

**income gearing:** see *interest cover*

**income in advance** is shown in the *balance sheet* as other payables. It represents monies that have been paid by a credit customer before the due date.

---

### Worked example

Tom McDonald has a financial year end on 28 February each year. He sublets part of his premises to James Janowski. The rental is £1200 per quarter payable in advance. James' first payment is due on 1 January 20*9; he pays on 6 January 20*9.

*Required:*

An extract from Tom McDonald's income statement for the year ended 28 February 20*9, and an extract from a balance sheet at that date.

*Solution:*

**Tom McDonald income statement extract for the year ended 28 February 20*9**

|  | £ |
|---|---|
| Gross profit | ***** |
| Add rent receivable | 800 |
| **Balance sheet extract at 28 February 20*9:** | |
| Current liabilities | |
| Payables | 400 |
| (Rent receivable paid in advance) | |

---

**income outstanding** is shown on the *balance sheet* as a receivable (debtor). It represents monies that are owed at the due date.

## Worked example

Ravi Lall has a financial year end on 30 June each year. He sublets part of his premises to Angus Lefevre. The rental is £3000 per quarter payable in advance. The first payment is due on 1 January 20*9; subsequent payments are to be made on 1 April, 1 July and 1 October. Angus paid his rent on 27 January 20*9 and has yet to make another payment.

### Required:

An extract from the income statement of Ravi Lall for the year ended 30 June 20*9 and an extract from the balance sheet at that date.

### Solution:

**Ravi Lall income statement extract for the year ended 30 June 20*9**

|  | £ |
|---|---|
| Gross profit | ***** |
| Add rent receivable | 6000 |
| **Balance sheet extract at 30 June 20*9** | |
| Current assets | |
| Receivables | 3000 |
| (Rent receivable owing) | |

**income statement** calculates a business's profit or loss for an *accounting period*. The statement shows the *gross profit* on the sales, plus any other incomes such as *discounts received*, rents received, *commission* received, profit on disposal of assets. All expenditure incurred during the same time period is then deducted. If incomes exceed expenditures then the business has made a profit. If, however, expenditures exceed incomes the business has incurred a loss.

At the end of each accounting period all revenue expense accounts are closed off by transferring the annual charge to the income statement. This means that the accounts are ready for entries in the new financial year.

For example: at the end of the year the rent account and the advertising account would be closed by transfers to the income statement. This example does not include any adjustments for accruals or prepayments.

| Rent | | | | Advertising | | | |
|---|---|---|---|---|---|---|---|
| Cash | 1100 | Inc statement | 4400 | Cash | 179 | Inc statement | 1369 |
| Cash | 1100 | | | Cash | 548 | | |
| Cash | 1100 | | | Cash | 126 | | |
| Cash | 1100 | | | Cash | 516 | | |
| | 4400 | | 4400 | | 1369 | | 1369 |

### Income statement extract for the year ended ******

| Rent | 4400 | Gross profit | **** |
|---|---|---|---|
| Advertising | 1369 | | |

Income statements are prepared on an accruals basis, not a cash basis. See **accruals concept** for examples of bookkeeping treatment of accrued income and accrued expenses. See also **prepayments of expenses** and **prepayments of income** for further examples.

The income statement can be prepared using either a **horizontal presentation** or a **vertical presentation**. The vertical presentation is the more usual layout used today. For example:

**Income statement for the year ended 31 August 20*9 (a vertical presentation has been used)**

|  | £ | £ | £ |
|---|---|---|---|
| Revenue |  |  | 87 912 |
| Less cost of sales |  |  |  |
| Inventory 1 September 20*8 |  | 4 203 |  |
| Purchases | 38 415 |  |  |
| Carriage inward | 234 | 38 649 |  |
|  |  | 42 852 |  |
| Less inventory 31 August 20*9 |  | 4 371 | 38 481 |
| Gross profit |  |  | 49 431 |
| Add discount received |  |  | 649 |
| Rent received |  |  | 1 000 |
|  |  |  | 51 080 |
| Less expenses |  |  |  |
| Wages |  | 28 566 |  |
| Carriage outwards |  | 139 |  |
| Rent |  | 4 400 |  |
| Rates and insurance |  | 3 561 |  |
| Advertising |  | 1 369 |  |
| Bad debts |  | 879 |  |
| Depreciation: | fixtures | 1 200 |  |
|  | van | 2 500 | 42 614 |
| Profit for the year |  |  | 8 466 |

**income statements of limited companies** are prepared by the **directors** of a limited company. They are used for management purposes i.e. to aid the directors and managers to run the company effectively and efficiently. These internal financial statements are prepared in great detail.

The statement is also prepared for **stewardship** purposes, i.e. to inform various **stakeholders** how the resources of the company are being used. The financial statements that are published and filed with the Registrar of Companies do not show details of every overhead or expense or the details of how revenue is made up. An example of an income statement is shown on the next page.

For internal use, details of how revenue; cost of sales; distribution costs; administration expenses and finance costs are made up would be shown.

**Sihon plc. Income statement for the year ended 31 December 20*9**

|  | £000 |
|---|---|
| Revenue | 2 700 |
| Cost of sales | (1 138) |
| Gross profit | 1 562 |
| Distribution costs | (478) |
| Administration expenses | (516) |
| Profit/(loss)from operations | 568 |
| Finance costs | (80) |
| Profit/(loss) before tax | 488 |
| Tax | (150) |
| Profit/(loss) for the year | 338 |

**income tax:** an annual tax on a person's income. The annual plan of how taxes are to be raised (together with planned government expenditure) is outlined in the Budget presented to Parliament each year. The proposals are made law through the resultant *Finance Act*.

Income tax is administered by Her Majesty's Revenue and Customs (HMRC), which is also responsible for *corporation tax* and *capital gains* tax. Routine administration throughout the country is carried out in 'districts'. The head of each district is an Inspector of Taxes who quantifies each person's liability. This now follows the process of self-assessment in the case of many taxpayers. When a person's tax liability is agreed, the tax is paid to the Collector of Taxes.

**incomplete records:** the generic term used to describe organisations that do not keep a full double-entry set of financial records. These organisations tend to be:
- small businesses that do most of their business on a cash basis
- clubs and societies (see *club accounts*)

As with the preparation of the *final accounts* of clubs and societies, there are four key stages used when preparing the accounts of cash-based businesses:
- prepare an opening *statement of affairs* (similar to an opening *balance sheet*)
- prepare a summary of the business bank account (often given in a question) and a cash summary
- prepare adjustment accounts (to take into account the *accruals concept*)
- prepare the financial statements

---

**Worked example**

Helmut Schott owns a delicatessen. He does not keep proper books of account. He supplies you with the following information for his financial year ended 31 August 20*9:

**Summarised bank account for the year ended 31 August 20*9**

|  | £ |  | £ |
|---|---|---|---|
| Balance 1 September 20*8 | 1 042 | Payments to creditors | 41 671 |
| Takings banked | 93 004 | Wages | 24 533 |
|  |  | Rent | 4 000 |

|  |  |
|---|---|
| Rates | 1 200 |
| Drawings | 12 000 |
| Other business expenses | 9 719 |
| Balance 31 August 20*9 | 923 |
| 94 046 | 94 046 |

All business takings were paid into the bank with the exception of:

|  | £ |
|---|---|
| Stationery | 670 |
| Drawings | 2 693 |

The following additional information is also available at 31 August:

|  | 20*8 | 20*9 |
|---|---|---|
|  | £ | £ |
| Inventories | 567 | 814 |
| Trade receivables | 437 | 210 |
| Trade payables | 1 720 | 2 181 |
| Rent owed | 200 | 300 |
| Rates prepaid | 48 | 112 |
| Fixtures at valuation | 10 000 | 9 000 |
| Vehicle at valuation | 6 000 | 3 000 |
| Cash in hand | 181 | 149 |

## Required:

An income statement for the year ended 31 August 20*9 and a balance sheet at that date.

## Solution:

**Stage 1** – prepare an opening statement of affairs. (Do this quickly as it is not part of the answer; it is part of your working papers – the order in which you list your assets and liabilities is not important.)

|  |  | £ |
|---|---|---|
| Assets – | bank | 1 042 |
|  | inventory | 567 |
|  | trade receivables | 437 |
|  | rates paid in advance | 48 |
|  | fixtures | 10 000 |
|  | vehicle | 6 000 |
|  | cash | 181 |
|  |  | 18 275 |
| Liabilities – | trade payables | (1 720) |
|  | rent owed | (200) |
| Capital – 1 September 20*8 |  | 16 355 |

**Stage 2** – prepare a bank account – no need; this is given in the question. Prepare a cash summary.

|  | £ |  | £ |
|---|---|---|---|
| Balance 1 September 20*8 | 181 | Stationery | 670 |
| Cash takings (missing figure) | 3 331 | Drawings | 2 693 |
|  |  | Balance 31 August 20*9 | 149 |
|  | 3 512 |  | 3 512 |
| Balance 1 September 20*9 | 149 |  |  |

## Stage 3 – prepare adjustment accounts.

| Trade receivables adjustment | | | | Trade payables adjustment | | | |
|---|---|---|---|---|---|---|---|
| Balance b/d | 437 | Cash | 93 004 | Cash | 41 671 | Balance b/d | 1 720 |
| Inc Stat |  |  |  |  |  | Inc Stat |  |
| (missing |  |  |  |  |  | (missing |  |
| figure) | 92 777 | Balance c/d | 210 | Balance c/d | 2 181 | figure) | 42 132 |
|  | 93 214 |  | 93 214 |  | 43 852 |  | 43 852 |
| Balance b/d | 210 |  |  |  |  | Balance b/d | 2 181 |

| Rent | | | | Rates | | | |
|---|---|---|---|---|---|---|---|
| Cash | 4 000 | Balance b/d | 200 | Balance b/d | 48 | I St (missing) | 1 136 |
| Balance c/d | 300 | I St (missing) | 4 100 | Cash | 1 200 | Balance c/d | 112 |
|  | 4 300 |  | 4 300 |  | 1 248 |  | 1 248 |
|  |  | Balance b/d | 300 | Balance b/d | 112 |  |  |

**Stage 4** – preparation of financial statement. - at last – what the question asked for.
Up to now no marks have been scored but all the hard work has been done.

### Helmut Schott income statement for the year ended 31 August 20*9

|  | £ | £ |
|---|---|---|
| Sales (92 777 + 3331) |  | 96 108 |
| Less cost of sales |  |  |
| Inventory 1 September 20*8 |  | 567 |
| Purchases | 42 132 |  |
|  | 42 699 |  |
| Less inventory 31 August 20*9 | 814 | 41 885 |
| Gross profit |  | 54 223 |
| Less expenses |  |  |
| Wages | 24 533 |  |
| Rent | 4 100 |  |
| Rates | 1 136 |  |
| Stationery | 670 |  |
| Other business expenses | 9 719 |  |
| Depreciation – fixtures | 1 000 |  |
| – vehicle | 3 000 | 44 158 |
| Profit for year |  | 10 065 |

## Balance sheet at 31 August 20*9

| | | | |
|---|---|---|---|
| Non-current assets | – Fixtures | 10 000 | |
| | Less depreciation | 1 000 | 9 000 |
| | Vehicle | 6 000 | |
| | Less depreciation | 3 000 | 3 000 |
| | | | 12 000 |
| Current assets | | | |
| Inventory | | 814 | |
| Trade receivables | | 210 | |
| Cash and cash equivalents (923 + 149) | | 1 072 | |
| Rates paid in advance | | 112 | |
| | | 2 208 | |
| Less current liabilities | | | |
| Trade payables | 2 181 | | |
| Other payables | | | |
| (Rent) | 300 | 2 481 | (273) |
| | | | 11 727 |
| Capital | | | 16 355 |
| Add profit | | | 10 065 |
| | | | 26 420 |
| Less drawings (12 000 + 2693) | | | 14 693 |
| | | | 11 727 |

**incremental costs** are the extra costs incurred when the level of activity increases within a business. Incremental costs are generally *variable costs* but in some cases an increase in activity may need to be supported by additional *fixed costs*, e.g. the rental of another workshop or the purchase of additional machinery.

Incremental costing shows the difference in costs which results from different levels of a business's activities. (See also *marginal costing*.)

**incremental revenue and expenditure** is the term used for the additional *revenue* and *expenditure* that will arise if a particular line of action is taken. For example, if a new machine is purchased:

> total business sales will rise from £300 000 to £370 000
>
> total business expenditure will increase from £185 000 to £211 000.

So:

> the incremental revenue is £70 000 (£370 000 – £300 000)
>
> the incremental expenditure is £26 000 (£211 000 – £185 000)

**incremental salary scales** give the employee regular annual salary increases, as in the teaching profession, the police force, etc.

**indirect costs** are expenses which cannot be identified directly with the end-product. They are also known as factory overheads. They include *indirect labour costs* and *indirect material costs*.

**indirect expenses** are any factory expenses that are not directly identifiable with the final product. Examples include factory rent and rates, *depreciation* of factory machinery, etc. They appear as factory overheads in a *manufacturing account*.

**indirect labour costs** are the costs involved in employing staff whose work cannot be directly identified with the final product. Examples include wages paid to maintenance engineers, the wages of supervisory staff, etc. These costs appear as factory overheads in a *manufacturing account*.

**indirect material costs** are the costs incurred in acquiring materials which cannot be directly identified with the final product. Examples include factory cleaning materials, machine lubricating oil, etc. These costs appear as factory overheads in a *manufacturing account*.

**inflation** is a sustained increase in the general level of prices within an economy.

**information technology (IT)** is the use of technology to acquire, store, process and distribute information. The technology used includes computers and telecommunications equipment.

**input tax** is the *VAT* that a business pays to a supplier, based on the total *invoice* price less any cash discount that might be available for prompt payment. The purchaser can claim this tax back.

**insolvent:** the term applied to a person (or business) who is unable to settle debts when they fall due.

**insolvent partner:** see *Garner v Murray (1904)*

**intangible assets:** non-physical assets, i.e. assets that cannot be seen or touched. Examples include *goodwill*, brand names and patents.

**intangible assets IAS 38:** this standard seeks to ensure that purchased goodwill and *intangible assets* are charged to the *income statement* in the time periods when they are depleted. Goodwill, and certain intangible assets, should therefore be capitalised and *amortised* through the income statement. Amortisation should usually take place over 20 years or less. It defines goodwill as 'the cost of acquisition less the aggregate fair value of the purchased … assets and liabilities'. Only intangible assets with a finite life should be amortised.

Goodwill should be included in the purchaser's *balance sheet* as an asset. Internally generated (inherent) goodwill should not be capitalised.

Internally developed intangible assets should only be capitalised where they have an ascertainable market value.

**integrated accounting system:** defined by *CIMA* as 'a set of accounting records which provides financial and cost accounts using a common input of data for all accounting purposes'.

**interest** is the charge made by a lender on a loan. A borrower has to pay for the use of the money borrowed. Interest is calculated as a percentage of the sum. (See *annual percentage rate*, *compound interest* and *simple interest*.)

**interest cover** measures a business's ability to service its long-term borrowing out of profits. A low interest cover would indicate to *shareholders* that *dividends* might be in jeopardy if profits are not maintained. The calculation is:

*FORMULA:* $\dfrac{\text{profit before interest and tax}}{\text{interest payable}}$

**Worked example**

James Hilton Ltd's profits before interest and tax are £160 000. Interest payments are £14 000 per annum.

*Required:*

Calculate the interest cover for James Hilton Ltd.

*Solution:*

$\text{interest cover} = \dfrac{\text{profit before interest and tax}}{\text{interest payable}} = \dfrac{£160\ 000}{£14\ 000} = 11.42 \text{ times}$

**interest on partners' capital accounts** is an appropriation of the profits of a *partnership*. It skews the profits towards the partner(s) who has more capital invested in the business.

It should be emphasised that this is not interest like that earned on a bank deposit account. Interest on capital is part of the way that partnership profits may be divided. Partners should not be credited with interest on capital as a right – it must be part of the *partnership agreement*.

Interest on capital should be credited to the partners' current accounts. The bookkeeping entries are:

**Debit:** Income statement          **Credit:** Partners' current account

**interest on partners' drawings** can be included in a *partnership agreement*. It is an attempt to deter partners from drawing out too much cash in the early part of the financial year. The bookkeeping entries are:

**Debit:** Partners' current account     **Credit:** Income statement

**interest payments** are a revenue expense. They should be shown in the business *income statement*. *Capital repayments* reduce the amount shown as outstanding on the *balance sheet*.

**inter-firm comparisons** of financial results can be used by managers as a performance indicator, or by potential investors as a means of deciding which business to invest in.

Inter-firm comparisons have value only if:

- the firms are in the same line of business – it would not be sensible to compare the financial results of a furniture manufacturer with the financial results of a motor vehicle manufacturer
- they use the same *accounting bases* – it would not be sensible to compare the financial results of a business whose managers used *straight-line methods* of depreciating their *non-current assets*, used *AVCO* to value closing *inventory*, and *provided for doubtful debts* at a rate of 5 per cent on *trade receivables* with a business using *reducing balance methods* of depreciation, using *FIFO* as the method for valuing closing *inventory*, and *providing for doubtful debts* at the rate of 1 per cent on *trade receivables*
- the businesses have a similar structure – it would not be sensible to compare the financial results of Jane Dixon's corner shop selling groceries with the results of Tesco

An effort must be made to ensure that, as far as possible, 'like with like' comparisons are made. Even so, it could be argued that this is impossible because each firm has:

- a different set of managers
- a different workforce
- a different set of market circumstances

**interlocking accounts** are defined by *CIMA* as 'a system in which the cost accounts are distinct from the financial accounts, the two sets of accounts being kept continuously in agreement by the use of *control accounts* or reconciled by other means'.

**internal audit:** see *audit*

**internal auditor** is a member of staff who examines in detail the efficiency of a business and how systems are being operated within the business. The results are checked against standards prescribed in the business's *strategic plan* or departmental action plans.

The results of the audit should enable managers to identify areas of weakness, which can be targeted for improvement. It can also highlight areas of good practice which could be adapted to make other parts of the business more efficient.

**internal financing** means obtaining or conserving cash resources from within a business. This can be done by:

- retaining profits ('ploughing back')
- running *inventory* down if possible without jeopardising future orders
- better credit control
- selling surplus *non-current assets*

**internal rate-of-return method of capital investment appraisal** takes the *time value of money* into account when making a *capital investment appraisal*. The internal rate of return represents the true interest rate earned by the investment over the course of its economic life. It is the discount rate that will cause the *net present value* of the investment to be zero.

The internal rate of return can be found by trial and error, by guessing a number of discount factors until the correct guess gives a net present value of zero.

## Worked example

The cost of capital for Damansara plc is 14%. The managers are considering a three-year project which will cost £100 000. The net cash flows from the project are expected to be:

|        | £       |
|--------|---------|
|        | £       |
| Year 1 | 40 000  |
| Year 2 | 45 000  |
| Year 3 | 50 000  |

The following are extracts from the present value tables for £1:

|        | 12%   | 14%   | 15%   | 16%   | 18%   |
|--------|-------|-------|-------|-------|-------|
| Year 1 | 0.893 | 0.877 | 0.870 | 0.862 | 0.847 |
| Year 2 | 0.797 | 0.769 | 0.756 | 0.743 | 0.718 |
| Year 3 | 0.712 | 0.675 | 0.658 | 0.641 | 0.609 |

## Required:

Calculate the internal rate of return on the new project being considered by Damansara plc.

## Solution:

Let us try 12%:

|              | Cash flows | Present value factor | Net present value |
|--------------|-----------|----------------------|-------------------|
|              | £         |                      | £                 |
| Year 0 (now) | (100 000) | 1                    | (100 000)         |
| Year 1       | 40 000    | 0.893                | 35 720            |
| Year 2       | 45 000    | 0.797                | 35 865            |
| Year 3       | 50 000    | 0.712                | 35 600            |
|              |           |                      | 7 185             |

The return is positive, so the internal rate of return is greater than 12%. Let us try 18%:

|        | Cash flows | Present value factor | Net present value |
|--------|-----------|----------------------|-------------------|
| Year 0 | (100 000) | 1                    | (100 000)         |
| Year 1 | 40 000    | 0.847                | 33 880            |
| Year 2 | 45 000    | 0.718                | 32 310            |
| Year 3 | 50 000    | 0.609                | 30 450            |
|        |           |                      | (3 360)           |

The return is negative, so the internal rate of return is less than 18%. Let us try 16%:

|        | Cash flows | Present value factor | Net present value |
|--------|-----------|----------------------|-------------------|
| Year 0 | (100 000) | 1                    | (100 000)         |
| Year 1 | 40 000    | 0.862                | 34 480            |
| Year 2 | 45 000    | 0.743                | 33 435            |
| Year 3 | 50 000    | 0.641                | 32 050            |
|        |           |                      | (35)              |

The return is negative, but only just, so the internal rate of return is just below 16%.

The project should be undertaken since the return on the project exceeds Damansara plc's cost of capital.

**International Accounting Standards (IASs)** are *accounting standards* that have been issued by the *International Accounting Standards Board* and are applicable internationally. This is to enable the users of accounts to be able to make judgements and comparisons based on the results of businesses from a range of countries.

**International Accounting Standards Board (IASB)** is a committee of accountants from many different countries whose brief is to try to harmonise the way that accounts are presented throughout the world.

**International Financial Reporting Standards (IFRSs)** are a set of financial reporting principles issued by the International Accounting Standards Board aiming to provide consistent practice in the preparation of financial statements.

**interpretation of accounts** is an attempt to explain what has happened to a business and to predict what might happen to the business in the future. The process must be careful and methodical. Data must be collected, ratios calculated and trends observed. Only then can analysis begin.

It can prove to be a very difficult task, since most users of accounts do not have access to the 'full' picture. They may have to use a set of *published accounts*. In order to interpret the results shown by the ratios and trends, a series of questions need to be answered:

- Has *profitability* increased or decreased? Has it improved or deteriorated?
- Has the sales margin increased or decreased? Has it improved or deteriorated?
- Has the proportion of turnover used to pay expenses increased or decreased? Has it improved or deteriorated?
- Has the *return on capital employed* increased or decreased? Has it improved or deteriorated?
- Are the changes due to increased profitability or to increased injections of capital?
- Has increased capital employed been as a result of internal financing or because of external financing?
- How has the *liquidity* position of the business changed?

These are just some of the questions that will help to interpret the calculations used in *ratio analysis*.

**inventory** is the international term now being used to describe raw materials, components, *work in progress* or finished goods held by a business that have not been disposed of during the financial year. Formally known as *stock*.

**inventories IAS 2** states that inventories should be valued at the lower of *cost* (the purchase price plus any costs incurred in bringing the product or service to its present location and condition) and *net realisable value* (the estimated selling price less any estimated costs required to get the product or service into saleable condition). This standard is applicable to all types of inventory.

**inventory account:** records receipts and issues of goods showing clearly the balance of inventory held. There is a different account for each different raw material and each different item carried in the business.

If all the transactions in every inventory account are totalled, they should agree with the total figures in the stores account. The stores account is, in essence, an inventory control account that records all receipts of all goods and all issues of all goods to the various departments.

| Description | | | | | | Number | | | |
|---|---|---|---|---|---|---|---|---|---|
| Stock levels | | Minimum reorder level | | | | Maximum reorder quantity | | | |
| Date | Detail | Stock level | | Stock issue | | Balance | | Allocated stock | Free stock |
| | | Quantity | £ | Quantity | £ | Quantity | £ | Quantity | Quantity |
| | | | | | | | | | |
| | | | | | | | | | |
| | | | | | | | | | |
| | | | | | | | | | |
| | | | | | | | | | |
| | | | | | | | | | |

The inventory account can be maintained by using either of the recognised methods of inventory valuation, such as FIFO and AVCO.

**inventory control** is necessary to make sure that the correct levels of inventory are maintained. Holding excessive goods is costly because:
- money must be spent to acquire the goods
- holding inventory represents idle money
- goods may deteriorate or be stolen

Holding insufficient goods can result in:

- lost orders
- loss of bulk order discounts
- greater administration costs

**inventory ledger:** the book containing all the inventory accounts.

**inventory losses:** see *loss of inventory*

**inventory record card** records changes in levels of each type of raw material or component held by a business. An appropriate entry is made on the card recording each movement of goods.

An inventory record card is very similar to an *inventory ledger* account, the only difference being that the record card does not usually show the prices of receipts and issues of goods. The allocated column shows goods that are not available for issue because they have been earmarked for a job that has not yet started. The source documents are:
- goods received: goods received notes
- goods issued: material/component requisition note

**inventory reorder level** indicates to the inventory (stock) controller when it is necessary to reorder certain raw materials or components. The inventory reorder level should ensure that the business always has sufficient goods to meet demands from the production department.

The calculation to determine the reorder level is:

> *FORMULA:*   maximum usage × maximum lead time

**Worked example**

A manufacturing business has a maximum usage of 2500 units of component ATX/51 per week. The supplier of the component has a maximum lead time of 5 weeks.

*Required:*

Calculate the reorder level for component ATX/51.

*Solution:*

> reorder level = maximum usage × maximum lead time
> = 2500 × 5
> = 12 500 units

To avoid cash being tied up in holding unnecessarily high levels of inventory, many businesses will set a maximum level of goods to be held at any one time. The calculation to determine the maximum levels of inventory to be held is:

> *FORMULA:*   reorder level − (minimum usage × minimum lead time) + reorder quantity

**Worked example**

The reorder level for component ATX/51 is 12 500 units. The business has a minimum usage of 650 units per week. The minimum lead time is 3 weeks. The reorder quantity is 10 000.

*Required:*

Calculate the maximum number of ATX/51 to be held at any one time.

*Solution:*

Maximum level of inventory to be held:

> reorder level   (minimum usage × minimum lead time) + reorder quantity
> = 12 500 − (650 × 3) + 10 000
> = 12 500 − 1950 + 10 000
> = 20 550 units of ATX/51

Minimum levels of goods to be held will allow the inventory controller to avoid running out of goods. The calculation to determine the minimum levels of inventory to be held is:

> *FORMULA:*   reorder level − (average usage × average lead time)

### Worked example

The reorder level for component ATX/51 is 12 500. The average usage is 1575 units per week. The average lead time is 4 weeks.

*Required:*

Calculate the minimum number of ATX/51 to be held.

*Solution:*

Minimum level of inventory to be held:

reorder level − (average usage × average lead time)

| 12 500 | − | (1575 | × | 4) |
|--------|---|-------|---|-----|
| = 12 500 | − | | 6300 | |

= 6200 units of ATX/51

In order to ensure that a business never runs out of goods, a safety level of goods should be maintained (these are also known as buffer stocks). If the business using component ATX/51 in the worked examples above required a buffer stock of 2000 units, the minimum level of inventory to be held would increase to 1110.

**investment analysts** are employed by stock broking firms to examine, in detail, the performance of businesses in certain sectors of the market.

**investment appraisal** is the process of determining the future *net cash flows* or *profitability* of a capital project. (See *accounting rate of return*, *payback method of capital investment appraisal*, *net present value method of capital investment appraisal*, and *internal rate of return*.)

**investment ratios:** see *dividend cover*, *dividend yield*, *earnings per share*, *gearing*, *interest cover* and *price/earnings ratio*.

**investments** are shown on a *balance sheet* as either *non-current assets* or *current assets*, depending on their nature. If a company intends to keep the investments on a continuing basis they should be treated as *non-current assets*, while investments to be held for a short time period should be shown as a current asset.

Investments are shown at cost. If the investments are listed on a recognised *stock exchange*, then the aggregate market price must be noted.

**investment trust:** a company whose business is to buy and sell other companies' shares. The shares of investment trusts can be purchased on the *stock market*.

**investor:** a person who puts money into shares, *bonds* or building societies or on deposit with some other financial institution.

Institutional investors are organisations, such as insurance companies and pension funds, that invest large sums of money in shares and bonds.

**invoice:** the document that is sent to a credit customer. It is sent by the seller to the customer demanding payment, usually within a stipulated time. (See *VAT invoice*.)

**invoice discounting** is a method used by a business to obtain early payment of *invoices*. The business sells its sales invoices at a discount to an invoice discounting company which will collect the full amounts due. The customer should be unaware of this arrangement.

**invoice factoring:** see *factoring*

**irr:** see *internal rate-of-return method of capital investment appraisal*

**irrelevant costs** are costs which should be ignored when making decisions between alternative courses of action. They are past or *sunk costs*. That is, they are costs undertaken some time ago and any future commitments will not affect them or be affected by them. Future *common costs* can also be ignored when deciding between alternative strategies.

**issued share capital:** the *nominal share capital* which has been issued to *shareholders.* This figure cannot exceed the *authorised share capital*.

**issue of debentures:** the bookkeeping entries are similar to those used for the *issue of shares*. The word 'debenture' should be substituted for the words 'share capital'.

**issue of shares:** the issue of shares is like any other contract – it requires an offer and an acceptance.

The invitation to treat is made by advertising and by the issue of a prospectus. The prospective *shareholders* (applicants) apply for shares and send cash with the application form. The company then allots shares to the applicants (now *allottees*). Any unsuccessful applicants will have their application moneys returned. The allottees send money due on allotment. Calls are made, and shareholders pay the calls when due.

These are the bookkeeping entries necessary to record a share issue:

| | Debit | Credit |
|---|---|---|
| On application | Bank | Application and allotment account |
| On allotment | Bank | Application and allotment account |
| Unsuccessful applicants | Application and allotment account | Bank |
| When allotment is complete | Application and allotment account | Share capital account |
| On call | Bank | Call account |
| When call(s) are complete | Call account | Share capital account |

**Worked example**

Howitt plc was formed with an authorised share capital of 500 000 ordinary shares of £1 each. 200 000 of these shares were offered to the public on the following terms:

50 pence on application

30 pence on allotment

20 pence on first and final call

*Note:*

There is only one call; the first is also the last call.

Applications were received for 371 000 shares. The directors decided to allot the shares to applicants for 300 000 shares on the basis of two shares for every three shares for which applications had been received. The balance of money received on application was to be applied to the amounts due on allotment. Unsuccessful applicants were repaid. All call money was received on the due date.

### Required:

Write up the journal (including cash) to record the above transactions in the books of Howitt plc.

### Solution:

### Journal

|  | £ | £ |
|---|---|---|
| Cash | 185 500 | |
|     Application and allotment | | 185 500 |
|         Monies received on application | | |
| Application and allotment | 35 500 | |
|     Cash | | 35 500 |
|         Monies returned to unsuccessful applicants | | |
| Cash | 10 000 | |
|     Application and allotment | | 10 000 |
|         Balance of cash from successful applicants due on allotment | | |
| Application and allotment | 160 000 | |
|     Ordinary share capital account | | 160 000 |
|         Transfer of successful applicants to ordinary share capital account | | |
| Cash | 40 000 | |
|     Call | | 40 000 |
|         Monies received on first and final call | | |
| Call | 40 000 | |
|     Ordinary share capital account | | 40 000 |
|         Transfer of call to ordinary share capital account, shares now fully paid | | |

**IT:** see *information technology*

### A–Z Online

Log on to A–Z Online to search the database of terms, print revision lists and much more. Go to **www.philipallan.co.uk/a-zonline** to get started.

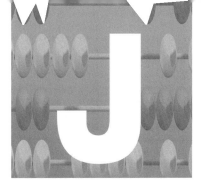

**JIT:** see *just-in-time (JIT) method of purchasing*

**job card:** see *time sheet*

**job costing:** the system of costing which allocates and *apportions* elements of cost to a job being undertaken to a client's specific instructions. A printer will use job costing when costing out the printing of invoices, letter headed stationery and business cards. Similarly, Tommy Davidson, a local builder, who has been employed to build a kitchen extension for the Graham household, will use job costing to arrive at the price the Grahams will have to pay.

**job sheet** (or card) records the quantities and values of raw materials, *direct labour*, direct expenses and any overheads used on a job. The job sheet is, in essence, an account for the job. When the job is complete, and the customer has been invoiced, the profit or loss can be calculated. Managers can compare the sheet with the original estimate.

**joint costs:** see *common costs*

**joint products** are the main products of a process that have their own high saleable value. In contrast, *by-products* arise as incidentals to the main production process and will not command the same high saleable value as the main product.

**journal** is a *book of prime entry*. It is also known as the journal proper. It is not part of the *double-entry bookkeeping* system. It is used to record the entries:

- in the *general ledger* when a firm starts in business
- used to close the ledgers down when a business ceases to trade
- when there is a purchase of *non-current assets* on credit
- when *non-current assets* are sold on credit
- required when making transfers from one ledger account to another
- required when correcting errors in ledger accounts

The use of the journal is necessary because:

- the entries above do not 'fit' into any other book of prime entry
- unusual transactions must be entered in a book of prime entry in the same way as all other transactions
- it reduces the likelihood of only using one entry in the double-entry system
- it reduces the likelihood of a fraud being perpetrated, since the journal is an integral part of the *audit trail*

**just-in-time (JIT) method of purchasing** is a method of *inventory control* that enables a business to reduce its holdings of goods to very low levels.

The purchaser arranges for materials and components to be delivered when they are required. The purchaser must be confident that the supplier can guarantee delivery and quality just before it is needed for processing. Many customers and suppliers are now linked by computer network, which enables orders to be placed when goods are required.

JIT purchasing reduces inventory-holding costs and, if the computer network is used, it can also reduce administration costs.

### Do you need revision help and advice?

Go to pages 259–72 for a range of revision appendices that include plenty of exam advice and tips.

**key factor:** see *limiting factor*

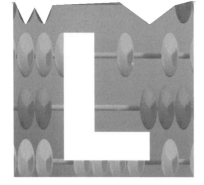

**labour budget** is prepared to determine the business's need for labour for production purposes in the future. It is a plan of the use and availability of labour hours.

### Worked example

Charlotte Jane has the following production budget.

|  | July | August | September | October |
|---|---|---|---|---|
| Production in units | 7000 | 8000 | 9000 | 8500 |

Each unit takes 5 hours to complete and Charlotte Jane has 40 000 hours of labour available each month.

### *Required:*

Prepare a labour budget for the four months ending 31 October.

### *Solution:*

|  | July | August | September | October |
|---|---|---|---|---|
| Production in units | 7000 | 8000 | 9000 | 8500 |
| Labour requirement | 35 000 hours | 40 000 hours | 45 000 hours | 42 500 hours |
| Surplus hours | 5 000 | | | |
| Shortfall in hours | | | 5 000 | 2 500 |

The budget shows that in July, Charlotte Jane can move labour to another process if required. In September and October she must employ new workers on a part-time basis, unless the shortfalls are persistent, in which case permanent staff should be employed. An alternative action could be to move workers who are currently not required from another department/process.

See also *manpower budget*.

**labour costs:** see *direct labour costs* and *indirect labour costs*

**labour efficiency variance:** see *direct labour efficiency variance*

**labour variance:** see *direct labour cost variance*

**labour wage rate variance:** see *direct labour rate variance*

**lead time:** the time that a supplier takes to deliver goods after receipt of an order.

**lease:** a written contract for the letting or renting of a building or piece of land. Vehicles and machinery can also be leased.

**ledger:** the book in which all the financial entries concerning a business are entered. The ledger is usually split into three parts:

- *purchases ledger*
- *sales ledger*
- *general ledger*

(See *division of the ledger.*)

**legacies** are monies (or assets) bequeathed to a club after the death of a member. They should be treated in a similar manner to *donations received*, i.e. credit to the income and expenditure account unless the bequest was made with a specific purpose in mind, or the amount involved is material (see *materiality*), in which case the legacy should be capitalised and shown separately on the club's balance sheet.

**legal entity** has a separate existence from that of its members. A *limited company* is regarded as having an existence in its own right. This means that a limited company can sue and be sued separately from its *shareholders*. The shareholders are not liable for the debts of the company beyond the amounts they have agreed to pay on their shares.

**lessee:** the person to whom a lease has been granted.

**lessor:** the owner of a good being leased.

**liabilities** are monies that are owed for goods and services supplied to a business, or for money borrowed by the business. (See *current liabilities* and *non-current liabilities*.)

**life membership:** permanent membership of a club offered in return for a one-off payment. The club benefits by having large payments which can be used for some extraordinary expenditure, e.g. to purchase the freehold of the grounds of the club or to refurbish a club house. The member benefits by having 'free' membership in subsequent years.

The committee of the club must remember that the annual income received in the future could be lower, and this will affect the future *cash flows* of the club.

The bookkeeping entries on receipt of payments for life membership are:

  **Debit:** Cash book                **Credit:** Life membership account

Each year a proportion of the life membership account is transferred to the *income and expenditure account*. The bookkeeping entries will then be:

  **Debit:** Life membership account     **Credit:** Income and expenditure account

**LIFO (last in first out)** cannot be used (see *IAS 2*).

**limited company:** an organisation that is a separate *legal entity* from its owners. The owners' (*shareholders'*) liability is limited to the shares that they hold in the company. Companies are either *private limited companies* (Ltd) or *public limited companies* (plc). Both types of limited company must register with the Registrar of Companies. Once registered, a private limited company can start to trade, and a public limited company will issue its *prospectus*. When the minimum capital has been raised, a public limited company can start to trade.

**limited liability** means that the liability of *shareholders* for the debts of a *limited company*, of which they are members, is limited to the amount they agreed to subscribe.

For example, if a shareholder purchases 500 £1 shares in a limited company, once he/she has paid this amount (plus any premium), he/she is not liable to make any further payments if the company goes into *liquidation*.

**limited liability company:** see *limited company*

**limited partner:** must register under the provisions of the Limited Partnership Act 1907, and, like the *shareholders* in a *limited company*, the limited partner's liability is limited to the amount of capital invested by him/her.

**limiting factor:** defined by *CIMA* as 'anything which limits the activity of an entity'. Also known as key factor.

A limiting factor could be:
- a shortage of materials
- a shortage of skilled labour
- a lack of productive capacity in a factory
- a lack of stock-holding facilities

It is essential that the managers use any limiting factor to obtain maximum advantage for the business.

**Worked example**

Bobtine plc manufactures four products that use the same type of skilled labour. At the moment there is a shortage of the skilled labour necessary to produce all four products. The following information relates to Bobtine plc:

| Product | A | B | C | D |
|---|---|---|---|---|
| Selling price per unit (£) | 160 | 200 | 250 | 300 |
| Maximum demand for the product | 4000 | 6000 | 5000 | 3000 |
| Material costs per unit (£) | 16 | 20 | 24 | 24 |
| Labour costs per unit (£) | 28 | 21 | 49 | 35 |
| Labour hours per unit | 4 | 3 | 7 | 5 |
| Other direct costs (£) | 10 | 7 | 12 | 9 |

The available skilled labour hours are restricted to 30 000 hours.

*Required:*

A calculation showing the level of production for each product which will maximise profits for Bobtine plc.

*Solution:*

Contribution earned per product:

| | A | B | C | D |
|---|---|---|---|---|
| Selling price per unit (£) | 160 | 200 | 250 | 300 |
| Marginal (variable) costs per unit (£) | 54 | 48 | 85 | 68 |
| Contribution per unit (£) | 106 | 152 | 165 | 232 |

| Contribution per hour of skilled labour used (£) | 26.50 | 50.67 | 23.57 | 46.40 |
|---|---|---|---|---|
| | $\left(\dfrac{106}{4}\right)$ | $\left(\dfrac{152}{3}\right)$ | $\left(\dfrac{165}{7}\right)$ | $\left(\dfrac{232}{5}\right)$ |
| Ranking | 3rd | 1st | 4th | 2nd |

Bobtine plc should produce 6000 units of product B and 2400 units of product D

total hours used 18 000
total hours used 12 000

All labour hours are now used.

This production pattern will maximise Bobtine plc's profits under these circumstances.

However, management may decide it wishes to keep providing a full range of products and so produce some of each product.

**liquidation:** see *bankruptcy*

**liquidity:** the ability of a business to gain access to sufficient cash or near-cash assets in order to meet everyday commitments. It is important for the day-to-day survival of a business; it is as important as *profitability*. Many businesses that go into *liquidation* do so, not because they are unprofitable, but because of their lack of liquidity.

Liquid assets are cash and cash equivalents, trade receivables and inventory.

**liquidity ratio:** see *acid test ratio*

**liquidity ratios:** see *acid test ratio* and *current ratio*

**loan:** money which has been lent and must be repaid at a date sometime in the future.

**loan capital:** part of the medium- to long-term capital of a *limited company* provided by either banks or *debenture* holders.

**loan interest:** the charge made by the provider of a loan for the use of the money. It is calculated as a percentage based on the capital borrowed. Interest on any type of loan is debited to the *income statement*.

**lodgements** are amounts paid into a business bank account. They are entered on the debit side of the *bank cash book* or in the debit *bank column* in a traditional *cash book*. The source document is a *bank paying-in slip*.

Lodgements are shown in the credit column of the business's bank statement.

**long-term finance** is finance that is either non-repayable, e.g. share capital, or needs to be repaid in more than one year, e.g. *debentures* repayable in 2025.

**long-term liabilities:** see *non-current liabilities*

**loss** occurs when the expenses of a business are greater than its incomes. Although it is preferable that a business makes a profit, a loss may be tolerated in the short term, but the situation cannot be sustained in the long run. How long a business can suffer losses without going into *liquidation* depends on the magnitude of its financial resources.

**loss leader** is a very popular item whose price is cut in order to attract customers. The supplier, generally a retail outlet, relies on the customer purchasing other full-priced products at the same time as the loss leader.

**loss of inventory:** goods that have been stolen. Such losses are often not apparent until the year end if a periodic inventory system of valuation used.

To calculate the value of goods that have gone missing during the financial year, an *income statement* is prepared using the figures that ought to apply and this is compared with the actual figures. The difference in closing inventories is assumed to be the goods that have been stolen.

### Worked example

Helen Shaw owns a beauty salon. Several boxes of expensive make-up have been stolen during the year, but she is unsure of the exact value of the stolen goods.

Make-up held at 1 June 20*8 was £387. Make-up held at 31 May 20*9 was £450. Purchases of make-up during the financial year were £18 221. Sales of make-up during the year amounted to £26 781.

All make-up sold in the salon carries a mark-up of 50%.

#### Required:

Calculate the value of goods stolen from Helen's salon.

#### Solution:

**Trading account for the year ended 31 May 20*9**

|  |  | Actual figures |  | As they should be |
|---|---|---|---|---|
|  |  | £ |  | £ |
| Sales |  | 26 781 |  | 26 781 |
| Less cost of sales |  |  |  |  |
| Inventory 1 June 20*8 | 387 |  | 387 |  |
| Purchases | 18 221 |  | 18 221 |  |
|  | 18 608 |  | 18 608 |  |
| Less inventory 31 May 20*9 | 450 |  | 754 |  |
| Stolen goods | 304 |  |  |  |
|  |  | 17 854 |  | 17 854 |
| Gross profit |  | 8 927 |  | 8 927 |

We can calculate the gross profit by taking 33.1/3% of sales, so cost of sales must be £17 854. By deduction, the closing inventory should be £754, but we are told that the make-up held at 31 May 20*9 was valued at £450. We can therefore assume that goods to the value of £304 had been stolen.

**Ltd:** an abbreviation for *private limited company*.

**lump sum:** an amount of money given as one single payment rather than in a number of instalments. On retirement, some pension schemes give a large one-off payment followed by regular monthly payments from the pension fund.

**machine hour rate method of absorbing overheads:** see *absorption*

**mainstream corporation tax** is the balance of a company's *tax liability* remaining after payment of *advance corporation tax (ACT)* during the relevant *accounting period*. It is paid by the company nine months after the end of its accounting period.

**make or buy decisions** are reached in a manufacturing business by the application of *marginal costing* principles. A business may decide to make its own product because:

- it is not produced by another manufacturer
- it is not produced by another manufacturer to the right specification
- the business does not wish to be reliant on another business
- the marginal costs of production are lower than the price quoted by the other manufacturer

### Worked example

O'Reilly Ltd produces tregs. The costings to produce tregs are:

|  | £ |
| --- | --- |
| Variable costs per unit | 28 |
| Fixed costs per unit | 13 |
| Total cost | 41 |

The managers of O'Reilly Ltd have been approached by a Spanish manufacturer who will supply tregs at a cost of £35.

### Required:

Advise the managers of O'Reilly Ltd whether they should continue to manufacture tregs or purchase them from the Spanish supplier.

### Solution:

O'Reilly Ltd should continue to produce tregs.

|  | Make | Buy |
| --- | --- | --- |
|  | £ | £ |
| Variable costs | 28 | 35 |
| Fixed costs | 13 | 13 |
| Total cost | 41 | 48 |

**management accounting** uses financial information:

- to make decisions affecting the future of a business
- to evaluate past decisions
- to make decisions about the allocation and use of a business's resources

Managers require information in order to formulate strategies, to plan and to control the business.

**management buy out:** the purchase of a business by its managers or, in the case of a *limited company*, the purchase of the company by its senior managers and *directors*.

**management by exception:** according to the *CIMA* definition, this is 'the practice of focusing on activities requiring attention and ignoring those that appear to be running smoothly'. *Variance analysis* facilitates management by exception since it highlights areas of business which deviate from the predetermined standards.

**management by objectives** seeks to establish personal targets for all levels of an organisation. These objectives are tested to see if the targets have been achieved within a given time span.

Departmental managers are set clearly identifiable, measurable work targets for all the members of his/her department. The targets are set by consultation with the job holder and his/her immediate superior. This involvement of personnel at all levels of the organisation should ensure that the organisational goals coincide with the managers' personal goals.

**management function of accounting:** accounting information is used to provide managers with information that will improve the performance of their business.

**management information systems** provide a variety of information which will enable the managers to run a business efficiently and effectively. The information is generally stored on a computer which can be accessed by managers and employees of all levels on a 'need to know' basis.

**management of trade payables:** although many people recommend delaying the payments made to suppliers for as long as possible, it is important to be aware of the dangers inherent in such a policy. Delays may result in:

- a damaged reputation resulting in a poor credit rating, a loss of credit facilities and a risk of losing suppliers
- loss of discounts
- risk of legal action

**manager's commission:** performance-related pay for the manager of a business or branch of a business. It is an incentive payment, usually paid as an addition to the manager's basic salary. The amount can be calculated as a percentage of the profits before *commission* is deducted or as a percentage of the profits after the commission is deducted.(See worked example opposite.)

**managing director (MD):** the *director* who is in charge of the day-to-day running of a whole *limited company*. The MD delegates responsibilities to the individual directors on the senior management team with regard to the running of the various sections of the business that they head. The managing director reports to the *chair of the board of directors.* (See *directors*.)

**Worked example**

Frump Ltd operates two retail branches, one in Dressley and the other in Kilton.

Clarry, the manager of the Dressley shop, is paid a basic salary plus 5% commission payable on annual profits earned by the branch before deduction of her commission.

Eddie, the manager of the Kilton shop, is paid a basic salary plus 5% commission based on annual profits earned by the shop after deduction of his commission.

Both shops earned a profit of £17 500 this year.

**Required:**

Calculate the commission due to Clarry and Eddie.

**Solution:**

Clarry's commission $= £17\,500 \times \dfrac{5}{10} = £875$

Eddie's commission $= £17\,500 \times \dfrac{5}{105} = £833.33$

**manpower budget:** this informs the personnel department what the manpower requirements for the organisation will be for the following year. Recruitment and training programmes can then address any staffing or skill shortages. The results of this exercise can then be fed into *production budget* and *cash budget*.

**manufacturing accounts** are the *financial statements* that are prepared to show all the factory costs involved in the production of a final product. The manufacturing account is divided into two sections. These correspond to the nature of the costs involved in the production process:

1 *prime cost* – all the *direct costs* associated with the product(s), e.g. raw materials, *direct labour*, royalties

2 *factory overheads* – all other costs associated with the manufacturing process

The two sections added together give the total production cost, which is transferred to the *income statement* so that the *cost of sales* figure can be ascertained.

Before transferring the total production cost to cost of sales, an inventory adjustment needs to be made for work in progress.

In a manufacturing business, there are three types of *inventory*:
- raw materials – an adjustment to the purchases of raw materials is necessary to determine the value of raw materials actually consumed in the production process
- partly finished goods (*work in progress*) – this adjustment is necessary in order to remove the prime costs and overheads that are included in the value of this type of unsold goods
- finished goods – the adjustment is necessary to calculate the value of goods sold at cost price

Manufacturing accounts are produced as part of the internal financial statements to aid management in their decision making.

## Worked example

The following balances have been extracted from the books of Tinkle plc, a manufacturing company:

|  |  | £000 |
|---|---|---:|
| Inventories at 1 September 20*8 | | |
| Raw materials | | 120 |
| Work in progress | | 37 |
| Finished goods | | 174 |
| Purchases | raw materials | 1 356 |
| | indirect materials | 37 |
| Factory wages | direct | 512 |
| | indirect | 106 |
| Office salaries | | 234 |
| Rent and rates | factory | 31 |
| | offices | 11 |
| Carriage | inward | 4 |
| | outward | 7 |
| Power | | 67 |
| Manufacturing royalties | | 9 |
| Heating and lighting costs | factory | 34 |
| | offices | 12 |
| Other indirect factory expenses | | 60 |
| Sales | | 2 693 |
| Machinery | | 950 |
| Office equipment | | 384 |

Additional information:

|  |  | £000 |
|---|---|---:|
| Inventories at 31 August 20*9 | | |
| Raw materials | | 135 |
| Work in progress | | 32 |
| Finished goods | | 180 |
| Depreciation | machinery 10% per annum | |
| | office 12.5% per annum | |

### Required:

A manufacturing account for the year ended 31 August 20*9.

### Solution:

## Tinkle plc manufacturing account for the year ended 31 August 20*9

|  | £000 | £000 |
|---|---:|---:|
| Inventory of raw materials 1 September 20*8 | | 120 |
| Purchases of raw materials | 1356 | |
| Carriage inward | 4 | 1360 |
| | | 1480 |
| Less inventory of raw materials 31 August 20*9 | | (135) |
| Raw materials consumed | | 1345 |

| | | |
|---|---:|---:|
| Direct wages | | 512 |
| Royalties | | 9 |
| Prime cost | | 1866 |
| Factory overheads | | |
| Indirect materials | 37 | |
| Indirect labour | 106 | |
| Factory rent and rates | 31 | |
| Power | 67 | |
| Factory heat and light | 34 | |
| Factory expenses | 60 | |
| Depreciation of machinery | 95 | 430 |
| | | 2296 |
| Work in progress 1 September 20*8 | | 37 |
| | | 2333 |
| Less work in progress 31 August 20*9 | | (32) |
| Production cost of completed goods | | 2301 |

Some manufacturing businesses transfer their goods from the factory at cost plus a certain percentage, or at what the goods might have cost if purchased from another manufacturer. This process will not increase the overall profits of the business, it will merely distinguish the profits earned by two separate **cost centres.**

**Inventories IAS 2** requires that inventories be shown in the **balance sheet** at cost of production prices. If a manufacturer uses a system of production cost plus a percentage **mark-up**, the *inventory* of finished goods includes an element of factory profit. This contravenes:

- the concept of **prudence**
- the **realisation concept**

so this profit needs to be eliminated in the **income statement** since the **net profit** will be overstated by the amount of the **unrealised profit**. The profit element included must also be eliminated from the **closing inventory** included in the **balance sheet** as a **current asset**, since all inventories should be valued at cost (or net realisable value if this is lower than cost), not cost plus a mark-up!

### Worked example

The balances shown in the previous example have been extracted from the books of Tinkle plc at 31 August 20*9. It is company policy to transfer manufactured goods to the company income statement at cost + 20%.

### Required:

Prepare the following for the year ended 31 August 20*9:

a) provision for unrealised profit account

b) an extract from the income statement for the year ended 31 August 20*9 showing the entry relating to the factory profit

147

c) an extract from the balance sheet at 31 August 20*9 showing the treatment of the provision for unrealised profit

*Solution:*

a) **Provision for unrealised profit account**

|          |        | Bal. b/d | 29 000 | £174 000 = 120% of cost of stock, so |
|----------|--------|----------|--------|---------------------------------------|
| Bal. c/d | 30 000 | Inc St   | 1 000  | £29 000 is the profit loading on £174 000 |
|          | 30 000 |          | 30 000 |                                       |
|          |        | Bal. b/d | 30 000 | £180 000 = 120% of cost of stock, so  |
|          |        |          |        | £30 000 is the profit loading on £180 000 |

b) **Tinkle plc income statement (extract) for the year ended 31 August 20*9**

|                                      | £000s  |
|--------------------------------------|--------|
| Gross profit on manufacturing        | 460.20 |
| Less provision for unrealised profit | 1.00   |
|                                      | 459.20 |

c) **Tinkle plc balance sheet (extract) at 31 August 20*9**

| Current assets | £000 | £000 | £000 |
|----------------|------|------|------|
| Inventories    |      |      |      |
| Raw materials  |      | 135  |      |
| Work in progress |    | 32   |      |
| Finished goods | 180  |      |      |
| Less provision for unrealised profit | 30 | 150 | 317 |

**manufacturing overheads:** all expenses incurred in running a factory other than those that are included in the *manufacturing account* under the *prime cost* heading. Manufacturing overheads include:
- *indirect material costs* – those materials which cannot be directly identified with the product(s), e.g. cleaning materials used in the factory
- *indirect labour costs* – wages which cannot be directly identified with the product(s), e.g. supervisory wages
- *indirect expenses* – other expenses which cannot be directly identified with the product(s), e.g. factory rent and rates, factory insurances, etc.

(See *manufacturing accounts*.)

**manufacturing profit:** see *manufacturing accounts*

**margin:** this term generally refers to the gross margin, and shows a business's gross profit as a percentage of the net sales. The margin can be improved by either purchasing (or manufacturing) cheaper goods or increasing the selling price to customers. It shows how many pence gross profit is earned out of every £ of sales. The calculation is:

$$FORMULA: \quad \frac{\text{gross profit}}{\text{sales}} \times 100$$

### Worked example

The following data refer to Wert & Co.:

|  | £ |
|---|---|
| Sales | 134 091 |
| Cost of sales | 56 859 |
| Gross profit | 77 232 |

### Required:

Calculate the gross margin earned by Wert & Co.

### Solution:

$$\text{gross margin} = \frac{\text{gross profit}}{\text{sales}} \times 100 = \frac{77\ 232}{134\ 091} \times 100 = 57.6\%$$

No comment can be made as to whether this is a good margin or not. Trends should be observed or comparisons made with other similar businesses.

**marginal costing:** a costing method based on the extra costs incurred and extra revenues generated by the production and sale of an additional item(s). It requires a clear distinction between *variable costs* and *fixed costs*. No attempt is made to allocate fixed costs to *cost centres* or *cost units*.

Marginal costing is used when:

- costing special one-off contracts or jobs (see *special-order pricing*)
- considering whether to make or buy a product (see *make or buy decisions*)
- choosing between competing alternative courses of action (see *competing courses of action*)
- when a business has a *limiting factor*
- calculating the *break-even point* for a product

(See *contribution pricing*.)

**marginal costs:** the extra costs involved in producing one additional unit of production. For example, Tocle & Son produce 1540 units of a product at a total cost of £34 723. When Tocle & Son produce 1 541 units the total cost rises to £34 947. The marginal cost of the marginal product is £224.

**marginal revenue:** the extra revenue generated by the sale of one additional unit of production.

**margin of safety:** the difference between the actual sales achieved, or forecast as achievable, and the break-even level of sales. The margin of safety indicates to management how far sales can fall before the business will move out of profit and into a loss-making situation. Clearly, the greater the margin of safety, the better for the business.

The margin of safety is generally expressed in units, but can be expressed in sales value or as a percentage of sales.

**Worked example**

break-even level of sales = £414 000

expected level of sales   = £1 380 000

*Required:*

The margin of safety expressed as a percentage of expected total turnover.

*Solution:*

Expected level of sales can drop by 70% before the break-even point is reached.

$$\text{margin of safety in percentage terms} = \frac{1\,380\,000 - 414\,000}{1\,380\,000} \times 100$$

$$= \frac{966\,000}{1\,380\,000} \times 100 = 70\%$$

For a worked example using graphical means, see **break-even point**.

**market analyst** makes a detailed examination and analysis of a market and then reports on his/her findings.

**marketing** is defined by the Chartered Institute of Marketing as 'the management process responsible for identifying, anticipating and satisfying customer requirements profitably'.

**market penetration pricing:** see *penetration pricing*

**market skimming pricing** occurs when a new product is launched. The manufacturer can charge a high price before competition reduces the market price. Manufacturers often justify this type of price setting as an attempt to recoup *research and development costs*, before competition reduces their margins.

**market value:** the price placed on a good by the forces of demand and supply prevailing in the market.

**mark-up** shows a business's *gross profit* as a percentage of the *cost of sales*. The mark-up of a business can be improved by either purchasing (or manufacturing) cheaper goods or increasing the selling price to customers.

It shows how many pence of gross profit has been added to each £ of the cost of the sales. The calculation is:

*FORMULA:* $\dfrac{\text{gross profit}}{\text{cost of sales}} \times 100$

**Worked example**

The following data refer to Wert & Co.:

|  | £ |
|---|---|
| Sales | 134 091 |
| Cost of sales | 56 859 |
| Gross profit | 77 232 |

*Required:*

Calculate the mark-up earned by Wert & Co.

*Solution:*

$$\text{mark-up} = \frac{\text{gross profit}}{\text{cost of sales}} \times 100 = \frac{77\ 232}{56\ 859} \times 100 = 135.83\%$$

**master budget:** an *income statement* and a *balance sheet* prepared from all the operational budgets. Examination questions will often ask for the preparation of a budgeted (or forecast) income statement and budgeted (forecast) balance sheet.

The preparation of the budgeted *financial statements* is no different from the preparation of a 'normal' set of financial statements, but remember that some budgets are prepared on a cash basis (*cash budget* ) whilst the master budget is prepared using the *accruals concept*.

**mastercard:** a credit card system.

**matching concept:** see *accruals concept*

**material costs:** see *direct material costs* and *indirect material costs*

**materiality:** if the inclusion or exclusion of information would mislead the users of a financial statement, then that information is material. For example, a business supplies the office junior with a ruler, costing 87 pence. The ruler will be used for, say, ten years. Theoretically, the ruler is a fixed asset and as such it should be depreciated over its useful economic life. Clearly, to do this would not be cost effective. The purchase is therefore treated as revenue expenditure and debited to office sundries. Doing this would not mislead a prospective investor, so it is not a material transaction.

On the other hand, if a computer system costing £180 000 was debited to office expenses, this would significantly change profits and would mislead the users of the accounts. This is therefore a material transaction.

**material price variance:** see *direct material price variance*

**material usage variance:** see *direct material usage variance*

**maximum number of partners** is generally 20. There are, however, a number of exceptions, e.g. solicitors and accountants.

**maximum number of shareholders** in a *public limited company* is determined by the number of shares issued.

**MD:** see *managing director*

**measured daywork** grades the efficiency of workers and pays them accordingly. A standard level of performance is agreed at 100%, and performance is then categorised into efficiency bands. If 100% were paid £7.50 per hour:
- efficiency band 90%–100% might be paid £6.00 per hour
- efficiency band 100%–120% might be paid £9.00 per hour

**medium-sized companies** are those that satisfy two of the following conditions:
- not more than £25.9 million turnover
- total assets of no more than £12.9 million
- average number of employees does not exceed 250

They are allowed certain 'filing exemptions' in the accounts that they submit to the *Registrar of Companies*. This is to protect them from rival businesses acquiring sensitive information.

Analyses of turnover and profit are not required, but the **balance sheet** must be prepared in full, and a **directors' report** must be filed with the accounts. (See **reporting requirements for medium-sized companies**.)

**members' equity:** the total of issued ordinary shares and permanent preferred shares plus all the **reserves**.

**memorandum accounts:** these are kept to give additional information about entries in the double-entry system. They are not, in themselves, part of the double entry system. For example, when **control accounts** are integrated into the double-entry system, **personal accounts** in the **purchase** and **sales ledger** will be kept as memorandum accounts only. If the personal accounts are part of the double-entry system, then the control account is kept as a memorandum account and is used only as part of the control system.

---

**Worked example**

Johnson purchases £176 goods from McTavish on credit.

*Required:*

The journal entries in Johnson's books to record the purchase if:

a) control accounts are integrated into the system

b) control accounts are not integrated

*Solution:*

**Journal**

|  | Dr | Cr |
|---|---|---|
|  | £ | £ |
| a) Purchases | 176 | |
| Purchase ledger control | | 176 |
| b) Purchases | 176 | |
| McTavish | | 176 |

---

**Memorandum of Association:** a document filed with the **Registrar of Companies** before a **limited company** can become incorporated. It defines the external relationship of the company to the outside world. The details filed include:
- the company's name, address and registered office
- share capital
- the company's objectives

**merchant bank** offers banking services to industry and businesses, and deals internationally.

**merger** takes place when a company issues its shares in exchange for the shares in another company. Sometimes a new company is formed and issues its shares to the **shareholders** in two or more 'old' companies. In neither of these circumstances has any cash changed hands. In both cases there is usually mutual agreement to the **takeover**.

**methods of inventory valuation** are used to value the **closing inventory** of a business in order to prepare the **financial statements**.

Some businesses keep very detailed records of receipts and issues of goods, making entries in the stores *ledger* after every transaction. This is known as a perpetual method and would be used by a business that needs to cost out its work very carefully. Most businesses using this method would have the system computerised.

Other businesses will calculate inventory only once, at the year end. This is known as a periodic method. The local mini-market or newsagents would probably use this method.

The overriding principle with regard to valuation of **inventory** is that inventory should be valued at the lower of **cost** or **net realisable value**. The following are the most frequently used methods of valuing the issues of goods from stores:

- **first in first out (FIFO)** – assumes that the first goods purchased will be the first ones to be delivered to the requisitioning department
- **weighted average cost method of inventory valuation (AVCO)** recalculates the average cost of goods held as inventory each time a new delivery of goods is received. Issues are then made at the weighted average cost

*Important note:* both methods described above are only methods of calculating the value of **closing inventory**, they are not necessarily methods of issuing goods to requisitioning departments.

### Worked example

Kitson Ltd purchases Vf/7 components to use in its manufacturing process. The following were the receipts and issues of the component during the month of January:

| | Receipts | | Issues | |
|---|---|---|---|---|
| 7 January | 6 @ £6 | | 10 January | 5 |
| 12 January | 10 @ £7 | | 19 January | 7 |
| 21 January | 8 @ £8 | | 28 January | 7 |

*Required:*

Calculate the value of closing inventory of component Vf/7 using:

i)     FIFO method of issuing goods from stores

ii)    AVCO method of issuing goods from stores

*Solution:*

| | | Receipts | Issues | Balance |
|---|---|---|---|---|
| i) | FIFO | | | |
| | 7 January | 6 @ £6 | | £36.00 |
| | 10 January | | 5 | 6.00 |
| | 12 January | 10 @ £7 | | 76.00 |
| | 19 January | | 7 | 28.00 |
| | 21 January | 8 @ £8 | | 92.00 |
| | 28 January | | 7 | 40.00 |
| ii) | AVCO | | | |
| | 7 January | 6 @ £6 | | 36.00 |
| | 10 January | | 5 | 6.00 |

153

| 12 January | 10 @ £7 | | 76.00 | (£6.91 ave cost) |
|---|---|---|---|---|
| 19 January | | 7 | 27.64 | (£6.91 × 4) |
| 21 January | 8 @ £8 | | 91.64 | (£7.64 ave cost) |
| 28 January | | 7 | 38.20 | (£7.64 × 5) |

Since each of the above methods gives a different closing inventory figure, it should be obvious that gross profits will differ according to the method used.

The advantages and disadvantages of each of the methods of *inventory* valuation are:

*FIFO:*

advantages:
- it is probably the method that the lay person would intuitively use
- issue prices are based on the prices that have actually been paid for the goods
- closing *inventory* values are based on the most recent prices paid
- it is an acceptable method from the point of view of the **Companies Act 1985**, **IAS 2** and for HMRC purposes

disadvantages:
- issues of goods are not at the most recent prices and this could influence the costing of work
- in times of rising prices, FIFO shows higher profit figures earlier – goes against the concept of prudence

*AVCO:*

advantages:
- prices are averaged so it recognises that issues from *inventory* have equal value to the business
- variations in issue prices are minimised, marked changes are ironed out
- it allows comparison of profit figures to be made on a more realistic basis
- closing *inventory* valuations are fairly close to the latest prices paid (the method is weighted towards the most recent purchases)
- it is an acceptable basis for the purposes of **IAS 2** and the **Companies Act 1985**

disadvantages:
- it requires a new calculation each time new goods are purchased
- the price charged for issues will not agree with the price paid to purchase the goods

**minimum disclosure requirements** for a *limited company* are stipulated by law. The main statutory requirements required by the **Companies Act 1985** are:
- an *income statement*
- a *balance sheet*
- a *directors' report*
- an *auditors' report*

All companies preparing *financial statements* that conform to *IFRSs* must also present a *statement of cash flows*.

**minimum shareholders** in a *public limited company* is two.

**minority interests:** if a *holding company* owns less than 100 per cent of the issued ordinary shares in its *subsidiary*, the shares that it does not hold are held by minority interests.

**minority shareholders** are *shareholders* who own less than half of the shares in a *limited company*.

**MIS:** see *management information systems*

**money measurement concept** states that only transactions that can be measured in monetary terms should be included in the business *books of account*. Because of their subjectivity it is extremely difficult to put a value on:
- managerial efficiency
- skill and efficiency of the workforce
- good customer relations

None of these can be included in the final accounts.

**mortgage:** a legal agreement whereby money is loaned to purchase property. The title deeds to the property are held by the *mortgagor*.

**mortgage debenture:** see *debentures*

**mortgagor:** the person or financial institution who is the lender of money to a mortgagee (the borrower) to purchase property.

**mutually exclusive project:** a project which when selected automatically excludes any other project(s) that may be under consideration.

M

**Are you studying other subjects?**

The *A–Z Handbooks (digital editions)* are available in 14 different subjects. Browse the range and order other handbooks at **www.philipallan.co.uk/a-zonline**.

**name:** a person who provides security for insurance arranged by a syndicate at Lloyds of London.

**narratives** are required when entries are made in a *journal*. This indicates to a reader why the entries are being made in the two *ledger* accounts. An entry in a journal to transfer an incorrect entry might read like this:

|  | Dr | Cr |
|---|---|---|
| T Phelps | 46 |  |
| T Philips |  | 46 |

Correction of error: Sales £46 to T Phelps incorrectly entered in T Philips account.

**National Insurance:** state insurance which pays for medical care, hospitals and social security payments.

**National Insurance contributions:** monies paid into the National Insurance scheme by both employers and employees.

**National Insurance number:** the number given to an individual as an identification for social security reasons.

**nationalised industries:** industries which are owned by the state. They are in the *public sector*.

**net asset value (NAV):** the total value of an organisation. It is calculated by deducting all external liabilities from all assets owned by the organisation.

---

**Worked example**

The business assets and liabilities of John Fallon are as follows:

Premises at book value £120 000; machinery at book value £30 000; vehicle at book value £18 000; inventory at cost £6000; trade receivables £1800; trade payables £1300; cash and cash equivalents £1200; non-current liability: mortgage £40 000.

*Required:*

Calculate the net asset value of John Fallon's business.

*Solution:*

|  | £ |
|---|---|
| Premises | 120 000 |
| Machinery | 30 000 |
| Vehicle | 18 000 |

| | | |
|---|---:|---:|
| Inventory | 6 000 | |
| Trade receivable | 1 800 | |
| Cash and cash equivalents | 1 200 | |
| | 177 000 | |
| Non-current liability: | | |
| Mortgage | 40 000 | |
| Trade payables | 1 300 | 41 300 |
| Net asset value | | 135 700 |

The net asset value is equal to the capital structure of the organisation. Also known as net worth.

**net asset value per share:** the *net asset value* of a *limited company* divided by the number of ordinary shares issued.

### Worked example

Ousby plc has an issued share capital of 800 000 ordinary shares of 25 pence each. The company has a net asset value of £184 000.

### Required:

Calculate the net asset value per share for Ousby plc.

### Solution:

$$\text{net asset value per share } \frac{£184\ 000}{800\ 000} = 23 \text{ pence per share}$$

**net book value:** see *carrying amount*

**net borrowings:** the borrowings of a business less any cash the business is holding in its bank accounts.

**net cash flow:** the difference between the cash received by an organisation and the cash being spent by the organisation.

**net current assets:** the excess of *current assets* over *current liabilities*, also known as working capital. If a business's current liabilities exceed its current assets, then this would be known as net current liabilities.

**net debt** is the borrowings of a *limited company* less its cash and liquid resources.

The calculation is: debentures + overdrafts – cash and cash equivalents

The net debt figure is needed in the reconciliation of net cash to movement in net debt in *statements of cash flow IAS 7*.

**net dividend per share:** the dividend per share after the deduction of any personal income tax.

**net loss:** the balance shown on the *income statement* when expenses incurred by a business exceed the *gross profit* earned by the business.

**net margin** shows a business's *profit for the year* as a percentage of net sales. It reveals how much the business earns out of every £1 of net sales, after all expenses have been met.

Net margin shows how efficiently the business's expenses are being controlled. To improve the ratio, the business must reduce the proportion of expenses paid out of every £1 turnover. The calculation is:

FORMULA: $\dfrac{\text{net profit}}{\text{sales}} \times 100$

## Worked example

The following is a summarised extract from the income statement for Gray & Co.:

|  | £ |
|---|---|
| Sales | 129 056 |
| Cost of sales | 57 330 |
| Gross profit | 71 726 |
| Less expenses | 49 702 |
| Profit for year | 22 024 |

### Required:

Calculate the net margin for Gray & Co.

### Solution:

$$\text{net margin} = \dfrac{\text{net profit}}{\text{sales}} \times 100 = \dfrac{22\ 024}{129\ 056} \times 100 = 17.07\%$$

**net present value method of capital investment appraisal** uses the present value of **net cash flows** (cash inflows minus cash outflows using today's price levels), less the initial investment. If the net present value of the investment is positive then the investment is acceptable; if the net present value is negative then the investment should be rejected on financial grounds. (Note: the business may still undertake the investment for non-financial reasons, e.g. to avoid redundancies in the workforce. See **social accounting**.)

When comparing mutually exclusive projects, a business should accept the investment(s) which gives the greatest net present value, and the investments giving the lower returns should be rejected.

## Worked example

Michelle Vogt is considering whether to purchase a new machine costing £20 000. She estimates that the future cash flows generated by the machine will be:

|  | Revenue receipts | Operating payments |
|---|---|---|
|  | £ | £ |
| Year 1 | 8 000 | 7 000 |
| Year 2 | 12 000 | 9 000 |
| Year 3 | 17 000 | 12 000 |
| Year 4 | 20 000 | 13 000 |
| Year 5 | 26 000 | 16 000 |

Her cost of capital is 10%. All costs are paid and all revenues are received on the last day of each year. The following is an extract from the present value tables of £1 at 10%:

|  | 10% |
| --- | --- |
| Year 1 | 0.909 |
| Year 2 | 0.826 |
| Year 3 | 0.751 |
| Year 4 | 0.683 |
| Year 5 | 0.621 |

**Required:**

Advise Michelle whether, on financial grounds, she ought to invest in the new machine.

**Solution:**

| Year | Cash flows | Present value factor | Net present value |
| --- | --- | --- | --- |
|  | £ |  | £ |
| 0 (now) | (20 000) | 1 | (20 000) |
| 1 | 1 000 | 0.909 | 909 |
| 2 | 3 000 | 0.826 | 2 478 |
| 3 | 5 000 | 0.751 | 3 755 |
| 4 | 7 000 | 0.683 | 4 781 |
| 5 | 10 000 | 0.621 | 6 210 |
|  |  |  | (1 867) |

Michelle should not buy the new machine since it would yield a negative net present value.

**net profit:** see *profit for the year*

**net profit margin:** see *net margin*

**net profit-to-sales ratio:** see *net margin*

**net realisable value:** see *methods of inventory valuation*

**net salary:** a person's income after tax, **National Insurance** and voluntary deductions have been deducted from their gross salary. It is also known as take-home pay.

**net worth:** see *net asset value*

**new issues:** previously unissued shares issued from the **authorised share capital** of a company. The issue can be to:
- the general public (for bookkeeping entries see **issue of shares**)
- existing **shareholders** as a bonus (scrip) issue (for bookkeeping entries see **bonus shares**), or
- existing shareholders as a **rights issue**

**next in first out (NIFO):** a method of valuing finished goods at the end of the **accounting period** which uses the replacement cost of the goods not their historical cost.

**NIFO:** see *next in first out*

**nominal accounts** are *general ledger* accounts that record incomes and expenses such as purchases, sales, wages, rent, business rates, etc.

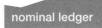

**nominal ledger:** the name given to the *general ledger* in computer programs.

**nominal share capital:** see *authorised share capital*

**nominal value of ordinary shares:** the face value or par value of shares. Once shares have been issued their market price can rise or fall. After a number of years it is unlikely that the *market value* will bear any resemblance to the nominal value. Any *rights issue* or issues to the general public are unlikely to be at the nominal value; the price will be fixed by the *directors* after reference to the current market price when the decision to raise more capital is taken.

**non-adjusting events** refers to events that occur after the balance sheet date, concerning conditions that did not exist at that time. They do not result in changes to the financial statements. If, however, they are material, a note to the financial statements is necessary to ensure that the financial statements are not misleading to any users of the accounts. See *events after the reporting period IAS 10*.

**non-controllable costs:** see *controllable costs*

**non-current asset register** is a record of all the *non-current assets* owned by a business. It lists all the important facts about all the assets of the business. The register shows:
- date of *acquisition*
- description
- cost
- unique registration number of each non-current asset
- location of each non-current asset
- method of depreciation to be applied
- *aggregate depreciation* to date
- *impairment losses*
- details of revaluations where necessary
- estimated useful life

and when disposed of:
- date
- proceeds
- authorisation for disposal

The total cost or valuation of all assets listed in the register should agree with the balance in the non-current asset accounts in the *general ledger*. Similarly, the totals of depreciation in the register should agree with the balances on the depreciation accounts in the general ledger.

The register is a detailed analysis of the *non-current asset* accounts. It is not part of the *double-entry bookkeeping* system; it is a memorandum book.

Physical checks of the assets held by a business should be made against the entries in the register.

**non-current asset replacement reserve:** a *revenue reserve* set aside out of profits to provide funds for the purchase of replacement assets in the future. It is essential that these funds are available in liquid form.

**non-current assets** are assets of a business that are held for more than one financial period. They are not purchased primarily to be resold; they are held to help generate profits for the business.

Non-current assets are listed in reverse order of *liquidity*, the most permanent coming first and ending with the non-current assets that can most easily be turned into cash. This is a typical list of non-current assets for a manufacturing business:

- land and buildings
- plant and machinery
- fixtures and fittings
- office equipment
- motor vehicles

Totals of non-current assets are usually shown in the *balance sheets* of *limited companies* under the headings:

- *property, plant and equipment*
- *tangible non-current assets*
- intangible non-current assets
- *investments*

The details are shown in the notes to the accounts; these include, for each type of asset:

- cost or valuation at the beginning and end of the year
- movements (purchases and sales)
- *depreciation* charge for the year, accumulated depreciation to date and the effect that any disposals have had on depreciation
- methods of depreciation used and the rates

**non-current asset turnover ratio:** the ratio of *revenue* to *non-current assets*.
If a business has non-current assets with a *carrying amount* of £100 000 and its annual turnover is £860 000, the non-current asset turnover ratio would be:

$$FORMULA: \quad \frac{sales}{book\ value\ of\ non\text{-}current\ assets} = \frac{860\ 000}{100\ 000}$$

$$= 8.6\ times$$

or £116.3 per £1000 of sales

This ratio measures the utilisation the business is obtaining from its investment in non-current assets. If the ratio is low compared with similar businesses, it would indicate that the managers may not be using their non-current assets to their full potential.

**non-current liabilities** are debts that are not due for payment within the next accounting period. They include long-term bank loans, mortgages and, in the case of limited companies, debenture stock.

**normal losses** are losses of materials in the normal production process which cannot be avoided. In certain processes liquids will evaporate, when producing timber-based products off-cuts of wood will be lost, etc. No matter how efficient or effective a production process, there will still be these kinds of uncontrollable waste.

**notice of coding** is sent to a taxpayer and his/her employer at the beginning of each tax year. The notice indicates the tax code to be used in calculating the tax to be deducted from the employee's gross pay. The tax code is based on the total of the *personal allowances*.

**notional expenses** are sometimes included in costings to ensure that expenses which should be included are charged to the job. For example, a manufacturing business might own its factory. A notional rent figure could be included in the costings to arrive at the total costs to be charged to a job.

**notional profit:** the value of certified work to date on a *contract*, less the costs involved on the contract to date, less some provision in anticipation of any unforeseen circumstances. The concept of notional profit is applied when a contract has already incurred large costs and the contract is still some way off completion.

**npv:** see *net present value*

**Aiming for a grade A\*?**

Don't forget to log on to **www.philipallan.co.uk/a-zonline** for advice.

**objectivity** avoids bias when making asset valuations. Assets are therefore valued at cost for *balance sheet* purposes. *Limited companies* do, from time to time, revalue certain assets to reflect current market price. (See *asset revaluation*.)

**omissions** are bookkeeping errors which will not be revealed by extracting a *trial balance*. They should be corrected by using the *journal*.

---

### Worked example

A purchase invoice for £57 received from Grant King has been destroyed. It has not been entered in the purchase day book.

*Required:*

Journal entries to rectify the error of omission.

*Solution:*

**Journal**

|  | Dr | Cr |
|---|---|---|
|  | £ | £ |
| Purchases | 57 |  |
| Grant King |  | 57 |

---

**on-cost:** an alternative name used for *fixed costs*.

**open cheque:** see *cheque*

**opening entries in a business's books** are recorded in the *journal*.

---

### Worked example

Tom has just purchased an existing business from Sarah. He has paid a purchase consideration of £85 000. He has used £45 000 of his own savings and he has borrowed £40 000 from his bank. The assets (at book value) taken over from Sarah are:

Premises £42 000; fixtures and fittings £17 500; vehicle £4200; and inventory £2600.

*Required:*

The journal entries required to open the ledger accounts in Tom's books of account.

*Solution:*

**Journal**

|  | Dr £ | Cr £ |
|---|---|---|
| Premises | 42 000 | |
| Fixtures and fittings | 17 500 | |
| Vehicle | 4 200 | |
| Inventory | 2 600 | |
| Goodwill | 18 700 | |
| Capital | | 45 000 |
| Bank loan | | 40 000 |
| | 85 000 | 85 000 |

**opening inventory:** the *closing inventory* from the previous financial period.

### Worked example

Refer back to the worked example for closing inventory. Mary McDougal is now in her second year of trading. Her year end is 30 November 20*9.

The entries on the debit side of her purchases account total £35 600.

The entries on the credit side of her sales account total £58 000.

Mary values her inventory on 30 November 20*9 at £6200.

*Required:*

Prepare an extract from the income statement and the inventory account as they would appear in the general ledger of Mary McDougal at the end of her second year of trading.

*Solution:*

At the end of Mary's second year of trading the inventory account would look like this:

**Stock**

|  | £ |
|---|---|
| Yr1 Income Statement | 4 500 |

If Mary extracted a trial balance, the balance on the inventory account would have to be shown since it is a balance in her general ledger. In a trial balance the opening inventory is always shown.

Mary's general ledger would show the following two accounts at 30 November 20*8:

**Income statement for the year ended 30 November 20*8**

|  | £ |  | £ |
|---|---|---|---|
| Inventory | 4 500 | | |

**Inventory**

|  | £ |  | £ |
|---|---|---|---|
| Yr1 Inc Stat | 4 500 | Yr2 Inc Stat | 4 500 |

Mary's inventory at the end of her second year of trading should now be entered in her inventory account in the general ledger.

**Income statement (extract) for the year ended 30 November 20*9**

| | £ | | £ |
|---|---|---|---|
| Inventory | 4 500 | Sales | 58 000 |
| Purchases | 35 600 | Inventory | 6 200 |
| Gross profit c/d | 24 100 | | |
| | 64 200 | | 64 200 |

**Inventory**

| | £ | | £ |
|---|---|---|---|
| Yr1 Inc Stat | 4 500 | Yr2 Inc Stat | 4 500 |
| Yr2 Inc Stat | 6 200 | | |

**open-market purchase:** purchase of shares in a recognised *stock market*.

**operating lease:** a short-term lease. There is no transfer of the risks and rewards of ownership to the lessee.

**operating statements** are used to summarise the *variances* that have been calculated using standard costing techniques. The statement reconciles the budgeted profit with the actual profit achieved:
- the statement starts with the budgeted profit
- the *favourable variances* are added
- the *adverse variances* are deducted
- the result is the actual profit

For the calculation of the variances see under the appropriate headings.

A standard cost operating statement could look like this:

**Sean Drew Ltd standard cost operating statement for the year ended 30 June 20*9**

| | | £ | £ | £ |
|---|---|---|---|---|
| Budgeted profit | | | | 16 700 |
| Sales volume variance | | | | (600) |
| | | | | 16 100 |
| Sales price variance | | | | 400 |
| | | | | 16 500 |
| Cost variances | | Adverse | Favourable | |
| Direct materials: price | | 600 | | |
| usage | | 100 | | |
| Direct labour: wage rate | | | 200 | |
| efficiency | | 50 | | |
| Variable production overhead: | expenditure | 400 | | |
| | efficiency | | 250 | |
| Fixed production overhead: | expenditure | | 800 | |
| | efficiency | 125 | | |
| | | 1 275 | 1 250 | (25) |
| Operating profit | | | | 16 475 |

165

| Less: | actual administrative overhead | 2 350 | |
|---|---|---|---|
| | actual selling and distribution overhead | 4 560 | 6 910 |
| | Actual profit | | 9 565 |

**operational costing:** the costing of the production processes involved in the manufacture of mass-produced products. The products are made to be held as inventory until an order is received. They are not made to a customer's specific requirements.

For example, costing might be made for the production of 10 000 boxes of matches. The total production costs are divided by 10 000 to arrive at the cost of producing one box of matches. Clearly, this is more sensible than trying to calculate the cost of producing one box.

**operational gearing:** a situation in which a business has high *fixed costs* which are financed by borrowings.

**opportunity cost:** the cost of making a decision in terms of the benefit lost by not using the resources in the next best alternative. (If resources are used, they are not available for use in another situation.) Opportunity cost is not necessarily a monetary cost, it is simply an opportunity forgone. For example, the cost of an evening visit to a relative could be an episode of *Eastenders* missed on television.

**ordinary share capital:** the total of all the issued shares held by the *ordinary shareholders*. It must be shown under the headings:
* *authorised share capital*
* *issued share capital*

The number of shares authorised and issued must be shown in the *balance sheet* or by way of a note to the accounts. The *nominal value* must also be stated.

**ordinary shareholders** are the owners of a *limited company*. The ordinary shareholders have:
* full voting rights at *shareholders'* meetings
* an interest in the net assets of the company
* an interest in the profits of the company (see *dividends*)

One company may own shares in another company. If a company owns more than 50 per cent of the ordinary shares in another company it can control that company. It can out-vote any shareholder or group of shareholders at any shareholders' meeting. (See *holding company* and *subsidiary company*.)

**ordinary shares** represent part ownership in a *limited company*. They are the most common type of share issued by a limited company. Every limited company has ordinary shares.

**organisation chart** shows as a diagram the structure of a business (see diagram opposite). Each job title is shown and formal lines of authority and responsibility are mapped. Very large businesses should have a chart for the business as a whole, as well as departmental or functional organisation charts.

Chains of command should be clear and each person should be answerable to only one other person. The chart should show:
* the different functions and departments
* main responsibilities (in the case of departmental charts)
* who reports to whom
* spans of control
* communication channels

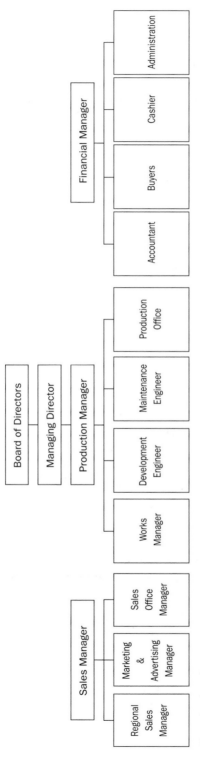

*Organisation chart*

**output-related pay schemes:** see *piece work*

**over-absorption of overheads** occurs when more units are produced than predicted in the budget. This means that more overheads are recovered than was intended.

### Worked example

In August, Brownlee Industries Ltd budgeted for overhead expenditure of £360 000 for department J on a budgeted output of 120 000 units. The budgeted overhead expenditure for department Q was £128 000 based on a budgeted output of 64 000 units.

*Required:*

a) Calculate the overhead absorption rate for departments J and Q based on the unit-produced method.

b) Calculate for each department the over- or under-recovery of overheads. Department J's actual output was 124 000 units. Department Q's actual expenditure was £129 000.

*Solution:*

a) overhead absorption rate for department J $= \dfrac{\text{overhead expenditure}}{\text{units produced}}$

$$= \dfrac{£360\,000}{120\,000} = £3$$

overhead absorption rate for department Q $= \dfrac{\text{overhead expenditure}}{\text{units produced}}$

$$= \dfrac{£128\,000}{64\,000} = £2$$

b) department J over-recovery = £12 000

$\left(124\,000 \text{ units} \times £3 \text{ recovery rate} = £372\,000 - \text{budgeted overheads } £360\,000\right)$

department Q under-recovery = £1000

$\left(\text{actual overheads} = £129\,000 - \text{budgeted overheads } £128\,000\right)$

These figures will be posted to an overhead adjustment account. At the financial year end a credit balance will be posted to the credit of the income statement. A debit balance on the overhead adjustment account will be posted to the debit of the income statement.

If the £12 000 over-recovery and the £1000 under-recovery were the only entries in the overhead adjustment account, at the financial year end the account would show the following entries:

**Overhead adjustment account**

|  | £ |  | £ |
|---|---|---|---|
| Under-recovery of overheads | 1 000 | Over-recovery of overheads | 12 000 |
| Income statement | 11 000 | | |
| | 12 000 | | 12 000 |

**overall recovery rate** can be used where a manufacturing business has a number of production departments. Rather than calculating an overhead recovery rate for each department, a recovery rate for the factory as a whole is calculated. It is also known as the blanket recovery rate. The calculation is:

FORMULA:   overall recovery rate $= \dfrac{\text{total factory overheads}}{\text{chosen absorption method}}$

### Worked example

Menny plc is a manufacturing company. The total overheads for the whole factory are estimated to be £67 165. The total labour hours worked in the factory for the month of February are estimated to be 28 340 hours.

### Required:

Calculate the overall recovery rate for February for Menny plc based on a direct labour hour rate method.

### Solution:

overall recovery rate $= \dfrac{\text{total factory overheads}}{\text{direct labour hour rate}} = \dfrac{£67\,165}{28\,340} = £2.37$

**overdraft** exists when, by arrangement with the bank manager, a business pays more from its current account than it has deposited. A bank overdraft will be a credit balance in the *bank columns* of the *cash book*, and a debit balance on the business's bank statement.

The balance according to the cash book will appear as a credit entry in the *trial balance* and as a *current liability* on the *balance sheet*.

**overhead absorption costing:** see *absorption costing*

**overhead efficiency variance** will be favourable if a business has saved money. The *variance* will be adverse if the overheads have cost more than was budgeted for. For a worked example, see *overhead variance*.

**overhead expenditure variance** will be favourable if a business has saved money. The variance will be adverse if the overheads have cost more than was budgeted for. For a worked example, see *overhead variance*.

**overheads** are described by *CIMA* as 'expenditure on labour, materials or services which cannot be economically identified with a specific saleable cost'. (See also *factory overhead expenses*.)

**overhead variance** is the difference between the standard overhead and the actual overheads incurred. The *variances* can be calculated for:
- *fixed overheads*
- variable overheads

The total *fixed production overhead variance* can be calculated by deducting the actual fixed production overheads from the flexed standard fixed production overheads. The calculation is:

FORMULA:   standard fixed production overhead charged to production $-$ actual fixed production overhead

**Worked example**

The budgeted and actual fixed overheads expenditure involved in the production of noddles is:

|  | Budgeted | Actual |
|---|---|---|
|  | £ | £ |
| Fixed overheads | 175 000 | 164 000 |
| Direct labour hours of input | 35 000 | 32 000 |
| Direct labour hours of output |  |  |
| (standard hours produced) | 35 000 | 31 000 |

*Required:*

Total fixed production overhead variance for the production of noddles.

*Solution:*

|  | £ |
|---|---|
| Standard fixed production overhead charged to production | 155 000 |
| Actual fixed production overhead | 164 000 |
| Adverse total fixed production overhead variance | 9 000 |

Fixed production overhead variance can be divided into:

1 Fixed production overhead expenditure variance – this identifies the portion of the total fixed overhead variance which is due to the actual fixed overhead expenditure differing from the budgeted fixed overhead expenditure. The calculation is:

> *FORMULA:* budgeted fixed overhead – actual fixed overhead

**Worked example**

Using the information given above for the production of noddles:

*Required:*

Calculate the fixed overhead expenditure variance.

*Solution:*

|  | £ | |
|---|---|---|
| Standard fixed overhead expenditure | 175 000 | |
| Actual fixed overhead expenditure | 164 000 | |
| Favourable expenditure variance (over-recovery) | 11 000 | favourable |

2 Fixed production overhead volume variance – this identifies the portion of the total fixed overhead variance that is due to actual production being different from the budgeted production. The calculation is:

> *FORMULA:* $\left(\begin{array}{l}\text{actual} \\ \text{production}\end{array} - \begin{array}{l}\text{budgeted} \\ \text{production}\end{array}\right) \times \begin{array}{l}\text{standard fixed} \\ \text{overhead rate}\end{array}$

## Worked example

Using the information given above for the production of noddles:

*Required:*

The fixed production overhead volume variance.

*Solution:*

The standard fixed overhead rate of £5 per hour is calculated on the basis of 35 000 direct labour hours. If exactly 35 000 hours are produced, then the total fixed overheads will be recovered. Actual labour hours are in fact only 31 000 hours so that actual production is 1000 standard hours less than budget. This means that £20 000 of fixed overheads will not be recovered.

$\Big($actual production − budgeted production$\Big)$ × standard fixed overhead rate

    31 000    −    35 000    ×    £5

= £20 000 adverse

3 Fixed production overhead volume variance – arises because the actual volume of output differs from the budgeted volume. The fixed overhead volume variance can be subdivided into:

- fixed overhead volume efficiency variance – this identifies the part of the overhead variance that might have been caused by the labour force having been more or less efficient than was anticipated when the budget was drawn up. The calculation is:

*FORMULA:*
$$\left( \begin{array}{ccc} \text{standard hours} & - & \text{actual hours} \\ \text{of output} & & \text{of input} \end{array} \right) \times \begin{array}{c} \text{standard fixed} \\ \text{overhead rate} \end{array}$$

## Worked example

Using the information given above for the production of noddles:

*Required:*

The fixed overhead volume efficiency variance.

*Solution:*

The actual number of input hours was 32 000 and so one could reasonably expect an output of 32 000 hours. In reality, only 31 000 hours were produced, so the output was 1000 hours less than it should have been. The business has actually lost 1000 hours at £5 per hour. This is £5000 that should have been absorbed.

$\Big($standard hour of output − actual hour of input$\Big)$ × standared fixed overhead rate

    32 000    −    31 000    ×    £5

= £5000 adverse

- fixed overhead volume capacity variance – this also indicates a reason why actual and budgeted production might be different. The variance could be caused by labour disputes, material shortages, machine breakdowns, lower demand for the product. The calculation is:

FORMULA: $\left(\begin{array}{c}\text{actual hour} \\ \text{of input}\end{array} - \begin{array}{c}\text{budgeted hours} \\ \text{of input}\end{array}\right) \times \begin{array}{c}\text{standard fixed} \\ \text{overhead rate}\end{array}$

## Worked example

Using the information given above for the production of noddles:

### Required:

The fixed overhead volume capacity variance.

### Solution:

The budget was drawn up under the assumption that direct labour hours of input would be 35 000 hours, whereas the actual hours of input were 32 000 hours. The difference of 3000 hours represents the under-utilisation of production capacity. The business has failed to absorb £15 000 of fixed overhead budgeted for because of the shortfall in direct labour hours of input.

$\left(\text{actual hour of input} - \text{budgeted hours of input}\right) \times \text{standard fixed overhead rate}$

$\quad\quad$ 32 000 $\quad\quad - \quad\quad$ 35 000 $\quad\quad \times \quad\quad$ £5

$= $ £15 000 adverse

The above variances can be seen more clearly in this diagram:

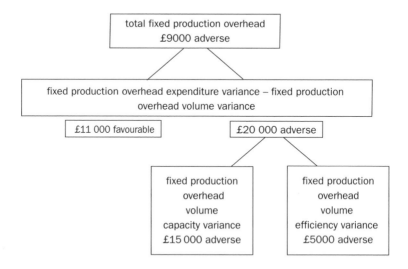

Variable production overhead variance can be divided into:

1 Variable production overhead expenditure variance – when actual cost differs from budgeted cost. It shows the difference between the flexed budgeted variable overhead and the actual variable total overhead incurred. The calculation is:

FORMULA: flexed budgeted variable overhead – actual variable overhead

2 Variable production overhead efficiency variance – arises through the efficiency of labour. It shows the difference between the standard hours of output and the actual hours of input. The calculation is:

FORMULA:
$$\left(\begin{array}{c}\text{standard hours}\\ \text{of output}\end{array} - \begin{array}{c}\text{actual hours}\\ \text{of input}\end{array}\right) \times \begin{array}{c}\text{standard variable}\\ \text{overhead rate}\end{array}$$

### Worked example

The following information applies to the variable overheads for producing remcors.
  Budgeted production of remcors was 80 000 units.
  Actual production of remcors was 60 000 units.

|  | £ | Hours |
|---|---|---|
| Budgeted variable overheads | | |
| (20 000 hours at £5 per labour hour) | 100 000 | |
| Actual variable overheads | 72 000 | |
| Standard labour hours | | 20 000 |
| Actual labour hours | | 18 000 |

### Required:

i) the total variable production overhead variance
ii) the variable production overhead expenditure variance
iii) the variable production overhead efficiency variance

### Solution:

i)

|  | £ | |
|---|---|---|
| Standard cost of production for variable overheads | 75 000 | |
| is 60 000 units at £1.25 per unit | | |
| Actual cost of production for variable overheads | 72 000 | |
| Total variable production overhead variance | 3 000 | favourable |

ii) To make a comparison between the actual variable production overhead and the budgeted variable production overhead, it is necessary to flex the budgeted figure. The actual variable production overhead was £72 000 from 18 000 hours of labour input, but for that level of activity nine-tenths (18 000/20 000) of £100 000 should have been spent.

|  | £ | |
|---|---|---|
| Budgeted flexed variable production overhead | 90 000 | |
| Actual variable production overhead | 72 000 | |
| Variable production overhead expenditure variance | 18 000 | favourable |

iii) The variable production overhead efficiency variance arises because 18 000 direct labour hours of input were required to produce 15 000 standard hours (three-quarters or 60 000/80 000 of 20 000). So 3000 hours longer were taken at £5 per labour hour, resulting in a £15 000 adverse variance.

$$\left(\text{standard hours} - \text{actual hours}\right) \times \text{standard variable production overhead rate}$$

|  |  |  |  |  |
|---|---|---|---|---|
| 15 000 | – | 18 000 | × | £5 |

= £15 000 adverse

**overtime:** time worked in excess of the contractually agreed hours.

**overtime premium** may be paid to workers who work *overtime*. The premium is usually expressed as 'time and a half' or 'double time' etc. 'Time and a half' means that the basic hourly rate is paid plus a premium of 50 per cent. 'Double time' means that the basic hourly rate is doubled. Overtime premiums might be paid for night work or weekend working.

**overtrading** occurs when a business attempts to finance expansion without securing the necessary long-term finance. This means large investment in *inventory* and *trade receivables* has to be financed by short-term credit from suppliers and from the bank in the form of *overdraft* facilities. The danger is that the suppliers and the bank may reach a point where they are no longer prepared to support the business. This may result in the business being forced into *liquidation*.

Overtrading is often evident in new businesses in high-growth sectors of the economy run by inexperienced management. It is also a problem experienced by businesses when the economy is moving out of a *recession*.

Negative *working capital* is a symptom of overtrading.

**owner's capital:** business finance provided by the owner(s).

**owner's equity:** the total of the issued ordinary share capital and all a company's *reserves*.

### A–Z Online

Log on to A–Z Online to search the database of terms, print revision lists and much more. Go to **www.philipallan.co.uk/a-zonline** to get started.

**Pacioli** was an Italian mathematician who wrote the first known book on *double-entry bookkeeping* in 1494. The underlying principles are the same as they were then, but many adaptations have been made to the basic model to suit the needs of today.

**paid-up share capital:** the part of the *called-up capital* for which a company has received money.

**parent undertaking:** the accounting term used to indicate that a business has the 'right to exercise a dominant influence' over a subsidiary undertaking. The influence may arise from:
- a right to appoint *directors*
- a control contract
- rights laid out in the *Memorandum* and *Articles of Association*

**pareto distribution theory:** also known as the 80/20 rule. The application of the rule states that about 80 per cent of the value of a business's stocks will be accounted for by approximately 20 per cent of the total quantity. Around 20 per cent of total customers will account for about 80 per cent of total turnover, etc.

The value of this theory to the managers of a business is that efforts are best concentrated on the key 20 per cent rather than the whole 100 per cent.

**partnership** exists when two or more persons join together in business with a view to profit.

**partnership accounts** are prepared in the same way as the accounts of any other business. The *financial statements* could include:
- a *manufacturing account*
- an *income statement*

These are all exactly the same as the financial statements of a *sole trader* or *limited company*. Because there is more than one owner, a partnership also needs to show how profits have been shared. See *partnership appropriation account*.

**Partnership Act 1890:** provisions come into force if a *partnership* does not have a *partnership agreement*. Section 24 of the Act states that in the absence of either an express or implied agreement:
- no partner is entitled to a partnership salary
- no partner is entitled to interest on capital
- no partner is to be charged interest on drawings
- profits are to be shared equally
- any loan made to the business by a partner will earn interest at the rate of 5 per cent per annum

**partnership advances** or loans made by a partner to a business should be kept separate from any injections of capital. They are treated *at arm's length*. The interest on the loan is debited to *the income statement* like any loan interest payable. The bookkeeping entries are:

**Debit:** Income statement　　　**Credit:** Partner's current account

Or if the interest has been paid to the partner(s):

**Debit:** Income statement　　　**Credit:** Partnership bank account

**partnership agreements** could be verbal or even implied by the conduct of the partner, but should be in writing to reduce the possibility of disputes or misunderstandings in the future.

A partnership agreement will generally cover the following accounting arrangements:
- the capital to be subscribed by each of the partners
- the rate of interest to be paid on any loans to the partnership by a partner
- the amounts of any salaries to be paid to partners
- the rate of interest, if any, to be given on partners' capital account balances
- the rate of interest, if any, to be charged on partners' drawings
- the ratio in which residual profits or losses are to be shared
- possibly some duties and responsibilities of the partners

**partnership appropriation accounts** show how a business's profits have been distributed amongst the partners. It is part of the income statement of a partnership.

---

**Worked example**

Trevor and Eunice are in partnership. They have capital account balances of £20 000 and £25 000 respectively. Their drawings for the year were: Trevor £26 439; Eunice £16 771. Their partnership agreement provides that:

　Trevor be paid a partnership salary of £2000 per annum

　Interest on capital be paid at 8% per annum

　Interest on drawings be charged: Trevor £160

Eunice £281

　Residual profits or losses are to be shared in the ratios 2:1 respectively.

　The profit for the year ended 31 October 20*9 was £41 762.

*Required:*

An extract from the income statement of the partnership for the year ended 31 October 20*9 showing the appropriations of profits.

*Solution:*

**Trevor and Eunice extract from the income statement for the year ended 31 October 20*9**

|  |  | £ | £ |
|---|---|---|---|
| Profit for the year |  |  | 41 762 |
| Add interest on drawings – | Trevor | 160 |  |
|  | Eunice | 281 | 441 |

|  |  |  |  |  |
|---|---|---|---|---|
|  |  |  |  | 42 203 |
| Less salary – | Trevor |  |  | 2 000 |
|  |  |  |  | 40 203 |
| Less interest on capital – | Trevor | 1 600 |  |  |
|  | Eunice | 2 000 |  | 3 600 |
|  |  |  |  | 36 603 |
| Share of profit – | Trevor | 24 402 |  |  |
|  | Eunice | 12 201 |  | 36 603 |

**partnership balance sheet** is similar, in most respects, to that of any other business. It shows the assets and liabilities of the *partnership*. The difference between the *balance sheet* of a partnership and that of a *sole trader* or *limited company* is in the capital section; there will be a capital account for each of the partners. The capital accounts may be *fixed* or *fluctuating*.

### Worked example

Using the information above regarding Trevor and Eunice.

*Required:*

A balance sheet extract showing the capital account details for both partners at 31 October 20*9. The partnership maintains fluctuating capital accounts.

*Solution:*

**Trevor and Eunice balance sheet extract at 31 October 20*9**

|  | £ | £ | £ |
|---|---|---|---|
| Capital accounts |  |  |  |
| Trevor: balance at 1 November 20*8 |  |  | 20 000 |
| Add salary |  | 2 000 |  |
| interest on capital |  | 1 600 |  |
| share of profits |  | 24 402 | 28 002 |
|  |  |  | 48 002 |
| Less drawings |  | 26 439 |  |
| interest on drawings |  | 160 | 26 599 |
|  |  |  | 21 403 |
| Eunice: balance at 1 November 20*8 |  | 25 000 |  |
| Add interest on capital | 2 000 |  |  |
| share of profits | 12 201 | 14 201 |  |
|  |  | 39 201 |  |
| Less drawings | 16 771 |  |  |
| interest on drawings | 281 | 17 052 | 22 149 |

The partners may have fixed capital accounts, in which case all appropriations of profit will be credited to partnership current accounts. (See *partnership current accounts* for an example.)

With current accounts and fixed capital accounts, a balance sheet extract might show:

| Capital accounts | Rodney | | 40 000 |
|---|---|---|---|
| | Stephanie | | 45 000 |
| | Theresa | | 30 000 |
| Current accounts | Rodney | 1 286 | 115 000 |
| | Stephanie | (603) | |
| | Theresa | 941 | 1 624 |

**partnership capital accounts:** see *capital accounts*, *fluctuating capital accounts*, *fixed capital accounts*. For a worked example, see *partnership balance sheet*.

**partnership current accounts** are credited with all appropriations of the partnership profits. The partners' *drawings* and any interest charged on those drawings are debited to the partners' current accounts.

### Worked example

Toni, Arnold and Beth are in partnership. The balances standing on their current accounts at 31 October 20*9 were:

| | £ |
|---|---|
| Toni | 452 Cr |
| Arnold | 34 Dr |
| Beth | 1673 Cr |

Their drawings for the year were:

| Toni | 16 742 |
|---|---|
| Arnold | 19 850 |
| Beth | 15 788 |

An extract from the partnership income statement for the year ended 31 October 2009 is shown:

| | | £ | £ |
|---|---|---|---|
| Profit for the year | | | 53 200 |
| Add interest on drawings – | Toni | 163 | |
| | Arnold | 410 | |
| | Beth | 87 | 660 |
| | | | 53 860 |
| Salary – Arnold | | | 5 000 |
| | | | 48 860 |
| Interest on capital – | Toni | 3 400 | |
| | Arnold | 800 | |
| | Beth | 2 450 | 6 650 |
| | | | 42 210 |
| Share of profits – | Toni | 14 070 | |
| | Arnold | 14 070 | |
| | Beth | 14 070 | 42 210 |

*Required:*

The partnership current accounts as they would appear at 31 October 20*9.

*Solution:*

**Partnership current accounts**

|  | Toni | Arnold | Beth |  | Toni | Arnold | Beth |
|---|---|---|---|---|---|---|---|
|  | £ | £ | £ |  | £ | £ | £ |
| Balance b/d |  | 34 |  | Balances b/d | 452 |  | 1 673 |
| Drawings | 16 742 | 19 850 | 15 788 | Salary |  | 5 000 |  |
| Int. on | 163 | 410 | 87 | Int. on cap'l | 3 400 | 800 | 2 450 |
| drawings |  |  |  |  |  |  |  |
|  |  |  |  | Sh. of profit | 14 070 | 14 070 | 14 070 |
| Balances c/d | 1 017 |  | 2 318 | Balance c/d |  | 424 |  |
|  | 17 922 | 20 294 | 18 193 |  | 17 922 | 20 294 | 18 193 |
| Balance b/d |  | 424 |  | Balances b/d | 1 017 |  | 2 318 |

**partnership dissolution** might occur when:

- a partner dies
- a partner retires
- a partner is bankrupt (see *bankruptcy*)
- the partners agree that the *partnership* should be terminated

On dissolution the partnership assets will be disposed of and the liabilities settled.
The settlement should be in the following order:

1 *trade payables*

2 partners' loans

3 partners' *capital accounts*

Unless an examination question indicates anything to the contrary, assume that the partnership will collect any monies due from receivables and will pay the partnership payables. Any loans to the partnership should be paid off, including loans made by any partner. Partners' loans should not be transferred into their capital accounts. Loans of any description are liabilities and must be settled before capital account balances.

All assets to be disposed of are debited to the *realisation account*. This means that the only accounts remaining in the partnership *books of account* will be the business bank account, the partners' current accounts, the partners' capital accounts and the realisation account.

Any current account balances should be transferred to the partners' capital accounts. The profit (loss) on dissolution is calculated and transferred to the partners' capital accounts. The bank balance should not be shared out in any prescribed way – the bank account should be used to balance off the partners' capital accounts.

## Worked example

David, Laura and Susan are in partnership sharing profits and losses 2:2:1. They agree to dissolve their partnership on 30 November 20*9. Their balance sheet on that date was as follows:

| Non-current assets | | £ | Capital accounts | | £ | |
|---|---|---|---|---|---|---|
| Premises | | 140 000 | David | | 80 000 | |
| Machinery | | 60 000 | Laura | | 70 000 | |
| Vehicles (3 cars) | | 14 000 | Susan | | 50 000 | 200 000 |
| | | 214 000 | | | | |
| Current assets | | | Current accounts | | | |
| Inventory | 16 000 | | David | | 3 000 | |
| Trade receivables | 7 000 | | Laura | | 1 000 | |
| Cash and Cash equ | 3 000 | | Susan | | 2 000 | 6 000 |
| | | 26 000 | | | | |
| | | | Loan – Susan | | | 25 000 |
| | | | Trade payables | | | 9 000 |
| | | 240 000 | | | | 240 000 |

The inventory was sold for £14 700 cash.

The premises and machinery were taken over by Lime Ltd. The purchase consideration was £240 000 being made up of 90 000 £1 ordinary shares. The partners have agreed that shares in Lime Ltd be distributed in the ratio of their last agreed capital account balances.

The vehicles were taken over by the partners at the following agreed valuations:

Car 1 by David valued at £3500
Car 2 by Laura valued at £6500
Car 3 by Susan valued at £1000
The trade receivables paid £6800 in settlement.
The trade payables accepted £8100 in settlement.
Costs of dissolution were £3950.

### Required:

The realisation account, cash account and the partners' capital accounts to close the partnership books of account.

### Solution:

#### Realisation account

| Discount allowed | | 200 | Discount received | | 900 |
|---|---|---|---|---|---|
| Premises | | 140 000 | Bank (inventory) | | 14 700 |
| Machinery | | 60 000 | Lime Ltd | | 240 000 |
| Vehicles | | 14 000 | Capitals (cars) | David | 3 500 |
| Inventory | | 16 000 | | Laura | 6 500 |
| Costs | | 3 950 | | Susan | 1 000 |

Profit on dissolution

| | | | |
|---|---|---|---|
| David | 12 980 | | |
| Laura | 12 980 | | |
| Susan | 6 490 | | |
| | 266 600 | | 266 600 |

### Capital accounts

| | David | Laura | Susan | | David | Laura | Susan |
|---|---|---|---|---|---|---|---|
| Realisation (cars) | 3 500 | 6 500 | 1 000 | Balances b/d | 80 000 | 70 000 | 50 000 |
| Lime Ltd – shares | 96 000 | 84 000 | 60 000 | Curr. accounts | 3 000 | 1 000 | 2 000 |
| | | | | Realis. profit | 12 980 | 12 980 | 6 490 |
| | | | | Cash | 3 520 | 6 520 | 2 510 |
| | 99 500 | 90 500 | 61 000 | | 99 500 | 90 500 | 61 000 |

### Bank

| | | | | | |
|---|---|---|---|---|---|
| Balance b/d | | | 3 000 | Loan – Susan | 25 000 |
| Trade receivables | | | 6 800 | Trade payables | 8 100 |
| Realisation – inventory | | | 14 700 | Costs | 3 950 |
| Capital accounts | David | | 3 520 | | |
| | Laura | | 6 520 | | |
| | Susan | | 2 510 | | |
| | | | 37 050 | | 37 050 |

*Note:*

Even though there are only 90 000 shares in Lime Ltd they have a value of £240 000. The partners will receive 36 000 shares, 31 500 shares and 22 500 shares respectively valued at £96 000, £84 000 and £60 000.

When a partner has a debit balance on his/her capital account after dissolution and he/she is insolvent, the ruling in *Garner v Murray (1904)* should be applied.

**partnership income statement** is no different from any other *income statement*. Note: if a partner has made a loan, any unpaid interest due on the loan should be debited to the partnership income statement, and be credited to the partner's current account. If the interest is actually paid to the partner, then debit the income statement and credit the partnership bank account.

**partnership retirement** means that the partnership ceases to exist on the retirement date (see also *retiring partner*). The following day the partnership recommences, with one fewer partner, as a new business. By way of example, Zack, Jack and Jill are in partnership. Jack retires on 30 June 20*9. Up to midnight on 30 June 20*9 the business has three owners – Zack, Jack and Jill. One microsecond after midnight the business has two owners – Zack and Jill.

When a partner retires (or dies) it is necessary to prepare an *income statement* up to the date of the retirement. It is also necessary to prepare another income statement for the period immediately after the retirement up to the 'normal' financial year end. (In examination questions, partners will retire or die at convenient times during the year!)

When a partner leaves a business it is necessary to have the business valued. It is no longer a going concern.

## Worked example

Zack, Jack and Jill are in partnership sharing profits 3:2:1. On 30 June 20*9 Jack retires from the partnership. The partnership balance sheet at that date is shown below.

### Zack, Jack and Jill balance sheet at 30 June 20*9

| | £ | | | £ |
|---|---|---|---|---|
| Premises | 150 000 | Capital | Zack | 90 000 |
| Machinery | 16 000 | | Jack | 63 000 |
| Vehicles | 31 000 | | Jill | 56 000 |
| Inventory | 4 350 | | | |
| Trade receivables | 9 150 | Trade payables | | 8 500 |
| Cash and cash equiv | 7 000 | | | |
| | 217 500 | | | 217 500 |

The following valuations have been agreed on 30 June 20*9 by the partners:

| | £ |
|---|---|
| Premises | 210 000 |
| Machinery | 8 000 |
| Vehicles | 19 000 |
| Goodwill | 26 000 |

Other assets and liabilities are valued at book value.

The partners agree that goodwill should not appear in the partnership books of account.

Zack and Jill have agreed to share profits and losses in their new partnership in the ratio 3:1.

### Required:

The partnership balance sheet immediately after Jack's retirement. The partnership has negotiated a bank loan in order to clear Jack's capital account balance.

### Solution:

#### Revaluation account

| | | £ | | £ |
|---|---|---|---|---|
| Machinery | | 8 000 | Premises | 60 000 |
| Vehicles | | 12 000 | Goodwill | 26 000 |
| Capitals | Zack | 33 000 | | |
| | Jack | 22 000 | | |
| | Jill | 11 000 | | |
| | | 86 000 | | 86 000 |

## Capital accounts

| | Zack | Jack | Jill | | Zack | Jack | Jill |
|---|---|---|---|---|---|---|---|
| | £ | £ | £ | | £ | £ | £ |
| Cash | | 85 000 | | Balances b/d | 90 000 | 63 000 | 56 000 |
| Balances c/d | 123 000 | | 67 000 | Revaluation | 33 000 | 22 000 | 11 000 |
| | 123 000 | 85 000 | 67 000 | | 123 000 | 85 000 | 67 000 |
| | | | | Bal's b/d | 123 000 | | |

### Zack and Jill balance sheet at 30 June 20*9 (after Jack's retirement)

| | £ | | | £ |
|---|---|---|---|---|
| Premises | 210 000 | Capital | Zack | 123 000 |
| Machinery | 8 000 | | Jill | 67 000 |
| Vehicles | 19 000 | | | |
| Goodwill | 26 000 | Loan | | 85 000 |
| Inventory | 4 350 | | | |
| Trade receivables | 9 150 | Trade payables | | 8 500 |
| Cash and cash equiv | 7 000 | | | |
| | 283 500 | | | 283 500 |

Goodwill should be written off so:

## Goodwill

| | £ | | | £ |
|---|---|---|---|---|
| Realisation | 26 000 | Capital | Zack | 19 500 |
| | | | Jill | 6 500 |
| | 26 000 | | | 26 000 |

Goodwill is written off in the partners' profit sharing ratios. There are now only two partners in the business sharing profits and losses 3:1, so:

### Zack and Jill balance sheet at 30 June 20*9 (after Jack's retirement)

| | £ | | | £ |
|---|---|---|---|---|
| Premises at valuation | 210 000 | Capital | Zack | 103 500 |
| Machinery at valuation | 8 000 | | Jill | 60 500 |
| Vehicles at valuation | 19 000 | | | |
| Inventory | 4 350 | Loan | | 85 000 |
| Trade rec | 9 150 | Current liabilities | | 8 500 |
| Cash and cash equiv | 7 000 | | | |
| | 257 500 | | | 257 500 |

**partnership salaries** are paid to partners who have a particular responsibility, skill or extra workload. Even though this benefit is called a salary it should be remembered that it is in fact part of the profits; it is not a salary like you or I may earn from our workplace.

The bookkeeping entries are:

**Debit:** Income statement    **Credit:** Partner's current account

If the salary has been paid to the partner during the financial year, the entries would be:

**Debit:** Income statement    **Credit:** Partnership bank account

**par value:** the face value or nominal value of a share. For example, £1 *ordinary shares* have a par value of £1. Ten pence shares have a par value of 10 pence.

**past costs:** see *irrelevant costs*

**payback method of capital investment appraisal:** one of the simplest and most frequently used methods of *capital investment appraisal*. It measures the length of time that is required for a stream of cash proceeds from an investment to recover the original cash outlay that was necessary to acquire that investment.

---

**Worked example**

Jackie Curran is considering the purchase of a machine for her business. There are currently two models that will suit her needs:

| | Machine CA 6<br>Cost £55 000<br>Estimated net cash flows | Machine NJ 4<br>Cost £65 000<br>Estimated net cash flows |
|---|---|---|
| | £ | £ |
| Year 1 | 20 000 | 25 000 |
| Year 2 | 22 000 | 28 000 |
| Year 3 | 25 000 | 32 000 |
| Year 4 | 28 000 | 35 000 |

*Required:*

Calculate the payback period for each machine.

*Solution:*

Machine CA 6 payback 2 years 6.24 months.
Machine NJ 4 payback 2 years 4.5 months.

---

The major criticism of the payback method of capital investment appraisal is that it does not take into account the *time value of money*. In order to overcome this criticism, many businesses use the method and discount the estimated *cash flows* by using the appropriate *cost of capital* for the business.

The discounted payback is the most commonly used method of capital investment appraisal in the UK. It is especially useful when a business is faced with *liquidity* constraints and requires a fast repayment from the investment. It is also used in conjunction with the *net present value* or the *internal rate-of-return* methods in order to determine which investments may require closer scrutiny.

## Worked example

Jackie's cost of capital is currently 11%. The following is an extract from the present value table of £1 at 11%:

|        | 11%   |
|--------|-------|
| Year 1 | 0.901 |
| Year 2 | 0.812 |
| Year 3 | 0.731 |
| Year 4 | 0.659 |

### Required:

Calculate the discounted payback for the two machines considered previously.

### Solution:

Machine CA 6

|        | Cash flows | Present value factor | Net present value |
|--------|-----------|---------------------|-------------------|
|        | £         |                     | £                 |
| Year 0 | (55 000)  | 1                   | (55 000)          |
| Year 1 | 20 000    | 0.901               | 18 020            |
| Year 2 | 22 000    | 0.812               | 17 864            |
| Year 3 | 25 000    | 0.731               | 18 275            |
| Year 4 | 28 000    | 0.659               | 18 452            |

The discounted payback for machine CA 6 is 3 years 0.55 months.

Machine NJ 4

|        | Cash flows | Present value factor | Net present value |
|--------|-----------|---------------------|-------------------|
| Year 0 | (65 000)  | 1                   | (65 000)          |
| Year 1 | 25 000    | 0.901               | 22 525            |
| Year 2 | 28 000    | 0.812               | 22 736            |
| Year 3 | 32 000    | 0.731               | 23 392            |
| Year 4 | 35 000    | 0.659               | 23 065            |

The discounted payback for machine NJ 4 is 2 years 10.1 months.

**PAYE (pay as you earn):** a method of collecting income tax. Income tax is deducted from the employee's wage by the employer. PAYE deductions are paid to the Revenue and Customs each month by the employer.

At the beginning of each tax year the Revenue and Customs allocates a code number to each taxpayer. The code number is based on the allowances claimed by the taxpayer (an allowance gives relief from paying tax).

**payee:** see *cheque*

**payment by results:** pay scheme that rewards workers for the actual numbers of units produced. (See *piece work*.)

**payroll analysis:** a summary of the payroll. It shows the totals of:
- gross pay
- employer's contribution to National Insurance
- employer's contribution to any pension funds

It also summarises the payroll costs to the business. It shows the total amounts payable to:
- Her Majesty's Revenue and Customs – for both employer's and employees' contributions for National Insurance and PAYE
- the pension fund – again both employer's and employees' contributions
- employees' net pay

**payroll on-costs** are the costs that a business has to bear because it is an employer. They are employer's *National Insurance contribution* and any *pension* costs borne by the employer.

**penetration pricing:** a strategy of employing low prices in order to gain a foothold in a new market. The same techniques may be used to force a competitor out of business. In this case it is known as destroyer pricing.

A *marginal costing* approach is adopted.

---

### Worked example

A British manufacturer enjoys a great deal of success with a product in the home market. The product sells for £36.00. The costs involved in the production of the good are:

| | |
|---|---|
| Variable costs per unit | £14.00 |
| Fixed costs per unit | £10.00 |

The manufacturer believes that there is a good potential market for the product in China.

*Required:*

Calculate the lowest price the manufacturer could charge in the Chinese market without lowering total business profits.

*Solution:*

The lowest price that could be charged is £14.00. This price would cover the manufacturer's marginal costs. The fixed costs are covered by British customers – they do not need to be recovered again. This could help to penetrate the new market. It could mean that other products bearing the same brand name may have an advantage. It might also mean that once consumer loyalty for the product is established in China the price can be increased.

A large manufacturer with ample resources can use the same tactic to force a competitor out of business.

---

**pension:** money paid to a person who no longer works. The payment is made on a regular basis by the state or by a privately run pension fund.

**PEP (personal equity plan):** a government-backed scheme to encourage share ownership and investment in UK incorporated companies. Individual taxpayers can each invest a certain amount of money in shares each year. Reinvested *dividends* are free of income tax and reinvested capital gains are free of capital gains tax.

**period costs** are costs which do not change when production levels change. They are time related. Examples include rent, rates and insurances.

**periodic inventory:** the term applied when *inventory* is valued at the end of a financial period. The method is probably used by your local newsagent or take-away. The person taking inventory makes a list of all goods held and then values each item or group of items. The list is then totalled to arrive at the value of inventory on that day.

Since *inventory* is only taken at the year end (a check of goods held may take place at other times if interim *financial statements* are prepared), there is little control over inventory movements. A major weakness of this method is that any theft or damage may lie undiscovered until the year end.

**periodicity** requires that regular reports are made to some users of the business accounts. The concept is now established in law:
- The *Companies Act* requires *annual reports* to be sent to the *shareholders*.
- Income tax legislation requires accounts to be submitted to the Revenue and Customs each year.

**perpetual inventory** revalues the value of *inventory* held each time there is a new purchase. Detailed records of goods received and issued are recorded in the store's *ledger* or on an *inventory record card*.

A perpetual inventory is used in modern supermarkets. Each time goods are scanned at the checkout the computerised stock record card is amended.

The worked examples shown for *methods of inventory valuation* are using perpetual methods.

**personal accounts** are in the names of people or other businesses. Personal accounts will be found in the *purchases ledger* if the people are suppliers of goods and services on credit. They will be found in the *sales ledger* if the people are credit customers.

**personal allowances** are relief from income tax. The allowances are presented to Parliament by the Chancellor of the Exchequer in the Budget. They become law in the subsequent Finance Act.

**personnel department:** the department in a business responsible for implementing manpower planning policies. It deals with:
- Recruitment – the department is responsible for hiring staff; making sure that staffing levels are sufficient to enable the business to achieve its objectives.
- Training – the department will generally have a budget allocation for this purpose. Close liaison with other departments is essential in this area to ensure that money is spent appropriately.
- Welfare – the department looks after the general well-being of the staff.
- Disciplining of staff.

**petty cash book:** used to record payments for small day-to-day expenses. It is kept using the *imprest system*. It is an extension of the main *cash book*, taking away many trivial cash transactions which would otherwise cause the main cash book to become overfull.

The petty cash book is written up using the *petty cash vouchers* as source documents.

The following is an example of how a petty cash book might be written up:

| £ | Date | Details | Voucher | Total | Postage | Trav. Exp. | Stati- onery | Sundry Exp. | Ledger | Folio |
|---|---|---|---|---|---|---|---|---|---|---|
Dr | | | | | | | | | | Cr
| 75.00 | 1 May | Cash | cb 72 | | | | | | | |
| | 1 May | Post | 1 | 14.00 | 14.00 | | | | | |
| | 6 May | Pins | 2 | 0.73 | | | 0.73 | | | |
| | 9 May | Rail tkt | 3 | 27.00 | | 27.00 | | | | |
| | 15 May | Post and | | | | | | | | |
| | | Envelopes | 4 | 15.61 | 14.00 | | 1.61 | | | |
| | 23 May | Tea & sugar | 5 | 1.04 | | | | 1.04 | | |
| | 28 May | J Brett | 6 | 7.88 | | | | | 7.88 | pl 82 |
| | | | | 66.26 | 28.00 | 27.00 | 2.34 | 1.04 | 7.88 | |
| | 31 May | Bal c/d | | 8.74 | gl 18 | gl 21 | gl 25 | gl 26 | | |
| 75.00 | | | | 75.00 | | | | | | |
| 8.74 | 1 June | Bal b/d | | | | | | | | |
| 66.26 | 1 June | Cash | cb 86 | | | | | | | |

There will be credit entries of £75.00 and £66.26 on pages 72 and 86 of the main cash book.

In the general ledger there will be debit entries in the postages account (on page 18), travelling expenses account (page 21), stationery account (page 25) and sundry expenses account (page 26).

There will also be a debit entry in J Brett's account on page 82 of the purchases ledger.

**petty cash vouchers** should be filled in each time money is given out of the petty cash float. The voucher should be signed by the person receiving the cash. If a receipt is obtained from outside the business, e.g. post office receipt for postage, bus or train tickets, etc., this can be stapled to the voucher. The petty cash vouchers are used to write up the *petty cash book*.

**piece rate:** the wage rate paid to workers for the production of one unit (or a batch of units).

**piece work:** workers are paid according to the number of units manufactured. The calculation of a worker's gross pay is:

*FORMULA:* number of units made × the piece rate per unit

This method does not pay *overtime* rates. Differential piece work sets different pay levels when set production targets are met.

**Worked example**

Hughes & Co. uses differential piece work pay rates based on the following:
Workers are paid 40 pence per unit until 300 units are produced.
Production of 301–400 units will attract a piece rate of 45 pence per unit.
Production of 401–500 units will attract a piece rate of 50 pence per unit.
This week Helen has produced 417 units and Douglas has produced 312 units.

*Required:*

Calculate Helen and Douglas's gross pay for the week.

*Solution:*

| Helen's gross pay | | Douglas's gross pay | |
|---|---|---|---|
| | £ | | £ |
| 300 × 40 pence = | 120.00 | 300 × 40 pence = | 120.00 |
| 100 × 45 pence = | 45.00 | 12 × 45 pence = | 5.40 |
| 17 × 50 pence = | 8.50 | | |
| | 173.50 | | 125.40 |

The advantages of piece work are:

- pay is proportionate to work completed
- pay is calculated easily
- time wasting is discouraged
- work is completed quickly
- it can lead to greater efficiency

The disadvantages are:

- it is not suitable for all types of work
- workers' earnings are reduced when production ceases, even in the event of a machine breakdown
- it can lead to rushed, substandard products being produced
- more supervision and quality control procedures are needed
- there may be problems in agreeing the levels of piece rates

**planning:** involves formulating the paths to be taken so that *business objectives* can be met. The business objectives can be either short or long term. Short-term or operational planning will manifest itself in various budgets. It will provide the foundations for the achievement of the strategic or corporate plan. Long-term planning is also known as corporate or *strategic planning*.

**plc** is the abbreviation for *public limited company*.

**point of separation:** see *common costs*

**posting** means entering financial transactions into ledger accounts from one of the *books of prime entry*. For example, the debit entry in Terry Yardley's account in the *sales ledger* has been posted from the *sales day book*. The totals of the sales day book are posted to the credit of the *sales account* in the *general ledger*.

**potential standards:** see *ideal standards*

**preference shares:** see *preferred shares*

**preferential creditors** must be paid before other creditors if a company goes into *liquidation*.

**preferred shares:** usually carry a fixed rate of *dividend*, and are entitled to repayment of capital in the event of the company being wound up. They do not normally have full voting rights. Voting is usually restricted to times when their dividends are in arrears. Preferred shareholders are given preferential rights to dividends but these will be paid only if profits are sufficiently large. They can be:

- cumulative – if the dividend on these shares is not paid in one year, then it accumulates and will be paid in the future when profits are sufficiently large; preferred shares are cumulative unless otherwise stated
- non-cumulative – if the profits are insufficient to pay a dividend there is no provision for the arrears to be made up in future years

Dividends are calculated as a set percentage on the nominal value of the shares (see *nominal value of ordinary shares*), generally half being paid as an interim dividend and the other half being paid at the year end as a final dividend. The capital on redeemable preferred shares will be repaid at some future date indicated in the title.

*Preferred shares* represent a safer form of investment than *ordinary shares* because of their prior claim to dividends and *capital repayment*.

*Preferred shares* that do not have a maturity date are now included in the *balance sheet* as part of the equity of a *limited company* but only if they are permanent preferred shares, i.e. not *redeemable preferred shares*.

**preliminary expenses** are the expenses incurred by a *limited company* on incorporation. They should not be capitalised but should be written off to the *income statement* when they are incurred. Also known as formation expenses.

**premium bonus pay schemes** reward time-efficient work. If a piece of work is expected to take eight hours to complete and a worker is able to complete it in six hours, a saving of two hours has been made. A bonus based on the hours saved will be paid to the worker as an addition to his/her basic gross pay.

The three best known versions of premium bonus schemes are:

- *Halsey premium bonus scheme*
- *Halsey–Weir premium bonus scheme*
- *Rowan premium bonus scheme*

**prepayment of income** occurs when income is paid in advance by the payer. A prepayment of income is shown as other payables under *current liabilities* in the *balance sheet*.

### Worked example

Josie sublets part of her premises at a rental of £720 per quarter, payable in advance. Her tenant takes up residence on 1 August 20*9, paying £720. He pays a further £720 on 4 November 20*9. Josie's financial year end is 31 December 20*9.

*Required:*

Write up Josie's rent receivable account for the year ended 31 December 20*9.

## Solution:

### Rent receivable

| 20*9 | | | | 20*9 | | | |
|---|---|---|---|---|---|---|---|
| 31 December | Income statement | 1200 | | 1 August | | Bank | 720 |
| 31 December | Balance c/d | 240 | | 4 November | | Bank | 720 |
| | | 1440 | | | | | 1440 |
| | | | | 2010 | | | |
| | | | | 1 January Balance b/d | | | 240 |

The income statement for the year ended 31 December 20*9 would show:

| | £ |
|---|---|
| Gross profit | **** |
| Rent receivable (added) | 1200 |

The balance sheet at 31 December 20*9 would show:

| | |
|---|---|
| Current liabilities | |
| Other payable (rent receivable) | 240 |

**prepayments of expenses** are payments made in advance of the *accounting period* to which they relate. Businesses pay insurance premiums in advance of the time covered by the insurance. *Business rates* are paid in advance. Unused stationery, packing materials and postage stamps are other examples of prepayments. Prepayments are shown as other receivables under *current assets* on the *balance sheet*.

### Worked example

Derek started in business on 1 January 20*8.

The following payments were made by Derek in his first year of trading:

10 January 20*8 Eden District Council £340 for the rating year to 31 March 20*8
23 January 20*8 Pendle Insurance Brokers £1394 insurance for the year to 31 December 20*8
17 April 20*8 Eden District Council £458 half year's payment for the rating year to 31 March 20*9
4 October 20*8 Eden District Council £458 second half year's payment for the rating year to 31 March 20*9
23 December 20*8 Pendle Insurance Brokers £1453 insurance for the year to 31 December 20*9

### Required:

The rates account and the insurance account as they would appear in Derek's books of account at 31 December 20*8.

### Solution:

| Rates | | | | | | Insurance | | | | | |
|---|---|---|---|---|---|---|---|---|---|---|---|
| 20*8 | | | 20*8 | | | 20*8 | | | 20*8 | | |
| 10 Jan | Bank | 340 | 31 Dec | Inc St | 1027 | 23 Jan | Bank | 1394 | 31 Dec | Inc St | 1394 |
| 17 Apl | Bank | 458 | | | | 23 Dec | Bank | 1453 | 31 Dec | Bal. c/d | 1453 |

| 4 Oct | Bank | 458 | 31 Dec | Bal. c/d | 229 | | 2847 | | 2847 |
|---|---|---|---|---|---|---|---|---|---|
| | | 1256 | | | 1256 | 20*9 | | | |
| 20*9 | | | | | | 1 Jan | Bal. b/d 1453 | | |
| 1 Jan | Bal. b/d | 229 | | | | | | | |

The income statement for the year ended 31 December20*8 would show:

| Expenses | £ |
|---|---|
| Rates | 1027 |
| Insurance | 1394 |

The balance sheet at 31 December 20*8 would show:

Current assets
Other receivables     1682

**presentation of financial statements IAS 1:** The standard sets out the format and content of *financial statements*. The standard is designed primarily for the financial statements of *limited companies*. Adoption of the terms and layouts outlined in the standard ensures that financial statements can be compared with previous years and with those of other businesses.

Limited companies must prepare a set of financial statements comprising:
1 an *income statement*
2 a *balance sheet*
3 a statement of cash flows
4 a statements showing changes in equity
5 a statement of accounting policies and explanatory notes

Comparative information from previous financial statements must be shown to aid the users of such statements.

It is a requirement that certain accounting concepts are applied when preparing *financial statements*. These are:
- the *going-concern concept*
- the *accruals concept*
- the concept of *consistency*
- the concept of *materiality*
- the application of further concepts
- *prudence*
- *business entity*
- *money measurement*
- *historic cost*
- duality (*dual aspect concept*)

IAS 1 requires that

- the name of the company is shown
- the period covered by the financial statements is shown
- the currency used is specified (also its magnitude, e.g. £000s)
- financial statements are separate from other information given in the company report

IAS 1 stipulates that certain details are to be included in the income statement.

An example is shown:

### Boxster plc income statement for the year ended 31 May 20*9

|  | £000 | £000 |
|---|---|---|
| Revenue |  | 49 000 |
| Cost of sales |  |  |
| Inventories 1 June 20*8 | 5 400 |  |
| Purchases | 24 100 |  |
|  | 29 500 |  |
| Inventories 31 May 20*9 | (5 700) | (23 800) |
| Gross profit |  | 25 200 |
| Distribution expenses | (1 020) |  |
| Sales and marketing expenses | (920) |  |
| Administrative expenses | (430) | (2 370) |
| Profit/(loss) from operations |  | 22 830 |
| Finance costs |  | (80) |
| Profit/(loss) before tax |  | 22 750 |
| Tax |  | (5 750) |
| Profit/(loss) for the year attributable to equity holders |  | 17 000 |
| **Statement showing changes in equity** |  |  |
| Balance at 1 June 20*8 | 49 950 |  |
| Profit for the year | 17 000 |  |
|  | 66 950 |  |
| Dividends paid | (8000) |  |
| Balance at 31 May 20*9 | 58 950 |  |

IAS 1 also stipulates that certain details be included in the balance sheet.

An example is shown:

### Boxster plc balance sheet at 31 May 20*9

|  | £000 | £000 | £000 | £000 |
|---|---|---|---|---|
| **Non-current assets** | **Valuation** | **Cost** | **Aggregate depreciation** | **Net** |
| Intangible |  |  |  |  |

| | | | |
|---|---|---|---|
| Goodwill | | 2 000 | 500 | 1 500 |
| Property, plant and equipment | | | | |
| Freehold land and buildings | 175 000 | | 15 000 | 160 000 |
| Machinery | | 48 000 | 16 000 | 32 000 |
| Fixtures and fittings | | 14 000 | 5 000 | 9 000 |
| | 175 000 | 64 000 | 36 500 | 202 500 |
| **Current assets** | | | | |
| Inventories | | | 5 700 | |
| Trade receivables | | | 6 030 | |
| Cash and cash equivalents | | | 670 | |
| | | | 12 400 | |
| *Total assets* | | | | 214 900 |
| **Current liabilities** | | | | |
| Trade payables | | | (3 700) | |
| Tax liabilities | | | (5 750) | |
| | | | (9 250) | |
| **Net current assets** | | | | 2 950 |
| | | | | 205 450 |
| **Non-current liabilities** | | | | |
| 8% debentures | | | | (100 000) |
| *Total liabilities* | | | | (109 250) |
| **Net assets** | | | | 105 450 |
| | | | | |
| **Equity** | | | | |
| **Authorised share capital** | | | | |
| 400 000 000 Ordinary shares of 50 pence each | | | | 200 000 |
| **Issued share capital** | | | | |
| 80 000 000 Ordinary shares 50 pence each fully paid | | | | 40 000 |
| **Capital reserves** | | | | |
| Share premium account | | | 5 000 | |
| Revaluation reserve | | | 1 500 | 6 500 |
| **Revenue reserve** | | | | |
| Retained earnings | | | | 58 950 |
| | | | | 105 450 |

Note that the total assets (£214 900 000) and total liabilities (£109 250 000) are included only as information and are not included in the balance sheet totals.

**present value** places a value for today on earnings or money to be received and expenses to be incurred at some future date. (See *net present value*.)

**price/earnings ratio (P/E)** makes a comparison between the earnings per share and the current market price of the share. It shows the number of years' earnings that a person is prepared to pay to buy the share.

The higher the ratio, the greater the confidence investors have regarding the prospects of the company, and the higher the market expectations of future profits and **dividends**. A high or low ratio can be judged only in relation to other businesses in the same sector of the market. The calculation is:

FORMULA:   $\dfrac{\text{current market price}}{\text{earnings per share}}$

### Worked example

The current market price of ordinary shares in Crampies plc is £4.67. The earnings per share is 28 pence.

**Required:**

Calculate the price earnings ratio for Crampies plc.

**Solution:**

$$\text{P/E ratio} = \frac{\text{current market price}}{\text{earnings per share}} = \frac{467 \text{ pence}}{28 \text{ pence}}$$

$$= 16.68 \text{ times}$$

**price elasticity of demand** measures by how much the quantity demanded of a product will change when the producer or the retailer changes the price.

**price elasticity of supply** measures by how much the quantity of a product supplied by producers will change if the market price changes.

**primary ratio:** also known as *return on capital employed (ROCE)*.

**prime cost:** the total of all *direct costs* incurred in producing the product(s) in a manufacturing business. (See *manufacturing accounts*.)

**private limited company:** a company whose *shareholders* are protected by *limited liability* but whose shares are not available for sale to the general public. If a private limited company needs more capital, the *directors* must find other people willing to invest in that company. As a result, many private companies are family businesses with members of the family or close friends owning all the shares.

**private sector** comprises all businesses owned by private individuals and not by the state. Marks and Spencer plc is in the private sector, and so is your local take-away. State-owned businesses are said to be in the *public sector*.

**private ledger:** part of the *general ledger* in which accounts of a confidential nature can be kept. The accounts might include *capital accounts*, and partners' current accounts in the case of a *partnership*, *drawings accounts*, loan accounts, *income statements*, etc.

**process costing** is applied to the costing of mass-produced products. It would be extremely difficult to cost the price of a rubber washer for use in a tap. Thousands of washers will have been produced from the same pieces of synthetic rubber, and all the washers will have gone through the same processing and machining, so it would be extremely difficult and time consuming to allocate costs to a single washer. It would be even more difficult to

**apportion** other overhead costs. (If 2 800 000 washers are produced in a week, and rent for the week is £932, rent apportioned = 0.00033 pence!)

Process costing solves this problem. **CIMA** defines process costing as 'the costing method applicable where goods or services result from a sequence of continuous or repetitive operations or processes. Costs are averaged over the units produced during the period'.

The cost of one washer can be ascertained by the formula:

*FORMULA:* $\dfrac{\text{total costs incurred in washer production for the period}}{\text{number of saleable washers produced in the period}}$

This method of costing is used when:
- one product is unable to be clearly distinguished from another during the process of manufacture, e.g. pencil erasers
- the product becomes a material or component in the next stage of production
- different products are produced during the same process
- **by-products** are produced during the main process of production

**product cost:** the total cost incurred in the manufacturing of a product. **CIMA** defines a product cost as 'the cost of a finished article built up from its cost elements'.

**production budget** is prepared to determine whether the required future levels of production needed to satisfy the anticipated level of predicted sales are attainable, to anticipate any problems that may arise and to enable management to take remedial action.

A production budget might look like this:

|  | May | June | July | August |
|---|---|---|---|---|
| Closing inventory of finished goods (units) | 30 | 90 | 50 | 10 |
| Sales | 270 | 180 | 200 | 230 |
|  | 300 | 270 | 250 | 240 |
| Less opening inventory | 100 | 30 | 90 | 50 |
| Units produced | 200 | 240 | 160 | 190 |

It can be seen that production varies between 160 units per month and 240 units per month. An even production flow to accommodate the required sales levels would look like this:

|  | May | June | July | August |
|---|---|---|---|---|
| Closing inventory of finished goods (units) | 50 | 90 | 110 | 100 |
| Sales | 270 | 180 | 200 | 230 |
|  | 320 | 270 | 310 | 330 |
| Less opening inventory | 100 | 50 | 90 | 110 |
| Units produced | 220 | 220 | 220 | 220 |

**production overheads:** also known as factory overheads. These are expenses incurred in the production of a final product which are not **direct costs.** It would be very difficult, if not impossible in the case of certain **indirect costs**, to identify these overheads with the goods being produced. Production overheads include supervisory wages, maintenance engineers' wages, **indirect material costs** and the **depreciation** of plant and machinery.

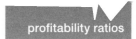

**productivity:** the measurement of the rate of output generated by each worker or each machine in a factory. The most common measure used is labour productivity. The greater the productivity rate, the lower the *unit costs* per hour. For example, if a worker on average produces 50 units per week and the pay rate is £300 per week, then the labour cost per unit is £6. If productivity rises and the worker now produces 55 units per week, then labour costs per unit fall to £5.45.

**productivity bonus:** extra pay given to workers when there has been an increase in productivity.

**productivity ratios** measure the amount of profit or sales that each employee generates. *Productivity* has always been regarded as a key indicator of the efficiency of an organisation. Often workers' pay deals are linked to increases in productivity.

*FORMULA:* $$\text{sales per employee ratio} = \frac{\text{sales}}{\text{number of employees}}$$

*FORMULA:* $$\text{profit per employee} = \frac{\text{net profit}}{\text{number of employees}}$$

It is not possible to say whether these figures are acceptable or not; this would depend on trends and managers' expectations of their workforce.

---

**Worked example**

Snodgrass & Co. made a profit for the year of £76 945 on a turnover of £864 967. It had an average of 532 employees during the year.

*Required:*

Calculate the sales and profit per employee ratios for Snodgrass & Co.

*Solution:*

$$\text{sales per employee} = \frac{\text{sales}}{\text{number of employees}} = \frac{864\ 967}{532}$$
$$= £1625.88 \text{ per annum}$$

$$\text{profit per employee} = \frac{\text{net profit}}{\text{number of employees}} = \frac{76\ 945}{532}$$
$$= £144.63 \text{ per annum}$$

---

**profit:** the excess of income over expenditure. This is not the same as the difference between cash received and cash paid out during a period. Profit is generally calculated by the managers of a business by preparing an *income statement* for a specified time period.

**profitability:** the ability of a business to make profits. Profits are necessary for the long-term survival of a business, but day-to-day survival depends on the business's *liquidity.*

**profitability ratios** allow comparisons to be made between businesses of differing sizes when undertaking *ratio analysis*. Ratios ignore absolute figures; figures are converted into percentages when undertaking profitability ratio analysis. The profitability ratios are:
- *mark-up* or gross profit/cost of sales
- *margin* or gross profit/sales
- *net margin* or profit for the year/sales
- *return on capital employed*

**profit and loss account:** see *income statement*

**profit for the year:** the excess of *gross profit* over expenditure. It is calculated on the *income statement* by deducting all business expenditure from the gross profit. Formerly known as net profit.

**profit maximisation** is often regarded as the prime motive for the existence of businesses. In reality, this may not be the case. Many *sole traders* and *partnerships* satisfice: that is, they find a level of income that suits their individual needs with regard to, say, leisure time, and merely work towards that, rather than trying to make the maximum amount of profit that the business is capable of.

**profit-related pay** links workers' pay to the profits earned by a business. This is designed to increase *productivity* in the workforce since bigger profits will mean greater *take-home pay* for the individual.

### Worked example

The 1600 workers of Gibbins plc have a profit-related pay scheme based on their pay plus an equal share of 0.04% of the annual company profits, which this year have reached £40 000 000.

*Required:*

Calculate the annual gross pay for Norman, who has a basic wage of £9500 and Greta, whose annual gross pay is £13 500.

*Solution:*

Norman will earn £10 500 and Greta will earn £14 500.
(0.04% of £40 000 000 = £1 600 000 to be shared between the 1600 workforce
= £1000 each)

**profit sharing ratio** in a *partnership* is equal unless there is a *partnership agreement* which states how profits are to be shared. This is laid down in the *Partnership Act 1890*. When a partnership agreement exists, the partners have decided how profits are to be shared.

The profit sharing ratio is calculated after partnership salaries and interest on capital have been taken into account, where applicable.

Change in profit sharing ratios of partners affects the structure of a partnership. When partners decide to alter their profit sharing ratios, one partnership ceases to exist and another 'new' partnership takes its place. This means that a revaluation of the partnership assets must take place so that the 'old' partners are credited with what are their dues, before the 'new' partners take over.

### Worked example

Wilson, Kepple and Betty are in partnership sharing profits and losses in the ratios 2:2:1 respectively. Their balance sheet at 31 March 20*9 was as follows:

|  | £ |  |  | £ |
|---|---|---|---|---|
| Premises at cost | 20 000 | Capital | Wilson | 30 000 |
| Machinery at cost | 18 000 |  | Kepple | 20 000 |

| Vehicle at cost | 15 000 | Betty | 15 000 |
|---|---|---|---|
| Inventory | 8 000 | | |
| Trade receivables | 4 000 | Trade payables | 3 000 |
| Cash and cash equivalents | 3 000 | | |
| | 68 000 | | 68 000 |

With effect from 31 March 20*9 the partners have agreed that profits should be shared equally. They further agree that goodwill should be valued at £36 000 on that date. Other assets are to be revalued as follows:

| Premises at | £80 000 |
|---|---|
| Machinery at | £4 000 |
| Vehicle at | £5 000 |

The partners agree that goodwill should not appear in the books of account.

### Required:

The accounts in the partnership books of account to record the change in the profit sharing ratios, and the balance sheet as it would appear immediately after the change.

### Solution:

#### Revaluation account

| | | | | |
|---|---|---|---|---|
| Machinery | | 14 000 | Premises | 60 000 |
| Vehicle | | 10 000 | Goodwill | 36 000 |
| Capitals | Wilson | 28 800 | | |
| | Kepple | 28 800 | | |
| | Betty | 14 400 | | |
| | | 96 000 | | 96 000 |

#### Capital

| | Wilson | Kepple | Betty | | Wilson | Kepple | Betty |
|---|---|---|---|---|---|---|---|
| Goodwill | 12 000 | 12 000 | 12 000 | Balance b/d | 30 000 | 20 000 | 15 000 |
| Balance c/d | 46 800 | 36 800 | 17 400 | Revaluation | 28 800 | 28 800 | 14 400 |
| | 58 800 | 48 800 | 29 400 | | 58 800 | 48 800 | 29 400 |
| | | | | Balance b/d | 46 800 | 36 800 | 17 400 |

### Wilson, Kepple and Betty balance sheet at 31 March 20*9
(after the change in profit sharing ratios)

| | | | | |
|---|---|---|---|---|
| Premises at valuation | 80 000 | Capital | Wilson | 46 800 |
| Machinery at valuation | 4 000 | | Kepple | 36 800 |
| Vehicle at valuation | 5 000 | | Betty | 17 400 |
| Inventory | 8 000 | | | |
| Trade receivables | 4 000 | Trade payables | | 3 000 |
| Cash and cash equivalents | 3 000 | | | |
| | 104 000 | | | 104 000 |

Note that goodwill has been written off to the capital accounts.

**profit sharing schemes** reward employees with a bonus based on the profits of a business. This type of bonus is designed to provide an incentive to the workforce, which should improve the results of the business.

**profit/volume chart** is prepared by some businesses to show the relationship between profits and levels of output. The conventional *break-even chart* does not show this clearly.

### Worked example

The following figures relate to trems:

| Sales of trems in units | 1 000 | 2 000 | 3 000 | 4 000 | 5 000 |
|---|---|---|---|---|---|
| | £ | £ | £ | £ | £ |
| Revenue | 8 000 | 16 000 | 24 000 | 32 000 | 40 000 |
| Variable costs | 4 000 | 8 000 | 12 000 | 16 000 | 20 000 |
| Fixed costs | 9 000 | 9 000 | 9 000 | 9 000 | 9 000 |

*Required:*

A profit/volume chart for trems showing clearly the break-even point for the product.

*Solution:*

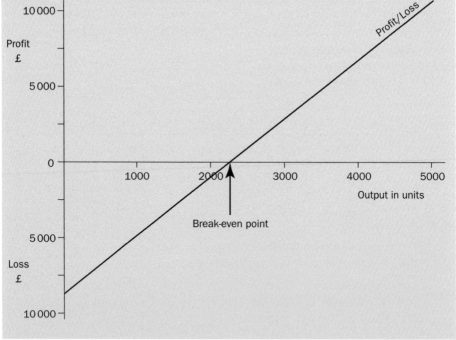

**profit/volume method of calculating break-even point:** see *profit/volume chart*

**profit/volume ratio (P/V):** see *contribution/sales ratio*

**progress payments** are payments made on account by a customer as a long-term *contract* progresses. (See **certification of work done**.)

**property, plant and equipment IAS 16** sets out how *tangible non-current assets* (excluding investment properties) should be treated. The standard allows a choice as to whether the tangible non-current assets are shown at cost or at revaluation. Cost includes the purchase price, any import duties, any costs incurred in making the asset fit for use plus any estimated costs of disposing of the asset at the end of its life. Revaluation is an amount at which the asset could be exchanged between knowledgeable and willing parties in an *at arm's length* transaction. In either case, whichever method is chosen, the asset should be shown less depreciation and impairment losses (in the case of revaluation this should include future depreciation and impairment losses based on the revalued amount). The objective of the standard is the consistent treatment of *tangible non-current assets* in the accounts.

The standard incorporates accounting for depreciation. All non-current assets, with the exception of freehold land, should be depreciated. The method chosen should reflect the way that the assets' economic benefits are consumed. An annual review must be undertaken to ensure that the method used is still appropriate and that the value of the asset is not overstated. It also allows the entity to charge no depreciation if the charge would be immaterial.

**prospectus** details the plans and anticipated profits of a *public limited company* and is issued to prospective *shareholders* in order to encourage them to purchase shares in a company. It is issued once the company has received its Certificate of Incorporation.

**provision:** an amount set aside out of profits for a known expense, the amount of which cannot be calculated with substantial accuracy. (See *provision for doubtful debts*, *provision for depreciation*.)

All provision accounts look the same; only the name and the calculations are different.

**Provision for ******\***

| | | | |
|---|---|---|---|
| | | Balance b/d at beginning of year | 1000 |
| Balance c/d at end of year | 1700 | Income statement | 700 |
| | 1700 | | 1700 |
| | | Balance b/d | 1700 |

You could insert the words 'depreciation of machinery', 'doubtful debts', 'discounts' or 'unrealised profit' in place of ******; the layout of the account would not change.

The *income statement* for the year would show as an expense:

$$
\text{Provision for} \begin{cases} \text{depreciation} \\ \text{bad debts} \\ \text{discounts} \\ \text{unrealised profits} \end{cases} 700
$$

The *balance sheet* would show one of the following:

| | | | |
|---|---|---|---|
| Non-current asset at cost | ***** | Trade receivables | ******* |
| less depreciation | 700 | less provision for bad debts | 700 |
| Trade receivables | ***** | Inventory of finished goods | ***** |
| less provision for discounts | 700 | less provision for unrealised profit | 700 |

**provision for bad debts:** another name used for *provision for doubtful debts*.

**provision for depreciation:** an amount set aside out of profits in each *accounting period* to reflect the cost of using the *non-current asset* in the generation of those profits. This is applying the matching or *accruals concept*. The bookkeeping entries are similar to those used to record *provision for doubtful debts*:

**Debit:** Income statement        **Credit:** Provision for depreciation of non-current asset

Often, the provision for depreciation is merely called 'depreciation'.

A different provision account should be used for each type of *non-current asset*.

**provision for discounts on trade receivables:** some businesses create a provision for discounts that they may allow credit customers on amounts owed at the end of the financial year. This is to take into account, in the period when the sales have taken place, the reduction in the value of the *trade receivables* caused by any discount that may be allowed for settlement within the agreed credit period.

The bookkeeping entries are similar to those used to record *provision for doubtful debts*:

**Debit:** Income statement        **Credit:** Provision for discount on trade receivables

**provision for doubtful debts:** an amount set aside out of profits to cover any outstanding debts, the recovery of which is in doubt. There are two main ways of calculating the amount of the *provision*. They are:

* by estimation based on past experience gained through knowledge of the particular business, its customers and the general economic business climate
* by drawing up an *ageing schedule of trade receivables*

The bookkeeping entries to record the provision are:

**Debit:** Income statement        **Credit:** Provision for doubtful debts

---

### Worked example

At the end of the first year of trading, Ann makes provision for doubtful debts at the rate of 5% on her trade receivables. Her outstanding trade receivables amount to £17 000.

At the end of the second year of trading she increases the amount of the provision to 6% on outstanding debts of £23 000. At the end of her third year of trading she reduces the amount of the provision to 4% on outstanding debts of £14 000.

*Required:*

a) The provision for doubtful debts account as it would appear in Ann's general ledger.
b) Extracts from the income statements showing the amounts transferred at the end of each year from the provision for doubtful debts account.

*Solution:*

Provision for doubtful debts account

| | | | | | |
|---|---|---|---|---|---|
| Year end 1 | Balance c/d | 850 | Year end 1 | Inc statement | 850 |
| | | | Start year 2 | Balance b/d | 850 |
| Year end 2 | Balance c/d | 1 380 | Year end 2 | Inc statement | 530 |
| | | 1 380 | | | 1 380 |

| | | | | | | |
|---|---|---|---|---|---|---|
| Year end 3 | Inc statement | 820 | Start year 3 | Balance b/d | 1 380 |
| Year end 3 | Balance c/d | 560 | | | |
| | | 1 380 | | | 1 380 |
| | | | Start year 4 | Balance b/d | 560 |

Income statement extract for the year ended year 1:
Provision for doubtful debts                (850)
Income statement extract for the year ended year 2:
Provision for doubtful debt                (530)
Income statement extract for the year ended year 3:
Overprovision for doubtful debts                820

**provision for unrealised profit:** see *manufacturing accounts* for a worked example. The bookkeeping entries are similar to those used to record **provision for doubtful debts**.

**provisions, contingent liabilities and contingent assets IAS 37:** this ensures that a provision is recognised only when it actually exists at the *balance sheet* date.

A **provision** is a liability of uncertain timing or amount.

A **contingent liability** is:
- either a possible obligation arising in the past that will be determined by some future event that may or may not occur. The existence of such an obligation will be confirmed only by some future event not wholly in the entity's control
- or a present obligation that is not probable or cannot be quantified reliably.

A **contingent asset** is a possible asset arising from past events, whose existence will be confirmed only by some future event that may or may not occur and which is outside the entity's control. This should be disclosed if an inflow of economic benefit is probable.

**prudence** states that, as accountants, we provide for losses as soon as they are anticipated, but we do not recognise profits until they are realised. In other words, it is much safer to understate rather than overstate profits.

The concept arises because certain items are, of necessity, estimates made when preparing periodic accounts, e.g. accrued expenses, prepaid expenses.

If managers or owners were over-optimistic it is possible that profits might be overstated, and this could result in the resources of the business being depleted by excessive *drawings* or excessive *dividends* being paid. Prudence is sometimes known as conservatism.

**public limited companies** are owned by their *shareholders*, who usually pay an amount when they apply for the shares, and the balance when the shares have been allotted to them (see *issue of shares*). If the company encounters financial difficulties, the shareholders cannot be required to contribute more than an agreed amount of capital. This could result in creditors not being paid what they are owed. To warn potential creditors, the company has to be more open about its affairs than the other forms of business ownership.

The shareholders put the day-to-day running of the company into the hands of *directors*.

**public sector** comprises organisations that are owned or funded by the state (e.g. the National Health Service) or local authorities (e.g. local libraries).

**published accounts** are distributed to the *shareholders* at the end of each financial year. They are also filed with the *Registrar of Companies*. All *limited companies* must distribute a set of accounts to the shareholders. However, *small* and *medium-sized companies* can file modified accounts with the Registrar of Companies.

A company draws up detailed *financial statements* for use by the managers of the business. If these were distributed to the shareholders, a copy could be used by competitors to undermine the business. A less detailed version of the accounts is therefore published, which affords the company some degree of protection.

The published income statements must comply with the provisions of the *Companies Act 1985*, schedule 4. This states the information that must be shown and how it should be shown.

**purchase order:** the business document used to place an order with a supplier. The responsibility for raising such a document lies with the purchasing department within the business. Usually the top copy of the order is sent to the supplier, a copy is kept by the purchasing department, another is sent to the accounts department and the bottom copy is sent to the goods inward department (or warehouse).

**purchase requisition:** a document raised by a department which wishes to make a purchase. It will be prepared and given to a manager for approval and signing. The requisition instructs the buying department to go ahead with the purchase.

**purchases day book** is a list of credit purchases. It is written up from the purchase *invoices* received from the suppliers of goods. When it is convenient, the purchases day book is used to post the individual purchases to the credit of the appropriate *personal accounts* in the *purchase ledger*, and the total purchases to the debit of the purchases account in the *general ledger*.

The purchase day book is not part of the *double-entry bookkeeping* system.

### Worked example

Debbie Crabbe has made the following purchases on credit. She has received purchase invoices from Smiley £170; from Hunt £35; from Priestley £216.

*Required:*

Write up Debbie's purchase day book and show the relevant postings to the ledger accounts.

### Solution:

**Purchases ledger**

**Smiley**

| £ | | £ |
|---|---|---|
| | PDB | 170 |

**Hunt**

| £ | | £ |
|---|---|---|
| | PDB | 35 |

**Priestley**

| £ | | £ |
|---|---|---|
| | PDB | 216 |

**Purchases day book**

| | £ |
|---|---|
| Smiley | 170 |
| Hunt | 35 |
| Priestley | 216 |
| | 421 |

**General ledger**

**Purchases**

| | £ | £ |
|---|---|---|
| PDB | 421 | |

**purchases journal:** see *purchases day book*

**purchases ledger** contains the accounts of all the credit suppliers of a business. The accounts are written up from the *purchases day book*.

**purchases ledger control account:** see *control accounts*

**purchases returns book:** see *purchases returns day book*

**purchases returns day book:** a *book of prime entry* in which goods returned to suppliers are entered. It is written up from the credit notes received from the supplier.

The book is used to post entries to:
- the debit side of the individual suppliers' accounts in the *purchases ledger*
- the credit side of the purchase returns (returns outward) account in the *general ledger*

### Worked example

Waqar Hasami has received the following credit notes:

J Bull £28; R Keane £51; T Klute £8 for goods he has returned to the supplier.

*Required:*

Enter the credit notes in the purchases returns day book and post to the appropriate ledger accounts.

*Solution:*

**Purchases ledger**

**J Bull**

| | £ | | £ |
|---|---|---|---|
| PRDB | 28 | | |

**Purchases returns day book**

| | £ |
|---|---|
| J Bull | 28 |
| R Keane | 51 |
| T Klute | 8 |
| | 87 |

**General ledger**

**Purchases returns**

| | £ | | £ |
|---|---|---|---|
| | | PRDB | 87 |

205

|  | R Keane | |
| --- | --- | --- |
|  | £ | £ |
| PRDB | 51 | |
|  | T Klute | |
|  | £ | £ |
| PRDB | 8 | |

**purchases returns journal:** see *purchases returns day book*

**purchases** are goods bought by a business for resale in the normal course of business. For Mr Choppe the butcher, sides of beef, pork and sausage skins are purchases. For W H Smith, books, pens and magazines are purchases.

**purchases account** in the *general ledger* is debited with goods bought by a business for resale in the normal course of business. Entries are posted to the debit of the account from:

- the *purchases day book* in the case of credit purchases; the credit entries will be found in the *personal accounts* of individual suppliers in the *purchases ledger*
- the *cash book* in the case of cash purchases (credit in *cash* or *bank columns*)

**purchases book:** see *purchases day book*

**Do you need revision help and advice?**

Go to pages 259–72 for a range of revision appendices that include plenty of exam advice and tips.

**quality of profit:** profit earned from cash sales is certain, whereas profit earned on credit sales is less certain because of the inherent risk that some customers may fail to pay. Profits earned can therefore be graded accordingly.

**quick ratio:** also known as the *acid test ratio* and the liquidity ratio.

**quotation:** a response made to a customer's enquiry. It is an offer to sell goods (or services) at the prices, terms and conditions stated in the quotation.

**ranking of projects** prioritises competing *capital expenditure* projects according to their financial desirability. Managers, with a limited capital expenditure budget, are often faced with a number of alternative projects. There is a need to list the projects in order, showing those that are likely to yield the best financial results. Managers may then make a decision as to where money should be best spent.

There may be a *limiting factor* that could affect the decision. This might be *direct materials* or *direct labour*.

**rate of inventory turnover** shows how many times on average a 'bundle' of goods was sold during the last *accounting period*. The speed of inventory turnover is an important efficiency ratio. In every 'bundle' of inventory held by a business, a large amount of cash and profit is tied up. A rapid turnover of goods will release this cash and profit quickly: the more often the business can sell its goods, the more benefit the business will get.

It might seem that the best rate of inventory turnover might be 365 per year. However, if inventory levels fall too low, it might result in lost customers if goods were not available when demanded. In some industries the need to hold large amounts of inventory for long periods has been almost totally eradicated with the use of the *just-in-time (JIT) method of purchasing* inventory. The calculation is:

$$FORMULA: \quad \text{rate of inventory turnover} = \frac{\text{sales}\left(\text{at cost}\right)}{\text{stock}^{*}}$$

*Inventory is obviously at cost, but which figure? We use an average!

---

**Worked example**

An income statement extract of Melanie Murphy is shown below:

|  | £ | £ |
|---|---|---|
| Sales |  | 217 000 |
| Less cost of sales |  |  |
|     Opening inventory | 13 000 |  |
|     Purchases | 106 000 |  |
|  | 119 000 |  |
|     Closing inventory | 11 000 | 108 000 |
| Gross profit |  | 109 000 |

**Required:**

Calculate Melanie's rate of inventory turnover.

**Solution:**

$$\text{rate of inventory turnover} = \frac{\text{cost of sales}}{\text{average stock}} = \frac{108\,000}{12\,000}$$

$$= 9 \text{ times or 40 days } \left(365/9\right)$$

Whether this is a good or bad rate of inventory turnover will depend on the type of product and previous years' rates, or comparison with similar businesses or with the rates prevailing in the industry as a whole.

**rate of return** measures the return that will accrue from a particular investment decision. A business might require a decision regarding investment in a capital project, or an individual might require a decision whether to invest in a savings account in a building society or a bank. A business would calculate the rate of return using one of the following methods of *capital investment appraisal*:

- *accounting rate of return*
- *internal rate of return*
- *net present value*
- *payback*

An individual would make an investment decision referring to the amount of interest or *dividend* which would come from the investment.

The rate of return is generally expressed as a percentage of the amount invested.

**ratio analysis:** a method of analysing the financial results of a business in order to measure its performance. The *final accounts* contain much financial information which can give an insight into the performance of the business. The ratios calculated from the accounts are used by:

- owners
- employees and trade unions
- bank managers
- competitors
- researchers
- press
- Her Majesty's Revenue and Customs
- *trade receivables* and *trade payables*
- pressure groups

The figures given are absolutes and as such do not give an indication of the efficiency or effectiveness of the organisation. The relationships between the figures give a better indication. We can then comment on whether the figures are better or worse than:

- trends in the results of the business over a number of years
- results of the business compared with the results of another business in the same business sector
- results of the business compared with the average results of all the businesses in the sector

**ratios:** the term applied to calculations used to compare the results of businesses using *ratio analysis*. The generic term 'ratio' is applied to results expressed in:

- ratios, e.g. current ratio might be 2.7:1
- percentages, e.g. the mark-up might be 37 per cent
- time, e.g. credit customers settle their debts in 34 days on average; *inventory* is turned over 14 times per year

See under the appropriate heading for particular ratios and their calculation. In an examination, always state the model or formula on which your calculations are based.

**real accounts** are *general ledger* accounts in which the purchase and sale of *non-current assets*, and cash and bank transactions are recorded. (In reality, for convenience the cash and bank accounts are kept separate from the general ledger.)

Real accounts include land and premises, machinery, vehicles, cash and bank.

**realisation account:** this is used to close the *books of account* and to record the sales of the assets of a *partnership* on dissolution. For a worked example showing the use of a realisation account, see *partnership dissolution*.

**realisation concept** states that revenue should only be recorded in the business *books of account* when the goods sold have been replaced by a debtor or by cash. Goods sent to a potential customer remain the property of the sender until the customer indicates that he/she has purchased the goods.

**realised profits** are recognised when a sale takes place and cash is received, or a debtor acknowledges the debt. *Unrealised profits* are not recognised until a contract of sale has been negotiated.

**receipts and payments account:** essentially a summary of all the cash receipts and cash payments made by a club or society during a financial year. It is the main source of information used in the preparation of *club accounts*.

**recession:** a time of high unemployment, of shortage of investment by businesses, and a general lack of confidence in the economy. It is officially defined as 'two successive quarterly periods of declining gross domestic product'.

**reciprocal services** are often provided by servicing departments for other departments within a business. For example, the maintenance engineers might service the catering machinery; the catering department might provide refreshments for the engineers. Similarly, the power-generating section might provide heating services for all departments; the personnel and wages departments might provide services for the power-generating department.

For accounting treatment, see *apportionment of reciprocal service overheads*.

**recoverable amount** is when the *fair value* of a *non-current asset* less any costs incurred in its sale is greater than its present value in use (the *net present value* of any future *discounted cash flows* expected to emanate from the asset).

**redeemable preferred share:** *preferred shares* that a company will buy back at some agreed time in the future. If an enterprise issues preferred shares that pay a fixed rate of *dividend* and are redeemable at some future date, the substance is that the company has a contractual obligation to pay the dividends and so the redeemable preferred share should be recognised as a *non-current liability*.

**redeemable shares:** shares that will be bought back by a company if the fact was stipulated when the shares were first issued. A company can issue redeemable shares of any class, if allowed in the *Articles of Association*. The redemption date may be:
- specified, as in the case of, say, 8 per cent redeemable preferred shares 2016 (these will be redeemed in the year 2016)
- at the discretion of the *shareholders* or of the company

**redemption of shares and debentures:** see *capital redemption reserve* for the bookkeeping entries.

**reducing balance method of calculating depreciation** calculates the annual *depreciation* charge on the *carrying amount* of the asset at the previous *balance sheet date*.

---

### Worked example

Akbar Smith purchased a new delivery vehicle on 1 January 20*8 for £18 000. It is his policy to charge depreciation on vehicles at 40% per annum using the reducing balance method of providing for depreciation.

*Required:*

i)   the provision for depreciation of delivery vehicle account

ii)  balance sheet extracts at 31 December 20*8 and 20*9

*Solution:*

**Provision for depreciation of delivery vehicle**

| 20*8 | | | 20*8 | | |
|---|---|---|---|---|---|
| 31 Dec bal c/d | 7 200 | | 31 Dec Inc St | 7 200 | |
| 20*9 | | | 20*9 | | |
| | | | 1 Jan bal b/d | 7 200 | |
| 31 Dec bal c/d | 11 520 | | 31 Dec Inc St | 4 320 | |
| | 11 520 | | | 11 520 | |
| | | | 1 Jan bal b/d | 11 520 | |

**Balance sheet extract at 31 December 20*8**

| Non-current asset | |
|---|---|
| Delivery vehicle at cost | £18 000 |
| Less depreciation | 7 200 |
| | 10 800 |

**Balance sheet extract at 31 December 20*9**

| Non-current asset | |
|---|---|
| Delivery vehicle at cost | £18 000 |
| Less depreciation | 11 520 |
| | 6 480 |

---

**refer to drawer** is written on a *cheque* when there are insufficient funds in the account to enable the bank to honour the cheque. The cheque is returned to the person on whose account it is drawn.

**Registrar of Companies** receives two documents when a business registers as a *limited company*. These documents are:
- *Memorandum of Association*
- *Articles of Association*

When the Registrar approves registration, the business becomes a limited company and is issued with its Certificate of Incorporation. This gives the company the status of a *legal entity* which is separate from the *shareholders*.

Once the minimum capital is raised, the Registrar issues the company with its Certificate of Trading. On receipt of this, a plc can trade.

It is also a requirement of the **Companies Acts** that copies of accounts and **annual reports** for incorporated businesses are lodged with the Registrar of Companies.

**relevant costs:** when making choices between two or more alternative policies, only *future differential costs* need to be considered; *sunk costs* should be disregarded. For example, Ruth is trying to decide whether she should travel by rail or use her own car in order to attend a meeting in Manchester. When she costs out the two methods she should ignore *depreciation*, insurance and road fund tax on her car since these have already been incurred. They are sunk costs and they should have no bearing on her decision.

**remittance advice:** the document that a customer sends to a supplier, listing all the *invoices*, less any credit notes, that are being paid at that time. The remittance advice is often attached to the statements sent out by the supplier. It can be torn off and sent back to the supplier with the appropriate payment.

**reorder levels:** see *inventory reorder level*

**reporting requirements for medium-sized companies** are less onerous than those for large companies. To be classified as a *medium-sized company*, two of the following criteria must be satisfied:
- a turnover not exceeding £25 900 000
- a *balance sheet* total not exceeding £12 900 000
- average number of employees not exceeding 250

The following concessions are allowed in the accounts to be filed with the **Registrar of Companies**:
- the *income statement* may show as its first item *gross profit* or *loss* – this is a combination of revenue, *cost of sales* and other operating incomes
- analyses of revenue and profit are not required

But
- the balance sheet must be reported in full
- the *directors' report* must be filed with the financial statements

**reporting requirements for small companies** are less onerous than those for large companies. To be classified as a small company, two of the following criteria must be satisfied:
- revenue not exceeding £6 500 000
- *balance sheet* total not exceeding £3 260 000
- average number of employees not exceeding 50

The following concessions are allowed in the accounts to be filed with the **Registrar of Companies**:
- *income statement* need not be filed
- a modified *balance sheet* may be filed

The minimum disclosures in the balance sheet are:
- *intangible assets*
- *tangible non-current assets*

- *investments (non-current assets)*
- *inventories*
- *trade and other receivables*
- investments (*current assets*)
- *called-up capital*
- *share premium account*
- *revaluation reserve*
- other *reserves*
- *retained earnings*

**research and development:** exploring new scientific methods of manufacturing and, generally, using the results to produce an end-product.

Research and development can be:
- pure research – no end-result was envisaged when the research was undertaken in the first place; its aim is to increase knowledge
- applied research – is directed towards a practical application, e.g. a cure for asthma
- development – is the application of knowledge gained in research to produce or improve a product or a process before it is marketed commercially

**research and development costs** are normally written off in the financial period in which they occur; they are treated as *period costs*. The costs might be carried forward and *amortised* over the useful life of the process, if they can be clearly identified with future commercial viability. (*IAS 38* deals with all intangible assets, including research and development)

**reserves:** the *Companies Acts* do not give a formal definition of a reserve. However, it is generally accepted that reserves do not include:
- *provisions for depreciation*
- provisions for known *liabilities*
- provisions for taxation charges

So, reserves are amounts set aside out of profits that are not provisions.

**retail price index:** a measure of the average level of prices of goods and services bought by final consumers. Each item in the index is given a weighting according to its relative importance in the total of consumers' expenditure. A base year is selected and the index is given a value of 100 at that time. Over time, price changes in the economy are measured and expressed as changes in the value of the index.

For example, if the index stood at 100 in 1985 and at 211 today, this would indicate that, on average, prices had risen by 111 per cent between 1985 and today.

**retained earnings:** the name given to the *revenue reserve* to which a *limited company*'s *retained profit* for the year is credited. This is a major regular source of long-term finance for a successful limited company. It is also known as retained profits. (See *statement of changes in equity*.)

**retained profits:** also known as retained earnings.

**retainer:** see *retention money*

**retention money:** money held back by a client after a long-term contract has been completed. This allows the client time to determine whether the contract has been completed satisfactorily. If it has not been completed to the satisfaction of the client, the money will be held until the work is complete. Retention money can also be held in case the contract is not completed by the date stipulated in the contract.

**retiring partner** means that a structural change has occurred in the ownership of a *partnership*. Before the partner's retirement date one business was in existence; after the retirement date 'new' partners emerge to start a 'new' business.

For example, Carrie, James and Maurice are in partnership. James retires on 30 April 20*9. Carrie, James and Maurice are the proprietors of the business until midnight on 30 April. One microsecond after midnight the proprietors of the business are Carrie and Maurice.

When a partner retires, the business is valued so that the departing partner can take his/her dues. This can sometimes cause a problem if the retiring partner has large capital and current account balances standing to his/her credit. To allow the partner to withdraw his/her balances as cash could cause severe liquidity problems for the business. To over-come this problem the new partnership might:
- borrow sufficient funds to pay the retiring partner
- transfer the balances to a loan account and repay the capital over a number of years
- take in a new partner and use his/her capital injection to pay the retiring partner

## Worked example

Yolande, Zena and Albert are in partnership sharing profits and losses 3:3:2. Yolande retired on 31 May 20*9. At that date the partnership balance sheet showed:

| | £ | £ |
|---|---|---|
| Non-current assets: | | |
| Premises | | 80 000 |
| Fixtures | | 12 000 |
| Vehicles | | 26 000 |
| | | 118 000 |
| Current assets: | | |
| Inventory | 9 000 | |
| Trade receivables | 13 000 | |
| Cash and cash equivalents | 1 750 | |
| | 23 750 | |
| Less current liabilities: | | |
| Trade payables | 6 750 | 17 000 |
| | | 135 000 |
| Capital accounts: | | |
| Yolande | | 50 000 |
| Zena | | 40 000 |
| Albert | | 40 000 |
| | | 130 000 |

Current accounts:

| | | |
|---|---|---|
| Yolande | 1 500 | |
| Zena | 2 150 | |
| Albert | 1 350 | 5 000 |
| | | 135 000 |

The partners have agreed the following asset values at close of business on 31 May 20*9:

| | £ |
|---|---|
| Premises to be revalued at | 150 000 |
| Fixtures to be revalued at | 7 000 |

Yolande will retain the business car she has been using at an agreed value of £7500 (it has a book value of £9000).

| | |
|---|---|
| The two remaining cars to be revalued at | 14 000 |
| Trade receivables are valued at | 12 500 |
| Goodwill to be valued at | 80 000 |

The partners have agreed that any balance remaining in Yolande's capital account be transferred to a loan account initially. No goodwill account is to remain in the partnership books of account. Profits and losses will be shared equally in the new partnership.

### Required:

i) Yolande's capital account showing the amount transferred to her loan account.
ii) The partnership balance sheet as it would appear on 31 May 20*9 after Yolande's retirement.

### Solution:

i)

**Capital account – Yolande**

| | | | |
|---|---|---|---|
| Vehicle | 7 500 | Balance b/d | 50 000 |
| Loan a/c | 96 500 | Current a/c | 1 500 |
| | | Revaluation a/c | 52 500 |
| | 104 000 | | 104 000 |

ii) **Zena and Albert balance sheet at 31 May 20*9**
(after Yolande's retirement):

| | £ | £ |
|---|---|---|
| Non-current assets: | | |
| Premises at valuation | | 150 000 |
| Fixtures at valuation | | 7 000 |
| Vehicles at valuation | | 14 000 |
| | | 171 000 |
| Current assets: | | |
| Inventory | 9 000 | |
| Trade receivables | 12 500 | |
| Cash and cash equivalents | 1 750 | |
| | 23 250 | |

| Less current liabilities: | | |
|---|---|---|
| Trade payables | 6 750 | 16 500 |
| | | 187 500 |
| Capital accounts: | | |
| Zena | | 52 500 |
| Albert | | 35 000 |
| | | 87 500 |
| Current accounts: | | |
| Zena | 2 150 | |
| Albert | 1 350 | |
| | | 3 500 |
| Loan account – Yolande | | 96 500 |
| | | 187 500 |

**return on capital employed (ROCE)** shows the percentage return on the capital invested in a business. There are a number of different measures for ROCE, so it is important in an examination to indicate to the examiner which measure you are using (if you have been given a choice). Write down the model that you are using.

ROCE is an important ratio (it is often called the primary ratio). Many of the other ratios are elements of the ROCE. The calculation is:

$$FORMULA: \quad \frac{\text{profit before interest and tax}}{\text{capital employed}} \times 100$$

*Capital employed* is:
- all share capital – *ordinary share capital* and preferred share capital
- all *reserves*
- any long-term *loans*
- *debentures* (in the case of a *limited company*)

Some users of accounts use the opening capital employed, some use the closing capital employed, and some use an average figure. For examination purposes, unless given precise instructions in the question, use the formula that you feel most comfortable with.

**Worked example**

Shuvelle and Bruce plc has a profit before interest and tax of £871 056 and capital employed of £4 000 000.

*Required:*

Calculate the return on capital employed for Shuvell and Bruce plc.

*Solution:*

$$ROCE = \frac{\text{profit before interest and tax}}{\text{capital employed}} = \frac{871\ 056}{4\ 000\ 000} \times 100 = 21.78\%$$

It is impossible to comment on whether or not this is a good ROCE. Clearly it should be as large as possible, but we really need previous years' figures or figures relating to the industry as a whole in order to make a judgement.

ROCE indicates how much profit has been earned by each £100 of long-term capital invested in a business. When comparing ROCE for different businesses, it is important to make sure that they are:

- in the same line of business
- using the same production techniques
- using the same accounting policies

The ratio can be used:

- by investors, when considering an investment opportunity
- by managers, when considering a capital investment decision – the project may be inappropriate if the cost of capital is greater than the ROCE
- when considering the purchase of a *subsidiary*
- in different departments of a business to assess their viability

Other versions of this ratio are:

- $\dfrac{\text{net profit before tax}}{\text{shareholders' funds}} \times 100$

- $\dfrac{\text{net profit after tax}}{\text{shareholders' funds}} \times 100$

- $\dfrac{\text{net profit after tax and preference dividend}}{\text{shareholders' funds excluding preference shares}} \times 100$

A major weakness of using ROCE and the *return on owners' equity* is that both ratios are based on the historic cost of the business's assets. If asset values are inaccurate then the capital employed figure must also be inaccurate.

**return on owners' equity:** a refinement of the *return on capital employed (ROCE)* calculation, measuring the return on the funds invested by the ordinary *shareholders*. The calculation is:

*FORMULA:*

$$\dfrac{\text{net profit before interest and tax but deducting preference dividends}}{\text{issued ordinary share capital} + \text{all reserves}} \times 100$$

The *profit* after deducting the *preferred share* dividend is the profit available for the ordinary shareholders before the deduction of interest and taxation.

**returns** are goods that have been sent back to the supplier because they are unsuitable in some way. The supplier will, generally, issue a credit note which the customer can set off against future purchases.

The bookkeeping entries can be seen under *purchases returns day book* and *sales returns day book*.

**returns inward:** see *sales returns day book*

**returns inward book:** see *sales returns day book*

**returns inward journal:** see *sales returns day book*

**returns inwards day book:** see *sales returns day book*

**returns outward:** see *purchases returns day book*

**returns outward book:** see *purchases returns day book*

**returns outward day book:** see *purchases returns day book*

**returns outward journal:** see *purchases returns day book*

**revaluation of assets** takes place when:
- there is a structural change in the ownership of a partnership, or
- the **directors** of a **limited company** believe that the **carrying amounts** values of some **non-current assets** are not representative of their **market value**.

**revaluation reserve** is created by the **directors** of a **limited company** when **non-current assets** are revalued upwards. It is a **capital reserve**, so it is not available for distribution as cash dividends. It can be used for the issue of **bonus shares**. **Sole traders** and **partnerships** do not create revaluation reserves. (See **going-concern concept**.)

---

**Worked example**

R Preston plc balance sheet extract at 30 November 20*9:

|  | £ | £ |
|---|---|---|
| Non-current assets |  |  |
| Premises at cost | 170 000 |  |
| Less depreciation | 12 000 | 158 000 |

The directors have recently had the premises valued by Maybins, a firm of professional valuers, at £210 000.

*Required:*

Journal entries to record the revaluation in the books of R Preston plc.

*Solution:*

**Journal**

|  | Dr | Cr |
|---|---|---|
|  | £ | £ |
| Premises | 40 000 |  |
| Provision for depreciation of premises | 12 000 |  |
| Revaluation reserve |  | 52 000 |

---

**revenue IAS 18** comprises sales of goods and services and receipts of interest, royalties and dividends. Revenue is recognised using the realisation concept.

**revenue expenditure:** expenditure on everyday running costs of a business.

**revenue receipts:** receipts received in the normal course of business, e.g. receipts from cash sales. Rent received, **commission** received, etc. are also revenue receipts. They are credited to an appropriate revenue account in the **general ledger**, i.e. rent receivable is entered on the credit side of the rent receivable account, not the credit of the rent payable account.

At the financial year end the accounts are closed by a transfer to the **income statement**:

**Debit:** The revenue received account        **Credit:** Income statement

**revenue reserves** are retained earnings that have been withheld from *dividend* distribution in order to strengthen the financial position of a company. Revenue reserves are a very important source of finance for *limited companies*.

The amount to be transferred to the reserve is debited to the *retained earnings* and credited to the appropriate *reserve* account. This reduces the amount of profits available for cash dividends. Revenue reserves are created at the discretion of the *directors*.

Revenue reserves are available for distribution to the *shareholders* in the form of cash dividends by debiting the reserve account and crediting the dividend payable account. Revenue reserves can also be used for the issue of *bonus shares*.

Examples of revenue reserves are:
- *non-current asset replacement reserve*
- *foreign exchange reserve*
- *general reserve*
- *retained earnings*

**reversal of entries:** see *errors not affecting the balancing of the trial balance*

**reverse order of liquidity:** see *non-current assets* and *current assets*

**rights issue of shares** is offered to existing *shareholders*. The right is to purchase a set number of new shares at a stated price. The number of shares that can be purchased by any one individual is based on their present holding. The rights issue might be one new share for every three already held, one for seven, etc. The right can be sold or given to another person if the shareholder does not wish to exercise his/her right.

The price of the shares is usually a little cheaper than the market price since the company does not have the same administrative expenses to pay on the issue.

The bookkeeping entries are exactly the same as the entries for an *issue of shares* to the public at large.

**Rowan premium bonus scheme** is used to reward *direct labour* for saving time during the production process. This method rewards the worker with a proportion of the time saved.

*FORMULA:*  $\text{proportion of time saved} = \dfrac{\text{time taken}}{\text{time allowed}} \times \text{time saved}$

**Worked example**

Alexandra is paid £7.00 per hour. The time allowed to complete a task is 10 hours. The actual time taken by Alexandra to complete the task is 7 hours.

*Required:*

Calculate the gross pay due to Alexandra after completing the task.

*Solution:*

$$\text{Alexandra's gross pay} = \left(7 \text{ hrs} \times £7.00\right) + \left(\dfrac{\text{time taken}}{\text{time allowed}} \times \text{time saved} \times \text{rate per hour}\right)$$

$$= \left(7 \text{ hrs} \times £7.00\right) + \left(70\% \times 3 \text{ hrs} \times £7.00\right)$$

$$= £63.70$$

**royalties** are an agreed amount of money paid to the inventor of a product or process or idea for the right of use. It is often a percentage of the revenue earned by the user. Royalties on a manufacturing process will appear in the *prime cost* section of the *manufacturing account*.

**running balance accounts:** *ledger* accounts where the balance is adjusted each time a transaction takes place. They are widely used, and rather than showing a traditional debit/credit layout, a three-column approach is used. You will probably have encountered this layout on your bank statement, if you have a bank account.

A traditional *sales ledger* account would be laid out like this:

### G Drood

| | | £ | | | £ |
|---|---|---|---|---|---|
| 1 May | Balance b/d | 416 | 15 May | Cash | 410 |
| 23 May | Sales | 1307 | | Discount allowed | 6 |
| 27 May | Sales | 198 | 25 May | Returns | 23 |
| | | | 31 May | Balance c/d | 1482 |
| | | 1921 | | | 1921 |
| 1 June | Balance b/d | 1482 | | | |

The running balance version of the same account is:

### G Drood

| | | Debit £ | Credit £ | Balance £ |
|---|---|---|---|---|
| 1 May | Balance | | | 416 Dr |
| 15 May | Cash | | 410 | 6 Dr |
| | Discount allowed | | 6 | 000 |
| 23 May | Sales | 1307 | | 1307 Dr |
| 25 May | Returns | | 23 | 1284 Dr |
| 27 May | Sales | 198 | | 1482 Dr |

**Are you studying other subjects?**

The *A–Z Handbooks (digital editions)* are available in 14 different subjects. Browse the range and order other handbooks at **www.philipallan.co.uk/a-zonline**.

**safety stock:** the amount of *inventory* held in excess of the normal expected usage. It is held to provide a buffer in case some unforeseen circumstance occurs, e.g. an urgent rush order or temporary difficulty in obtaining goods from suppliers.

**salaries** are payments, usually monthly, made to administrative employees with a contract of employment.

**sales:** now included as part of *revenue* in *financial statements*.

**sales account** records the value of goods sold to customers during a financial year. The sales account is a *nominal account* and is found in the *general ledger*.

Sales may be:

- cash sales – these occur when a customer exchanges cash or a cheque, immediately, for the goods sold. The bookkeeping entries are:

  **Debit:** Cash                              **Credit:** Sales account in general ledger

- credit sales – payment for the goods sold takes place at some future time. The bookkeeping entries are:

  **Debit:** Customers' account in sales ledger    **Credit:** Sales account in general ledger

When large numbers of credit sales take place, the credit sales are entered in a *sales day book* prior to entry in the double-entry system.

The sales that are recorded in the sales account are those that form the normal trading activities of the business.

Sales of *non-current assets* are recorded in an *asset disposal account*.

For example, J Last owns a shoe shop. The sales account is credited with sales of shoes, trainers, shoe polish, etc. The asset disposal account is credited with the sale of an old display unit.

**sales analysis book:** a breakdown of sales by product. It is often used in businesses that sell a number of different products. It enables management to see the level of sales for each particular product line. The analysis facilitates the compilation of departmental *financial statements*. (See *columnar day books* and *departmental accounts*.)

**sales book:** see *sales day book*

**sales budget** shows predicted sales and the revenues that they are expected to generate for the budget period. It is generally the first budget to be prepared, since most businesses

S

are sales led. Once the sales budget has been prepared, the other budgets can be prepared taking into account what is shown by the sales budget.

A sales budget can be subdivided into analysis columns which show information that is important to that particular business. Analysis can be into:

- products
- national or international regions
- departments
- sales representatives and sales office
- customers (in the case of a business with a few large customers)

**sales day book:** a list of **credit sales**. It is written up from copy **sales invoices** sent to customers when a sale is completed. When it is convenient, the sales day book is used to post debit entries in the **personal accounts** in the **sales ledger** and a credit entry in the **sales account** in the **general ledger**. The sales day book is not part of the double-entry system.

---

**Worked example**

Frank Lumley has sold goods on credit to P Kew £51, R Hess £89, J Kay £410.

**Required:**

Write up Frank's sales day book and show the relevant postings to the ledger accounts.

**Solution:**

| Sales ledger | | | Sales day book | | General ledger | | |
|---|---|---|---|---|---|---|---|
| **Kew** | | | | £ | **Sales** | | |
| | £ | £ | Kew | 51 | | £ | £ |
| SDB | 51 | | Hess | 89 | | SDB | 550 |
| | | | Kay | 410 | | | |
| **Hess** | | | | 550 | | | |
| | £ | £ | | | | | |
| SDB | 89 | | | | | | |
| **Kay** | | | | | | | |
| | £ | £ | | | | | |
| SDB | 410 | | | | | | |

---

**sales forecasts:** estimates of anticipated sales for the next time period based on the information available. They are used as the main basis for the preparation of the **sales budget**. Amongst other things, a sales forecast draws on:

- market research
- representatives' field reports
- trade sources for specific business intelligence
- general economic forecasts

to determine the budgeted demand for sales of the product(s).

Once the volume of sales has been forecast, total sales revenue can be forecast by taking into account the business's pricing policy.

**sales invoice:** the formal demand sent to a credit customer asking for payment for goods sold. The *invoice* will generally show:

- seller's name and address
- purchaser's name and address
- seller's *VAT* number (if VAT registered)
- date of invoice/tax point
- description of items sold
- the quantity and price of individual items sold
- details of trade discount if applicable
- invoice total plus VAT (the rate should be indicated)
- the amount payable
- details of cash discounts available
- date when amount is due

**sales journal:** see *sales day book*

**sales ledger:** contains the accounts of all the business's credit customers. Cash sales do not appear in this ledger. The entries in the sales ledger are posted from the *sales day book*.

The sales ledger is also known as the debtors' ledger since any balances outstanding on any of the accounts are amounts owed by debtors.

**sales ledger control account** checks the arithmetic accuracy of all entries posted to the *sales ledger*. (See *control accounts*.)

**sales margin variance** is the difference between the budgeted profit from sales and the actual profit from sales. It is used to analyse the performance of the sales department.

The total sales margin variance calculation is:

*FORMULA:*

actual profit based on standard unit costs − budgeted profit based on standard unit costs

This can be subdivided into:

- sales margin price variance:

  *FORMULA:*

  (actual margin based on standard unit costs − standard margin based on standard unit cost) × actual sales volume

- sales margin volume variance:

  *FORMULA:*   (actual sales volume − budgeted volume) × standard profit margin

**Worked example**

Brittas plc produces and sells a single product, the inkle. The standard costs of producing an inkle total £48. The standard selling price of an inkle is £65. The budget based on standard cost for an output of 100 000 inkles is shown below:

|  | £ |
|---|---|
| Sales | 6 500 000 |
| Total standard cost | 4 800 000 |
| Budgeted profit | 1 700 000 |

The actual results show:

Sales 95 000 units at £66 each      6 270 000

*Required:*

i) total sales margin variance for inkles

ii) sales margin price variance for inkles

iii) sales margin volume variance for inkles

*Solution:*

i)      £

| | |
|---|---|
| Actual sales revenue | 6 270 000 |
| Standard cost of sales (95 000 × £48) | 4 560 000 |
| Actual profit margin | 1 710 000 |
| Actual profit margin | 1 710 000 |
| Budgeted profit margin | 1 700 000 |
| Total sales margin variance | 10 000    favourable |

ii) The change in the selling price of inkles has led to an increase in the profit margin of £1 per unit (the change in price has increased profit from £17 per unit to £18 per unit). Actual sales volume of 95 000 gives a favourable sales margin price variance of £95 000.

$$\Big(\text{actual margin} - \text{standard margin}\Big) \times \text{actual sales volume}$$

£18    –    £17     ×     95 000

= £95 000 favourable

iii) A comparison of budgeted sales volume with actual sales volume shows by how much sales have deviated from budget. When multiplied by the standard profit margin, the result will show how much the change in volume of sales has impacted on profits. Budgeted sales were 100 000 units, but actual sales were only 95 000 units. The reduction in sales of 5000 units has reduced profit by £17 per unit = £85 000.

$$\Big(\text{actual sales volume} - \text{budgeted sales voulume}\Big) \times \text{standard profit margin}$$

95 000    –    100 000     ×     £17

= £85 000 adverse

**sales variance:** the difference between standard sales revenue and actual sales revenue. The variance is made up of:

- *selling price variance*
- sales volume/profit variance

### Worked example

The budgeted sales for shrids was 17 000 units at a selling price of £900 each. The actual sales volume was 16 875 at a selling price of £895 each. The standard cost per unit was £500.

*Required:*

*Calculate:*

    a) the selling price variance

    b) the sales volume profit variance

    c) the total sales variance

*Solution:*

We need to use a modified grid, as shown in *direct labour variance*.

standard quantity × standard profit

}= sales volume profit variance

actual quantity × standard profit

actual quantity × standard price

}= selling price variance

actual quantity × actual price

So:

sq × sp 17 000 × 400 = £6 800 000

}= £50 000    adverse sales
volume profit variance

aq × sp 16 875 × 400 = £6 750 000

aq × sp 16 875 × 900 = £15 187 500

}= £84 375    adverse selling
price variance

aq × ap 16 875 × 895 = £15 103 125
total sales variance    £134 375

**sales volume/profit variance:** see *sales variance*

**sales returns book:** see *sales returns day book*

**sales returns day book:** a record of goods that have been returned by customers. It is written up from copy credit notes that have been sent to customers. When it is convenient, the returns are posted from this day book to the credit of the *personal accounts* in the *sales ledger* and the debit of the sales returns (*returns inward*) account in the *general ledger*.

#### Worked example

Pam Deli has had some goods returned as unsatisfactory. She has issued the following credit notes to her customers: Tomkins £18, Cubby £139, Sapper £46.

*Required:*

Write up Pam's sales returns day book and show the relevant postings to the ledger accounts.

*Solution:*

| Sales ledger | | Sales returns day book | | General ledger | |
|---|---|---|---|---|---|
| **Cubby** | | | £ | **Sales returns** | |

| | £ | | £ | Tomkins | 18 | | £ | | £ |
|---|---|---|---|---|---|---|---|---|---|
| | | SRDB | 139 | Cubby | 139 | SRDB | 203 | | |
| | | | | Sapper | 46 | | | | |
| **Sapper** | | | | | 203 | | | | |
| | £ | | £ | | | | | | |
| | | SRDB | 46 | | | | | | |
| **Tomkins** | | | | | | | | | |
| | £ | | £ | | | | | | |
| | | SRDB | 18 | | | | | | |

**sales returns journal** see *sales returns day book*

**Saloman v Saloman and Company Ltd 1897** confirmed the distinction between a company and its *shareholders*. A *limited company* has a legal status separate from that of its owners, and as such, from that date, limited companies became separate *legal entities*.

**savings banks** accept deposits, and customers receive interest on those deposits.

**scrip issue:** see *bonus shares*

**secured loan:** a loan which has an asset pledged as security for the loan. Some *debenture* stock is secured, with the assets of the company pledged as security. If the company were to go into *liquidation*, the assets would be sold and used to repay the debenture holders. If there was a surplus after paying the debenture holders, the remaining cash would go towards paying off the preferred *shareholders* and finally the ordinary shareholders.

**sellers' market** occurs when there is a limited supply of particular goods and a large demand. This means that sellers can demand high prices for their goods.

**selling price variance:** see *sales variance*

**semi-variable costs:** costs which cannot be classified as either *fixed costs* or *variable costs* because they contain an element of both. An example of a semi-variable cost is the charge for electricity consumption. The standing charge is the fixed cost element – it must be paid even when no electricity is used. The variable element is the charge based on the number of units of electricity used.

**sensitivity analysis** tries to measure outcomes if the variables in a forecast were to change. Many projects involve long time periods and the commitment of large sums of money, so reliable forecasting is difficult. Sensitivity analysis attempts to determine how sensitive the outcome of a project is to changes in future costs and receipts.

**separate valuation principle** is a fifth fundamental *accounting concept* identified in the *Companies Act 1985*. It states that when valuing an asset or liability for *balance sheet* purposes, each component item of the asset or liability must be valued separately and then aggregated.

**service cost centres** are non-productive departments which provide a service to production departments. Examples include maintenance, personnel, canteen.

**service costing** can be applied to:
- the provision of support functions in a manufacturing business
- the costing involved in a business in the service sector of the economy, e.g. transport

The costing techniques are similar to those applied to any other department in a business; costs are allocated and apportioned using the usual methods. The costs allocated and apportioned to a service department will be absorbed by the departments that use the service (see *apportionment of service cost centre overheads*).

For the techniques used for apportioning the costs of departments providing reciprocal services, see *apportionment of reciprocal service costs*.

In the case of a business in a service sector of the economy, overheads will be recovered in the same way as they are recovered in a manufacturing business by the use of an appropriate method of absorption.

**service departments** support the activities of other departments, e.g. personnel, finance, technical support, maintenance, etc.

**set of financial statements:** IAS 1 lists these as *balance sheet*, *income statement*, *statement of changes in equity*, *statement of cash flows*, *accounting policies*, explanatory notes.

**shareholders:** the owners of a *limited company* by virtue of owning shares in that company. A company's share capital is, generally, divided into:
- *ordinary shares*
- *preferred shares*

**shareholders' funds** are made up of:
- the share capital of the company, plus
- all *reserves*

Note that, when using IAS terminology, equity capital comprises *ordinary shares* and *preferred shares*, provided they are irredeemable, plus all reserves. Redeemable preferred shares are not part of the equity capital of a company. If a company is wound up, all the equity capital remaining is distributed, after the preferred shareholders have been settled, to the ordinary shareholders.

**share premium account** arises when shares are issued by a *limited company* at a price greater than par. The extra amounts received are credited to a share premium account.

---

### Worked example

A limited company issues 100 000 shares with a nominal value of £1 at a price of £4.50.

*Required:*

The entries in the company's general ledger.

*Solution:*

| Cash | £ |
| --- | --- |
| Ordinary share cap'l | 100 000 |
| Share premium acc. | 350 000 |

| Ordinary share capital | £ |
| --- | --- |
| Cash | 100 000 |

| Share premium account | £ |
| --- | --- |
| Cash | 350 000 |

The share premium account is a **capital reserve**. It cannot be used for cash dividend purposes It can be used to:

- issue **bonus shares**
- write off **preliminary expenses**
- provide any premium payable on the **redemption of shares** (but only if the share premium account was originally created by the issue of those shares)

**shift premium:** see *shift work*

**shift work:** if a business operates its production process 24 hours per day, the day will generally be split into three shifts. A different group of workers will work each shift, ensuring that 24-hour production is maintained.

The workers who are required to work on the evening and night shifts will generally be paid a shift premium to compensate them for working unsocial hours.

**short-term planning** identifies the building blocks or the components of any long-term planning that an organisation may undertake.

**simple interest** is calculated on the capital sum borrowed when a loan is agreed. No further calculations of interest are made.

> **Worked example**
>
> Percy borrows £700 from Shark & Co. The simple interest charge is 12%. The loan has to be repaid in 24 equal instalments.
>
> $$\text{Percy will pay } \frac{£700 \times 112\%}{24} = £32.67 \text{ per month}$$
>
> This is in fact greater than 12% since after the first month Percy should only be charged interest on £667.33.

(See *annual percentage rate (APR)* and *compound interest*.)

**simplified method of apportioning overheads of reciprocal service departments:** also known as the *elimination method of apportioning overhead costs of reciprocal services*.

**single-entry bookkeeping:** a method of recording financial transactions that relies on the use of the **cash book** as the main source of information for preparing the *financial statements*. It is mainly used in the preparation of financial statements for:

- small cash-based businesses
- clubs and societies

In the cash book, debit entries are made for receipts of cash and cheques, credit entries are made for cash and cheque payments. The 'opposite' double entries are not made in a *ledger*. (See *incomplete records*.)

**sinking fund** is built up by investing regular amounts of money in order to provide a set amount to meet a future need like the purchase of a new machine, or the repayment of a loan.

**small companies:** by definition, small companies must fulfil two of the following criteria:

- a turnover not exceeding £6 500 000
- *balance sheet* total not exceeding £3 260 000
- average number of employees not exceeding 50

They are allowed 'filing exemptions' in the accounts that they file with the **Registrar of Companies**. This is to protect their interests from rival businesses. (See **reporting requirements for small companies**.)

**social accounting** takes note of the fact that not all accounting decisions are taken on purely financial grounds. The **money measurement concept** states that only transactions that can be recorded in cash terms are entered in the business **books of account**. This means that many things that have a direct bearing on the conduct and results of the business are missing from the financial statements.

Profitability is of vital importance to all businesses, but there has been a move in recent years to consider the impact that business has on society at large. We are all consumers, perhaps employees, and we all live in an environment which is influenced in many ways by the business world. Social accounting recognises that a business which fails to consider the social implications of its policies may well find that some of those policies are counterproductive, and that **profitability** might be affected. An unhappy workforce could cause a fall in **productivity**. Similarly, a business which pollutes a locality may find that turnover falls through bad publicity. In 1995, for example, many consumers throughout Europe refused to purchase Shell products because of the company's proposal to dispose of the Brent Spar oil platform in the North Sea.

**software** is used to instruct computer **hardware** how to perform. Programs are contained in magnetic form on floppy disks. When a disk is inserted into the disk drive, the instructions on it are read by the computer and used by the operator. Programs can be transferred from the software onto hard disk so that they are ready for use at any time.

Software packages for accounting include:
- *spreadsheets*
- *sales* and *purchases ledger accounts*
- (general) *nominal ledger accounts*
- payroll
- inventory records
- *financial statements*

**sole trader:** a type of business ownership where the business is owned and controlled by one person.

**solvency:** the ability to pay all outstanding debts when they fall due.

**source documents:** the primary sources of information that are used to make entries into the subsidiary books, e.g. purchase invoices are used to write up the purchases day book; copy sales invoices are used to write up the sales day book etc.

**sources of finance:** the various ways in which funds can be raised for business use. These are important, since a business cannot function in either the short run or the long run without adequate finance.

Short-term finance depends to a large extent on a business's ability to manage its working capital well. Good management of working capital will ensure sufficient cash resources to pay everyday running expenses. A good **rate of inventory turnover** will release cash tied up in the goods on a regular basis.

A short **trade receivables' payment period** will also bring cash quickly into the business on a regular basis. Credit sales now form a large proportion of many businesses' turnover.

S

Outstanding balances in the **sales ledger** represent cash tied up in *trade receivables*. This cash is actually providing finance for the business's customers.

If there is a lack of short-term finance, a business may have to resort to:
- disposal of surplus stocks
- *factoring*
- negotiating **overdrafts**

Long-term financing can take the form of:
- issuing new shares for cash
- issuing **debentures**
- grants from local and central government and from the EU

Cash may be conserved for use in other areas of the business by using:
- credit terms for the purchase of assets
- *hire-purchase* agreements
- leasing arrangements
- sale and lease back

**special-order pricing** uses *marginal costing* techniques to arrive at a decision whether to accept a special 'one-off' order or not. If the order gives a positive contribution and the following conditions hold, then it should be accepted:
- the order should not displace other business
- there must be spare capacity in the production department
- regular customers must not be aware of the customers receiving the special price
- special prices should not set a precedent for future pricing
- the special-price customer should not be in a position that will allow them to sell to others at below regular price

A negative contribution might be acceptable:
- to keep skilled workers
- to keep machinery working
- in order to stimulate full-price orders in the future

### Worked example

Clough Engineering manufactures one product, the yut. The following information relates to the production of yuts:

|  |  | £ |
|---|---|---|
| Selling price per yut |  | 200 |
| Costs per unit: | direct materials | 45 |
|  | direct labour | 63 |
|  | fixed costs | 18 |

There is spare capacity in the factory.

A German retailer has indicated that he is willing to purchase 1000 yuts, but he is only prepared to pay £120 per unit.

**Required:**

Advise the managers of Clough Engineering whether or not they should accept the order.

*Solution:*

The order ought to be accepted. It makes a positive contribution of £12 per unit.

$$\text{contribution} = \text{selling price per unit} - \text{variable costs per unit}$$
$$= £120 - £108\left(45 + 63\right)$$
$$= £12$$

**speculator:** a person who buys and sells securities or commodities in the expectation that a change in the price will earn him/her a profit. (See *bear* and *bull*.)

**split-off point:** see *common costs*

**spreadsheet:** a computer program into which numerical data can be inputted. It can be used to build statistical and financial models. A template composed of rows and columns is set up as memory cells and, by the use of formulae entered into these cells, calculations and changes to models can be made. The spreadsheet can be observed on screen or it can be printed out as a hard copy.

Spreadsheets are used in businesses to:
- budget
- appraise different courses of action
- estimate and prepare quotations, etc.

Spreadsheets are particularly useful to observe changes to a model through calculations known as 'what if', e.g. 'what would be the effect on revenue if prices were increased by, say, 3%, 3.5%, 4% etc?' Spreadsheet packages also have the facility to produce graphics.

**staff appraisal** aims to assess staff within the grading of their job. An immediate superior is required to put a value on specified qualities of each employee. Such a scheme would have a direct bearing on promotions and inter-departmental transfers.

**stakeholders:** people and organisations that stand to gain or lose by the activities of a business. The stakeholders contribute directly in some way to the success or failure of the business. Stakeholders in a business include:
- owners (shareholders)
- management
- workforce
- customers
- suppliers
- lenders
- banks
- community

*Social accounting* recognises that businesses have a responsibility to the stakeholders.

**standard costing** sets levels of costs and revenues which ought to be achievable when reasonable levels of performance are used, together with efficient working practices, to manufacture a product. It deals with costs and revenues that ought to occur. It is a carefully prepared prediction of what should happen to individual costs and revenues if everything goes according to plan.

S

standard hour

Standard material cost, standard labour cost and standard overhead cost are compared with actual material cost, actual labour cost and actual overhead cost. Any differences between standard cost and actual cost is called a *variance.*

For worked examples of the calculation of total variances and sub-variances, see *direct labour variance, direct material variance*, *sales variance* and *overhead variance*.

**standard hour** measures the quantity of work that can be achieved at a standard level of performance in one hour. A standard hour may be 12 standard units: that is, a manager will expect a worker to produce 12 standard units of output in one hour's work.

**standard minute** measures the quantity of work that can be achieved at a standard level of performance in one minute. If a standard hour were 12 standard units, then a standard minute would be 0.2 standard units per minute.

**standard setting** is undertaken when a standard cost system is introduced into a manufacturing business. The cost accountant needs to prepare standards for materials, labour and overheads. Information with regard to quantities will be needed from the production departments. Specifications will be given on:

| Materials | Labour | Overheads |
|---|---|---|
| type | grade | production methods |
| quantities | numbers | sequence of operations |
| | | machines required |
| | | tools required |

The prices will be determined by:

| buyers | personnel | absorption rates |
|---|---|---|
| | trade union | |

**standing orders:** payments made automatically by a bank on behalf of customers. They are for set figures and may be paid on a weekly, monthly or annual basis by the bank. If the amount to be paid is likely to be variable then a direct debit arrangement with the creditor and bank is a more appropriate method of payment.

**statement of account** summarises the transactions that have taken place between a supplier and a customer, generally over an agreed period (usually one month). All *invoices* sent to the customer, all monies received plus *discounts allowed* and all returns are individually itemised on the statement.

The statement of account is a copy of the customer's account in the supplier's *sales ledger*. The customer checks the statement against the supplier's account in the *purchases ledger*. If there is a difference then remedial action can be taken by the party who has made the error. Any corrections are recorded on the next statement.

**statement of affairs** is identical to an opening *balance sheet*. It is prepared for a business that does not keep a full set of accounting records. Technically, the statement cannot be called a balance sheet (a sheet showing balances) since, by definition, the business does not have any ledger balances – it does not have *ledgers* because it has *incomplete records*.

**statement of cash flows IAS 7:** shows how cash has been generated by a *limited company* and how cash has been spent in the financial year. It is a historical document prepared together with the *income statement* and *balance sheet* in order to give a more complete picture of the financial position, performance and financial adaptability of the company.

The standard sets out the structure of the statement using the following headings:
- net cash (used in)/from operating activities
- cash flows from investing activities
- cash flows from financing activities

A total cash inflow or (outflow) must be shown for each heading.

A statement of cash flows shows information that is not available from scrutiny of the *income statement* and *balance sheet*. It concentrates on *liquidity*, which is important for business survival. The inability to generate cash resources is the single biggest reason for many businesses going into *liquidation*.

Remember that the profit generated by a business is not necessarily the same as the cash generated by that business.

## Worked example

### Balance sheets at 31 December 20*9 and 31 December 20*8 for Mose and Catt plc

|  | 20*9 |  | 20*8 |  |
|---|---|---|---|---|
|  | £000 | £000 | £000 | £000 |
| Non-current assets at cost | 4 368 |  | 3 478 |  |
| Less depreciation | 1 045 | 3 323 | 1 060 | 2 418 |
| Current assets |  |  |  |  |
| Inventory | 1 534 |  | 1 481 |  |
| Trade receivables | 596 |  | 639 |  |
| Cash and cash equivalents | 1 121 |  | 846 |  |
|  | 3 251 |  | 2 966 |  |
| Current liabilities |  |  |  |  |
| Trade payables | (745) |  | (720) |  |
| Taxation | (624) |  | (540) |  |
|  | (1 369) |  | (1 260) |  |
| Net current assets |  | 1 882 |  | 1 706 |
|  |  | 5 205 |  | 4 124 |
| Non-current liabilities |  | (800) |  | (1 000) |
|  |  | 4 405 |  | 3 124 |
| Equity |  |  |  |  |
| Issued share capital |  | 2 000 |  | 1 750 |
| Share premium account |  | 1 000 |  | 875 |
| Retained earnings |  | 1 405 |  | 499 |
|  |  | 4 405 |  | 3 124 |

### Statement of changes in equity

|  | £000 |
|---|---|
| Issued share capital |  |
| Balance at 1 January 20*9 | 1 750 |

233

| | | |
|---|---|---|
| Issue of shares | 250 | |
| Balance at 31 December 20*9 | 2 000 | |
| Share premium account | | |
| Balance at 1 January 20*9 | 875 | |
| Issue of shares | 125 | |
| Balance at 31 December 20*9 | 1 000 | |
| Retained earnings | | |
| Balance at 1 January 20*9 | 499 | |
| Profit for year | 1 306 | |
| | 1 805 | |
| Dividends paid | (400) | |
| Balance at 31 December 20*9 | 1 405 | |

*Note:* during the year non-current assets costing £600 000 that had been depreciated by £375 000 had been sold for £300 000. Dividends of £400 000 were paid during the year. Debenture interest of £70 000 was also paid during the year.

### Required:

A statement of cash flows for the year ended 31 December 20*9.

### Solution:

**Mose and Catt plc statement of cash flows for the year ended 31 December 20*9**

| | £000 | £000 |
|---|---|---|
| **Profit before interest and income taxes** | 2 000 | |
| Adjustment for depreciation | 360 | |
| Profit on disposal of non-current assets | (75) | |
| Increase in inventories | (53) | |
| Decrease in trade receivables | 43 | |
| Increase in trade payables | 25 | |
| Interest expense | (70) | |
| Income taxes paid | (540) | |
| **Net cash (used in)/from operating activities** | | 1 690 |
| **Cash flows from investing activities** | | |
| Purchase of non-current assets | (1 490) | |
| Proceeds from sale of non-current assets | 300 | |
| **Net cash (used in)/from investing activities** | | (1 190) |
| **Cash flows from financing activities** | | |
| Proceeds from issue of share capital | 375 | |
| Repayment of debenture stock | (200) | |
| Dividends paid | (400) | |
| **Net cash (used in)/from financing activities** | | (225) |
| **Net increase/(decrease) in cash and cash equivalents** | | 275 |
| Cash and cash equivalents at beginning of year | | 846 |
| Cash and cash equivalents at end of year | | 1 121 |
| **Reconciliation of net cash to movement in net debt** | £000 | |

| | |
|---|---|
| Increase in cash during period | 275 |
| Cash used to re-purchase debentures | 200 |
| Change in net debt | 475 |
| Net debt at 1 January 20*9 | (154) |
| Net debt at 31 December 20*9 | 321 |

Statements of cash flows – uses

The statement shows:

- how positive and negative cash flows have been generated during the year
- major financing activities for the year
- how the company met its obligation to service loans and to pay dividends
- why reported profits differ from related cash flows during the year

**statement of changes in equity** details changes that have taken place in share capital and reserves during the financial year.

### Worked example

The following balances are given for Simpkins plc

| | At 1 January 20*9 £000 | At 31 December 20*9 £000 |
|---|---|---|
| Equity | | |
| Ordinary share capital | 1 000 | 1 200 |
| Preferred shares | 2 000 | 2 000 |
| Share premium account | 500 | 600 |
| Revaluation reserve | 100 | 350 |
| Retained earnings | 1 750 | 2 700 |

*Required:*

Prepare a statement of changes in equity for the year ended 31 December 20*9.

*Solution:*

| Retained earnings | £000 |
|---|---|
| Balance at 1 January 20*9 | 1 750 |
| Profit for the year | 1 350 |
| | 3 100 |
| Dividends paid | (400) |
| Balance at 31 December 20*9 | 2 700 |
| Ordinary share capital | |
| Balance at 1 January 20*9 | 1 000 |
| Share issue | 200 |
| Balance at 31 December 20*9 | 1 200 |
| Share premium account | |
| Balance at 1 January 20*9 | 500 |

| | |
|---|---|
| Ordinary share issue | 100 |
| Balance at 31 December 20*9 | 600 |
| Revaluation reserve | |
| Balance at 1 January 20*9 | 100 |
| Revaluation of land and buildings | 250 |
| Balance at 31 December 20*9 | 350 |

**statement of comprehensive income:** IAS terminology for income statement.

**statement of financial position:** IAS terminology for balance sheet.

**statements:** methods used to convey information. They are often asked for in examination questions. Candidates should be aware that statements can be presented in many different guises:

- *income statements*
- written statements
- computations, e.g. calculation to show a change in profits.

Choose the most appropriate way that you think will convey the information required clearly to a reader, but use the heading outlined in the question.

**statutory accounts** are the financial statements required by law that must be filed at Companies House.

**stepped costs** remain fixed until a certain level of business activity is reached. Costs then rise to a higher fixed level and remain there until the next level of activity requiring a change is reached.

### Worked example

Hanif owns a small engineering business which manufactures electrical generators. The maximum output is limited to 1000 generators per week. Hanif employs quality controllers on weekly contracts. They can inspect 250 generators per week. Each quality controller earns £300 per week.

*Required:*

A graph showing the budgeted costs of employing quality controllers.

*Solution:*

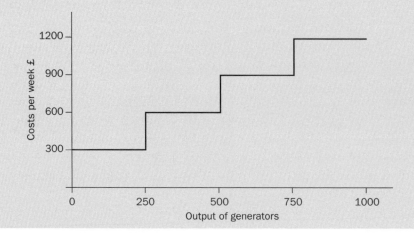

**stewardship:** the term applied to the responsibility that managers have for the management of resources within a business on behalf of the owners. An accountant must report periodically the state of affairs of the business to the owners.

**stock:** see *inventory*

**stock account:** see *inventory account*

**stock control:** see *inventory control*

**stock exchange:** the marketplace where stocks and shares are bought and sold. Much of the business of the stock exchanges is to deal in second hand shares and government securities.

**stock ledger:** see *inventory ledger*

**stock losses:** see *loss of inventory*

**stock market:** see *stock exchange*

**stock outs:** occasions when certain goods are required for production purposes but stores or suppliers are unable to supply at that time.

**stock record card** see *inventory record card*

**stock reorder level:** see *inventory reorder level*

**stocks and shares:** the generic term covering all *ordinary shares*, *preferred shares*, loan stocks and *debentures*.

**stockturn:** see *rate of inventory turnover*

**stock turnover:** see *rate of inventory turnover*

**stock valuation:** see *methods of inventory valuation*

**straight-line method of calculating depreciation** is calculated by spreading the net cost of purchasing a *non-current asset* over its expected economic life (any anticipated residual value should be deducted from the initial cost to arrive at the net cost). Intuitively, this is the method that most people would choose as a method of depreciating non-current assets. It is also called the equal instalment method.

---

**Worked example**

Litt Ltd purchases a machine at a cost of £120 000. It is expected to have a useful economic life of 4 years. It can then be sold for £20 000 for scrap.

*Required:*

Calculate the annual depreciation charge using the straight-line method.

*Solution:*

$$\text{straight-line method} = \frac{\text{cost} - \text{scrap value}}{\text{years of use}}$$

$$= \frac{£120\ 000 - £20\ 000}{4}$$

$$= £25\ 000 \text{ per annum}$$

S

237

**straight piece work:** see *piece work*

**strategic planning:** formulation of a long-term plan of action which, when in place, will help an organisation to achieve the long-term objectives identified by the senior management team. Also known as corporate planning.

**structural changes in partnerships:** changes to a *partnership agreement* which can take the form of:
- the *admission of a new partner*
- the retirement or death of an existing partner (see *partnership retirement*)
- an agreed change in the *profit sharing ratios* of the partners

In each of these cases, one partnership ceases to exist when the change takes place, and immediately after the change a new partnership starts up. This means that when the structural change takes place there must be a revaluation of the business assets and liabilities so that the 'old' partner(s) are credited with their dues.

**subjectivity:** the use of personal judgements or assumptions rather than facts. This must be avoided in the writing up of the *books of account* and when preparing financial statements. Accounting is concerned only with those facts that can be given a monetary value (see *money measurement concept*).

To avoid individual bias in the accounting world, many areas have been standardised by the issue of:
- *International Accounting Standards*
- *International Financial Reporting Standards*

**subsidiary books:** see *purchases day book*, *purchases returns day book*, *sales day book*, *sales returns day book*, *journal* and *cash book*

**subsidiary budgets:** the departmental and functional budgets which are collated by the budget officer and summarised into the master budget.

**subsidiary company** has more than 50 per cent of its *ordinary shares* held by a *holding company*. For example, Sayret Ltd has an issued share capital of 620 000 ordinary shares of 50 pence each. Likfor plc acquires 312 000 of Sayret's ordinary shares for £923 760. Since more than 50 per cent of Sayret Ltd's ordinary share capital is now owned by Likfor plc, Sayret Ltd is a subsidiary company and Likfor plc is the holding company. If Likfor plc purchased the remaining 308 000 ordinary shares in Sayret Ltd, Likfor plc would hold all the voting shares in Sayret Ltd. Sayret Ltd would become a wholly owned subsidiary company of Likfor plc.

The *Companies Act 1985* gives the following definition: 'a company is a "subsidiary" of another company, its "holding company", if that other company:
- holds a majority of the voting rights in it; or
- is a member of it and has the right to appoint or remove a majority of its *board of directors*; or
- is a member of it and controls alone, pursuant to an agreement with other shareholders or members, a majority of the voting rights in it; or
- if it is a subsidiary of a company which is itself a subsidiary of that other company'

**substance over form:** ensures that financial statements observe the commercial substance of transactions rather than just their legal form. In the vast majority of cases, the commercial substance of the transactions is likely to be the same as their legal form. The main applications are when:

- an asset is being acquired using a hire purchase contract
- a transaction is only part of a series of transactions and the single transaction can only be fully understood as part of the whole series
- a transaction includes options and it is very likely that the company will exercise one of the options

**sunk costs:** costs which have occurred some time ago and any future decisions taken by the business will not incur those costs again. In the process of decision making, they are *irrelevant costs*.

For example, a business may incur market research costs in order to determine whether or not to produce a new product. Whether the business goes ahead with production of the new product or not, the expenditure has been incurred. The market research costs are a sunk cost and should now be disregarded when costing out the budget on which the decision will be based.

**superannuation:** a pension.

**super profits:** the excess profits earned by a business after an imputed *return on capital employed* and an imputed wage have been deducted. They are sometimes used as a basis for valuing the *goodwill* of a business.

---

### Worked example

Lesley is a self-employed builder. Her profit for the year is £48 000. She has £85 000 capital invested in the business. She could earn £14 000 working for another building firm.

*Required:*

Calculate Lesley's annual super profits.

*Solution:*

|  | £ | £ |
|---|---:|---:|
| Annual profit | | 48 000 |
| Less imputed earnings in other employment | 14 000 | |
| Less imputed interest on capital employed | 4 250 | 18 250 |
| Annual super profits | | 29 750 |

The rate of interest chosen was 5% but this would clearly depend on the alternative investment opportunities available to Lesley at the time.

To value Lesley's goodwill, £29 750 might be multiplied by some agreed figure. If Lesley and the purchaser agreed, goodwill might be valued at 2 years' purchase of super profits, i.e. £29 750 × 2 = £59 500.

---

**suspense account** is used to balance a *trial balance*. It is a temporary account where the difference is held until errors are located and corrected.

In the real world, errors may not be found. If the difference in the suspense account is not material then the error can be written off, unless there are suspicious circumstances involved. £200 difference would be material for some small businesses, so every effort would be made to find and correct the error(s). £2000, on the other hand, could be an insignificant amount for a large multinational company and may therefore be written off.

## Worked example

Tracy Kennedy extracted a trial balance from her ledgers at the close of business on 31 August 20*9. The trial balance totals failed to agree. The debit side of the trial balance exceeded the credit side by £491. During September 20*9 Tracy found the following errors:

1  The advertising account had been undercast by £100.
2  A cheque received from Jibe & Co. for £345 had been posted to the debit of Jibe & Co.'s account in the sales ledger.
3  Discounts allowed, £54, had been posted to the credit of the discount received account as £45.
4  Goods returned by Gerat plc, £87, had been completely omitted from the books of account.

### Required:

i) journal entries necessary to correct the errors

ii) the suspense account used to correct the errors

### Solution:

i)  **Journal**

|  | Dr £ | Cr £ |
|---|---|---|
| Advertising | 100 | |
| Suspense | | 100 |
| Suspense | 690 | |
| Jibe & Co. | | 690 |
| Discount received | 45 | |
| Discount allowed | 54 | |
| Suspense | | 99 |
| Returns inward | 87 | |
| Gerat plc | | 87 |

ii)

**Suspense**

| | £ | | £ |
|---|---|---|---|
| Jibe & Co. | 690 | Trial balance difference | 491 |
| | | Advertising | 100 |
| | | Discount received | 45 |
| | | Discount allowed | 54 |
| | 690 | | 690 |

*Note:* The trial balance difference is entered in the suspense account on the same side as the difference in the trial balance.

**SWOT analysis** might be part of a business's long-term planning process. The analysis seeks to identify:

- strengths
- weaknesses
- opportunities
- threats

to the achievement of the strategic plan. Management should then implement actions which will maximise the strengths and opportunities identified, while efforts are made to minimise the weaknesses and threats.

A four-box format makes the analysis a useful visual aid for discussion purposes:

| strengths | weaknesses |
|---|---|
| opportunities | threats |

**systems analyst** specialises in analysing a process such as stock control to see if it can be done more efficiently and effectively using a computer program.

**Aiming for a grade A\*?**

Don't forget to log on to **www.philipallan.co.uk/a-zonline** for advice.

S

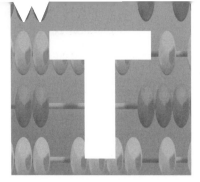

**table A:** model *Articles of Association* for a *limited company*, as set out in the *Companies Act 1985*.

**table B:** model *Memorandum of Association* for a *limited company*, as set out in the *Companies Act 1985*.

**tactical planning** plans how resources will be utilised in an organisation in order to achieve specific objectives in the most efficient and cost-effective way.

**take-home pay:** see *net salary*

**takeover** occurs when one business acquires a controlling interest in another. In the case of a *limited company*, the bidder has to purchase more than 50 per cent of the issued *ordinary share* capital.

**tangible non-current assets** are shown in company balance sheets under the heading of *property, plant and equipment IAS 16.* These are physical assets such as:

- land and buildings
- plant and machinery
- fixtures and fittings
- office equipment
- motor vehicles

**taxation:** see *income tax* and *corporation tax*

**tax avoidance:** trying to pay as little tax as possible by using legal tax loopholes.

**tax deductible** are legitimate expenses that can be deducted from income or profits before tax is calculated.

**tax evasion:** illegal avoidance of paying tax.

**tax liability:** individuals who are resident in the UK are liable to pay tax on income no matter where it is earned. Non-residents can be liable to pay UK tax on income if it is derived from the UK.

**tax point** is the time when goods and services are said to be supplied for the purposes of calculating *value-added tax*. It is generally the date of issue of the VAT invoice. If a VAT invoice has not been issued within fourteen days of despatch of the goods, the tax point is the date on which the goods were despatched.

**tenders** are submitted by suppliers to a client showing what is included in the terms of the contract, how much the contract will cost and how long the contract will take. The client will decide which tender to accept based on the criteria laid down in the initial invitation for tenders.

**time rate:** the amount of pay to be earned for one hour's work, e.g. £6.40 per hour.

**time-related pay schemes** calculate a worker's gross pay by multiplying the hours worked in a week (as recorded on the *clock card*) by the agreed time rate for each hour.

---

**Worked example**

An employee works for 38 hours. The hourly rate of pay is £8.00 per hour.

*Required:*

Calculate the employee's gross weekly wage.

*Solution:*

gross weekly wage = hours worked × time rate = 38 × £8.00 = £304

---

**time sheet** (or job card) records the number of hours an employee spends on each task during each working day. The total hours recorded on the time sheet should correspond with the hours shown on the *clock card*. Any difference between the two is idle time (unproductive time). Idle time might be due to:

- the time taken to get from the time recorder to the workstation
- machine breakdown
- delay in receiving raw materials or components
- maintenance of machinery

Idle time means lost production while overheads are still being incurred. Managers must be aware of the extent of idle time in order to be able to take steps to reduce it as far as is practicable.

**time value of money** means that money received or paid in the future has not the same value as money paid today. Ask yourself, would you rather win £100 000 on Saturday night's national lottery, or £100 000 on the lottery in 2047? Would you rather settle a £100 debt today or in 15 years' time? The concept is used in capital investment appraisal techniques.

**total cost** is composed of all *variable costs* + all *fixed costs*.

**total factory cost** is composed of:

    *FORMULA:*   factory direct costs + factory indirect costs + factory overheads

These are all brought together when a business prepares a *manufacturing account*.

**trade and other payables** is shown on the balance sheet as a *current liability* and comprises the total of *trade payables* plus 'other payables'. 'Other payables' are the amounts owed by the business for services provided to the business but not yet paid for, e.g. an electricity bill received but not yet paid.

**trade and other receivables** is shown on the balance sheet as a *current asset* and comprises the total of *trade receivables* plus other receivables. 'Other receivables' are amounts owed to the business for payments made in advance by the business, e.g. a prepayment for business rates or insurance.

**trade discount:** an amount allowed as a reduction in price when goods are supplied to other businesses. Trade discount is not allowed when the goods are sold on to the general public. Purchases are recorded in the *books of account* net of trade discount.

For example, if you or I purchase a bathroom suite it may cost £750. When Mr Tapp the local plumber purchases the same type of bathroom suite to install in a customer's bathroom, he might only pay £500. The difference is £250 trade discount. VAT is calculated on the net amount of Mr Tapp's purchase, i.e. on £500.

**trade investments** consist of small holdings of issued shares in other companies (less than 20 per cent). They are held to:

- earn *dividends*
- appreciate, ultimately giving a capital profit
- gain a foothold in another company as a possible start to gaining control in the future

**trade payables** are debts owed to suppliers of goods for resale. They are shown on a *balance sheet* under the heading of *current liabilities*. Amounts owing for services are shown as 'other payables'.

**trade payables budget:** a forecast of the amounts that will be owed each month to creditors. It will be linked to the raw materials budget (and any other relevant budgets, e.g. capital expenditure budget) and the cash budget.

The trade payables budget could look similar to the following:

**Trade payables budget**

|  | February £ | March £ | April £ |
|---|---|---|---|
| Balance b/fwd (*creditors end of January) | *4 563 | 4 863 | 5 455 |
| Credit purchases | 16 432 | 16 712 | 18 051 |
|  | 20 995 | 21 575 | 23 506 |
| Cash paid to creditors | 15 823 | 15 661 | 15 968 |
| Discounts received | 309 | 459 | 901 |
| Balance c/fwd | 4 863 | 5 455 | 6 637 |

**trade payables payment period** measures the average time a business takes to pay its credit suppliers. The calculation is:

$$FORMULA: \quad \text{trade payables payment period} = \frac{\text{trade receivable} \times 365}{\text{credit purchases}}$$

so if credit purchases for the year were £89 567 and trade payables at the year end were £7894, the trade payables' period payment period would be:

$$\frac{7894 \times 365}{89\ 567} = 33 \text{ days} \quad (32.17 \text{ but always round up})$$

Whether this is good or bad will depend on:

- trend – is this a longer or shorter time than in previous years?
- trade receivables – are trade receivables paying sooner or later than trade payables are being paid?

Generally, the longer this time period the better for the business; however, care must be taken not to alienate suppliers.

**trade receivables:** amounts owed to a business by credit customers who have not yet settled their account. They are shown in the *balance sheet* as *current assets*. Amounts owed for services paid in advance are shown as *prepayments*.

**trade receivables budget:** a forecast of amounts owed to a business at the end of each month by credit customers. It will be linked to the *production budget* and the *cash budget*.

The budget could look similar to the following example.

|  | June £ | July £ | August £ |
|---|---|---|---|
| Balance b/fwd (*trade receivables at end of May) | *16 731 | 20 137 | 25 333 |
| Credit sales | 43 789 | 58 051 | 49 003 |
|  | 60 520 | 78 188 | 74 336 |
| Cash received from credit customers | 39 875 | 51 980 | 47 435 |
| Discounts allowed | 508 | 875 | 761 |
| Balance c/fwd | 20 137 | 25 333 | 26 140 |

**trade receivables payment period:** a measure of the average time that credit customers take to pay outstanding balances.

The calculation is:

$$FORMULA: \quad \text{trade receivables payment period} = \frac{\text{trade receivables} \times 365}{\text{credit sales}}$$

So if credit sales for the year were £604 722

And the trade receivables at the year end were £51 493

$$\text{The trade receivables payment period would be} = \frac{51\ 493 \times 365}{604\ 722} = 32 \text{ days}$$

(31.35 but always round up)

This appears to be acceptable although many businesses would like outstanding trade receivable balances to be cleared in 30 days.

Whether the payment period is acceptable will depend on:
- trend – is this a longer or shorter time than in previous years?
- trade payables – are trade payables being paid more or less quickly than trade receivables are settling their debts?

Generally, the shorter this time period the better. However, this calculation gives an average collection time that could mask the fact that some balances may have been outstanding for some considerable time.

**trading account** is part of the income statement. It compares the value of sales at cost price with the actual value obtained from customers. The main activity of a trading business is to purchase goods and sell them on at a higher price. The difference between sales and the cost of the same sales is *gross profit*.

The trading account was traditionally the warehouse account and included in its format certain warehouse expenses. The majority of trading organisations now have limited warehousing space, so examination questions now rarely test the treatment of these expenses. However, the following worked example does include warehouse rent so that the reader can see where and how any warehouse expenses are dealt with.

## Worked example

Rosemary Butt owns a hardware shop. She supplies the following information at 30 April 20*9:

|  | £ |
|---|---|
| Purchases | 47 659 |
| Sales | 89 655 |
| Returns inward | 411 |
| Returns outward | 871 |
| Carriage inward | 544 |
| Carriage outward | 769 |
| Warehouse rent | 4 000 |
| Inventory 1 May 20*8 | 2 451 |
| Inventory 30 April 20*9 | 2 769 |

### Required:

An extract from the income statement showing clearly the cost of sales and gross profit for the year ended 30 April 20*9.

### Solution:

**Rosemary Butt income statement extract for the year ended 30 April 20*9**

|  | £ | £ | £ |
|---|---|---|---|
| Sales |  |  | 89 655 |
| Less returns inward |  |  | (411) |
|  |  |  | 89 244 |
| Less cost of sales |  |  |  |
| Inventory 1 May 20*8 |  | 2 451 |  |
| Purchases | 47 659 |  |  |
| Carriage inward | 544 |  |  |
|  | 48 203 |  |  |
| Less returns outward | (871) | 47 332 |  |
|  |  | 49 783 |  |
| Less inventory 30 April 20*9 |  | (2 769) |  |
|  |  | 47 014 |  |
| Plus warehouse rent |  | 4 000 | 51 014 |
| Gross profit |  |  | 38 230 |

Carriage outward is a revenue expense that is shown in the main body of the income statement.

**trading assets:** also known as *current assets*.

**transfer pricing** generally takes place in vertically integrated businesses. Goods are passed from one branch or department of a business to another to undergo further processing. The goods are passed on, not at cost, but at a transfer price that includes a mark-up.

Overall, the aggregate profit earned by the business is not affected. The profits are allocated to individual branches or departments. The policy of transfer pricing will have a direct influence on the individual branch or department's reported performance.

**transfers** between ledgers are recorded in the journal, for example:

Journal

|  |  | Dr | Cr |
|---|---|---|---|
|  |  | £ | £ |
| Dretly | PL 26 | 410 |  |
| Dretly | SL 57 |  | 410 |

Debit balance in Dretly's account in the sales ledger set off against his account in the purchases ledger.

**trend analysis** is used to analyse the results of a business over a number of years. This technique is usually used over a five- or ten-year time scale. The main advantage is that it is easy to get a general picture of the trends in items highlighted in the accounts. The main disadvantage is that the figures may not be adjusted to take into account price inflation.

**trend extrapolation** seeks to predict future results by reference to the trends observed in past results. For example, examine the following revenue figures:

|  | £000 |
|---|---|
| 20*5 | 128 |
| 20*6 | 140 |
| 20*7 | 156 |
| 20*8 | 132 |
| 20*9 | 180 |

Apart from 20*8, the trend is that turnover is increasing at around 10 per cent per annum. If we extrapolate the trend to 20*0, we would expect turnover to be around £200 000.

**trial balance:** a summary of all balances extracted from all the *ledgers* of a business. It is used as an arithmetic check on the accuracy of the entries in the whole *double-entry bookkeeping* system. If the trial balance totals agree it does not necessarily mean that the system is error free. There are errors which will not be revealed by extracting a trial balance. (See *errors not affecting the balancing of the trial balance*.)

**true and fair view:** the *directors* of a *limited company* must produce an *income statement* that shows a true and fair view of the company's results, and a *balance sheet* that shows a true and fair view of its financial position. One of the directors must sign the balance sheet, indicating that they have fulfilled this responsibility.

The *auditors* have to verify that the accounts show a true and fair view before the accounts are presented to the *shareholders* at a general meeting. When the accounts are adopted by the shareholders they can be filed with the *Registrar of Companies*.

**unavoidable costs** are incurred by businesses whether business activity takes place or not.

**uncalled capital:** see *called-up capital*

**under-absorption of overheads** occurs when fewer units of a product are produced than was predicted in the budget. This means that not all the expected overheads are recovered. For an example, see *over-absorption of overheads*.

**underwriting:** the acceptance of a business risk in return for a fee. Lloyd's of London has a worldwide reputation for accepting insurance risks of all kinds.

*Merchant banks* form a syndicate which guarantees that a share issue will be completely sold by agreeing to purchase all the shares which are not subscribed to by the general public.

**undistributed profits:** profits that have been retained within a business. They increase the *retained earnings* in the books of a *limited company*. The retained earnings are an aggregate of all previous years' undistributed profits. The retained earnings are a *revenue reserve*; they are available to issue cash *dividends*. The undistributed profits belong to the *ordinary shareholders*.

**unfavourable variances** occur when actual results are worse than the results predicted in a budget. If the *variance* has reduced the profit that was predicted in the budget, the variance is said to be an *adverse variance*. If, however, the variance increases the profit that was predicted in the budget, then the variance is favourable (see *favourable variances*).

**uniform business rate:** a form of local taxation levied on business properties.

**unit cost:** the average of all the costs involved in the production of one unit of a good or service. Unit cost is calculated by:

$$FORMULA: \quad \text{unit cost} = \frac{\text{total production costs}}{\text{number of units produced}}$$

It is used in *process costing* where it would be impractical to try to find the cost of one small unit of production. Imagine trying to allocate, *apportion* and then absorb all the costs involved in the production of a child's lollipop retailing at 5 pence, or a cylinder head gasket for a Ford Mondeo.

Unit costs could be enrolled students in a college, a keg of beer in a brewery, bed occupation in a hospital or a kilowatt hour (kWh) in electricity generation.

**unpresented cheques:** cheques that have not yet been cleared and debited to the business account at a bank. They occur because of the time delay between the writing of a cheque (when it is also entered in the **bank column** of the business **cash book**) and the cheque being entered on the bank statement by the bank. An example of an unpresented cheque is one that has been paid to a supplier, but who for some reason has not yet paid the cheque into his/her bank account; or it has been paid into the supplier's bank account and the cheque is still in the bank cheque clearing system. (See **bank reconciliation statement**.)

**unrealised profit:** see *realised profits* and *provision for unrealised profits*

**unsecured creditor:** a person or business who is owed money but has no security from the debtor for the debt.

**unsecured loan:** a loan that has been made without security. (See **secured loans**.)

**unsocial hours payment:** see *shift work*

**users of financial reports** are generally, but not always, interested in the survival of a business and its ability to generate profits and cash. The usefulness of the financial reports depends on the ability to compare the results with other businesses and earlier years. This means that the users are reliant on the reports being prepared with a consistent approach to all the *accounting concepts and conventions.*

The users of financial reports include:

- management
- auditors
- Her Majesty's Revenue and Customs
- employees
- trade unions
- credit customers
- credit suppliers
- bank managers and other providers of finance
- researchers
- press
- pressure groups
- students

Competitors will use the accounts as a means of gaining information which might benefit them in their fight for a greater market share. (See *ratio analysis*.)

C

**valuation of inventory:** see *methods of inventory valuation*

**value added:** *CIMA* defines value added as 'sales value less the cost of purchased materials and services. This represents the worth of an alteration in form, location or availability of a product or service'. Also known as *added value*.

**value-added statement** shows the value added to the goods and services acquired by an organisation in order to generate its sales revenue. The statement also shows how the value added has been distributed among the employees, the *shareholders* and other providers of finance, how much has been paid to the government in taxes and how much has been retained in the business.

In recent years, some limited companies have incorporated a value-added statement into their annual *published accounts*. Here is an example of a value-added statement:

Trasker plc value-added statements for the years to 28 February

|  | | 20*9 | | 20*8 |
| --- | --- | --- | --- | --- |
|  | | £000 | | £000 |
| Revenue | | 6 187 | | 4 754 |
| Purchases of materials and services | | 3 078 | | 2 358 |
| Value added | | 3 109 | | 2 396 |
| Applied as follows: | | | | |
| To pay employees | | 1 873 | | 1 546 |
| To pay suppliers of capital | | | | |
| interest on loans | 28 | | 23 | |
| dividends to shareholders | 90 | 118 | 80 | 103 |
| To pay government – corporation tax | | 345 | | 216 |
| To provide for maintenance of assets | | | | |
| and expansion of business | | | | |
| depreciation | 48 | | 42 | |
| retained earnings | 725 | 773 | 489 | 531 |
| Value added | | 3 109 | | 2 396 |

**value-added tax (VAT):** a tax levied on the final consumer of goods and services. With the exception of certain services that are exempt, all business transactions are subject to VAT. Each time value is added in a stage of production, the tax is added and charged to the business undertaking the next stage of production. Each business can claim back from Her Majesty's Revenue and Customs the tax paid, with the exception of the final consumer, who bears the tax based on the final invoice price.

**variable costs:** costs which change in direct relation to levels of business activity.

**variable overhead absorption rate:** the means by which the variable factory overheads are absorbed into the product cost(s). The variable factory overheads might be absorbed in a labour-intensive business by use of budgeted *direct labour* hours:

FORMULA:    $\dfrac{\text{budgeted variable overheads}}{\text{budgeted direct labour hours}}$

In the case of a capital-intensive industry, the calculation could be:

FORMULA:    $\dfrac{\text{budgeted variable overheads}}{\text{budgeted machine hours}}$

**variance analysis** investigates differences that occur when actual costs are different from *standard costs*. It enables managers to identify problem areas which need investigating in order that remedial action can be taken. (See *standard costing*.)

**variances** arise when there is a difference between actual and budgeted figures. Variances are reported to heads of department and highlight departures from budgets. They are often used as a measure of managerial effectiveness. (See *direct material variance*, *direct labour variance*, *sales variance*, *sales margin variance*, *overhead variance*.)

**VAT:** see *value-added tax*

**VAT account in general ledger** shows the *VAT* charged by suppliers (input tax) on the debit side of the account and VAT charged to customers (output tax) on the credit side of the account. At the end of the quarter, when the VAT return is sent to Her Majesty's Revenue and Customs (HMRC), the account will show a debit balance if inputs have been greater than outputs, or a credit balance if the outputs are greater than inputs. The debit balance will be wiped out when the cheque is received from HMRC. The credit balance will disappear when the business settles the liability with HMRC.

If there is a balance on the VAT account in the *general ledger* at the end of the *accounting period*, it will be shown on the business *balance sheet* as either a *current asset* (debit balance) or a *current liability* (credit balance).

**VAT invoice:** an *invoice* that details the *VAT* included in a transaction. It is essential if a registered business wishes to claim relief from the VAT paid to suppliers. A copy of the invoice must be retained for possible inspection by Her Majesty's Revenue and Customs. A VAT invoice shows:
- invoice number
- tax point
- supplier's name, address and VAT registration number
- customer's name and address
- description of the goods supplied in sufficient detail for identification purposes
- rate of VAT applicable to each type of good referred to on the invoice
- total amount of the invoice payable excluding VAT
- amount of cash discount to be allowed, if any
- total amount of VAT chargeable

**VAT payment:** the payment of tax collected by a business to Her Majesty's Revenue and Customs. It should be made one month after the relevant quarterly period.

**VAT returns:** a record of the VAT involved in the transactions undertaken by a business. They are submitted to Her Majesty's Revenue and Customs for a quarterly period.

**vertical financial analysis** considers only one year's set of financial statements. All the components of the financial statements are expressed as a percentage of a selected figure. For example, all the items in the *income statement* can be expressed as a percentage of revenue. All *balance sheet* items might be expressed as a percentage of, say, capital employed.

## Worked example

The following is the income statement for the year ended 30 June 20*9 for Tony Jones Ltd:

|  |  | £000 |
|---|---|---|
| Revenue |  | 1 678 |
| Less cost of sales |  | 748 |
| Gross profit |  | 930 |
| Less expenses |  |  |
| distribution costs | (189) |  |
| administration costs | (320) |  |
|  |  | (509) |
| Profit for the year on ordinary activities |  | 421 |

**Required:**

A vertical financial analysis of the income statement for the year ended 30 June 20*9 for Tony Jones Ltd, using revenue as the basis of calculation.

**Solution:**

Tony Jones Ltd vertical financial analysis of the income statement for the year ended 30 June 20*9:

|  |  | £000 | % |
|---|---|---|---|
| Revenue |  | 1678 | 100.0 |
| Less cost of sales |  | 748 | 44.6 |
| Gross profit |  | 930 | 55.4 |
| Less expenses |  |  |  |
| distribution costs | (189) |  | (11.2) |
| administration costs | (320) |  | (19.1) |
|  |  | (509) | (30.3) |
| Profit for the year on ordinary activities |  | 421 | 25.1 |

This type of analysis is also known as common size statements. The advantages of vertical analysis include:

- businesses of different size can be compared
- it identifies changes in expenses relative to revenue (or significant changes in structure of balance sheet)
- since figures are based on only one year's figures, inflationary distortions are eliminated

Disadvantages of vertical analysis:

- when making *inter-firm comparisons*, care must be taken to compare like with like
- size of business is ignored, but this is important in analysing performance

**vertical ledger accounts:** many businesses record entries into the *ledger* using a vertical layout. The presentation is similar to that seen on a bank statement. The accounts generated by computer are often in this format.

This is a copy of Tracy Minall's account in Hilary's sales ledger using a traditional layout and a vertical layout:

| Tracy Minall | | | |
|---|---|---|---|
| 7 Jan Cash | 150 | 3 Jan Purchases | 174 |
| 28 Jan Rets | 23 | 16 Jan Purchases | 98 |
| 31 Jan Bal c/d | 99 | | |
| | 272 | | 272 |
| | | 1 Feb Bal b/d | 99 |

| Tracy Minall | | | |
|---|---|---|---|
| | Dr | Cr | Bal |
| 3 Jan Purchases | | 174 | 174 |
| 7 Jan Cash | 150 | | 24 |
| 16 Jan Purchases | | 98 | 122 |
| 28 Jan Returns | 23 | | 99 |

**vertical presentation of financial statements** is widely used today. It is probably easier for the lay person to understand a set of *financial statements* presented in this way rather than in the traditional horizontal format used in the past. The vast majority of *limited companies* use a vertical presentation when publishing their *annual reports and accounts*.

A vertical presentation of an *income statement* could look like this:

**John Lumley income statement for the year ended 31 October 20\*9**

| | £ | £ | £ |
|---|---|---|---|
| Sales | | | 173 502 |
| Less returns inward | | | (1 497) |
| | | | 172 005 |
| Less cost of sales | | | |
| Inventory 1 November 20*8 | | 8 467 | |
| Purchases | 93 551 | | |
| Less returns outward | (4 792) | 88 759 | |
| | | 97 226 | |
| Less inventory 31 October 20*9 | | (10 005) | (87 221) |
| Gross profit | | | 84 784 |
| Add  discount received | | 512 | |
| commission received | | 750 | 1 262 |
| | | | 86 046 |
| Less expenses | | | |
| Discount allowed | | (2 918) | |
| Rent and rates | | (7 500) | |
| Wages | | (46 853) | |
| Gas and electricity | | (4 710) | |
| Printing, stationery and advertising | | (5 636) | |
| Insurances | | (4 981) | |
| Depreciation  office equipment | (2 300) | | |
| vehicles | (7 500) | (9 800) | (82 398) |
| Profit for the year | | | 3 648 |

**wage methods of calculation:** see under various methods. Examples include the *Halsey premium bonus scheme*, *piece work*, etc.

**warehouse costs:** costs incurred in the holding of goods. They are a *cost of sales* expense shown in the *income statement*. Warehouse expenses are found in the *general ledger*. At the end of the *accounting period* these *nominal accounts* are closed by transferring the balance to the business *income statement*.

---

**Worked example**

Tom Damansara opened a mini-market on 1 August 20*8. During the year ended 31 July 20*9, the following expenses had been incurred in running his warehouse:

Warehouse rent paid on 3 August 20*8: £4500; warehouse rent paid on 17 February 20*9: £4500.

Warehouse insurance paid on 1 August 20*8 for period 1 August 20*8 until 31 December 20*8: £670; warehouse insurance paid on 2 January 20*9 for the year ended 31 December 20*9: £1200.

*Required:*

The warehouse rent account and the warehouse insurance account showing clearly the transfer to the income statement for the year ended 31 July 20*9.

*Solution:*

| Warehouse rent | | | | | Warehouse insurance | | | | |
|---|---|---|---|---|---|---|---|---|---|
| 20*8 | | £ | | £ | 20*8 | | £ | 20*8 | £ |
| 3 Aug | Cash | 4 500 | | | 1 Aug | Cash | 670 | | |
| 20*9 | | | 20*9 | | 20*9 | | | 20*9 | |
| 17 Feb | Cash | 4 500 | 31 Jul Inc st | 9 000 | 2 Jan | Cash | 1 200 | 31 Jul Inc st | 1 370 |
| | | | | | | | | 31 Jul Bal. c/d | 500 |
| | | 9 000 | | 9 000 | | | 1 870 | | 1 870 |
| | | | | | 1 Aug | Bal. b/d | 500 | | |

In the income statement there will be two debit entries immediately after the cost of sales figure for: warehouse rent – £9000; warehouse insurance – £1370.

Under the heading 'current assets' in Tom Damansara's balance sheet will appear: Other receivables (Insurance prepaid): £500

---

**wastage** makes up the major source of material losses in a manufacturing business. Wastage has no value – it cannot be sold. Scrap does have a value and produces some revenue for the business.

**weighted average cost method of inventory valuation (AVCO):** see *methods of inventory valuation*

**wholly owned subsidiary company:** see *subsidiary company*

**winding up:** the term used when a business goes out of existence (see *bankruptcy*). The winding-up procedure, when a company goes into *liquidation*, is a complex subject. The major concern is that during the winding-up process everyone involved should be treated in the fairest way possible.

**work certified:** an interim valuation of work done on a long-term *contract*. The interim valuation is undertaken by a professional valuer. The valuation then forms the basis upon which progress payments are made by the customer. It would be very unfair to expect the contractor to wait until the contract was completed before any payment was made; conversely it would be equally unfair to expect the customer to pay the whole amount at the start of the contract. Part payments based on work certified is a compromise which should suit both parties.

**working capital:** see *net current assets*

**working capital cycle:** the time taken between making payment for goods taken into the business and the receipts of cash from the customers for the sale of the goods. The shorter the time between the business laying out the cash for the purchase of goods and the collection of the cash for the sale of the goods, the better for the business.

The cycle is calculated by adding the *rate of inventory turnover* (in days) to the *trade receivables payment* (collection) *period* (in days), and deducting the *trade payables payment period* (in days).

**Worked example**

The following is an extract from the income statement of Sandra Neal for the year ended 31 May 20*9:

|  | £ | £ |
|---|---|---|
| Sales |  | 970 365 |
| Less cost of sales |  |  |
| Inventory 1 June 20*8 | 40 132 |  |
| Purchases | 437 561 |  |
|  | 477 693 |  |
| Inventory 31 May 20*9 | 42 462 | 435 231 |
| Gross profit |  | 535 134 |
| Additional information: |  |  |
| All purchases and sales are on credit. |  |  |
| Trade receivables at 31 May 20*9 | 76 438 |  |
| Trade payables at 31 May 20*9 | 36 281 |  |

*Required:*

Calculate Sandra Neal's working capital cycle.

*Solution:*

| | | |
|---|---|---|
| inventory turnover in days | 35 | $\dfrac{\text{cost of sales}}{\text{average stock}} = 10.54$ times per year |
| trade receivables' collection period in days | 29 | $\dfrac{\text{debtors} \times 365}{\text{credit sales}}$ |
| | 64 | |
| trade payables' payment period in days | 31 | $\dfrac{\text{creditors} \times 365}{\text{credit purchases}}$ |
| working capital cycle in days | 33 | |

The shorter the cycle, the lower the value of working capital to be financed by other sources. The cycle can be reduced by:

- increasing the rate of inventory turnover by reducing the levels of goods held
- speeding up the rate at which **trade receivables** pay
- taking longer to pay **trade payables**

**working capital ratio:** see *current ratio*

**work in progress:** *inventory* of partly finished goods. In any manufacturing business there will be three distinct types of inventory:

- inventory of raw materials and components waiting to go through the production process
- inventory of finished goods waiting to be despatched to the customer
- inventory of goods that are only part way through the production process – work in progress

In the *financial statements* of a manufacturing business, work in progress is treated like any other type of inventory. *Opening inventory* is added and *closing inventory* is deducted.

Total production cost in a *manufacturing account* is made up of *prime cost* plus factory overheads. Opening work in progress is added to this figure, and closing work in progress is deducted. The result is the amount to be transferred to the *income statement*.

### Worked example

James John owns a manufacturing business. The following information relates to his financial year end 30 April 20*9:

| | £ |
|---|---|
| Prime cost | 506 781 |
| Factory overhead costs | 307 374 |
| Work in progress 1 May 20*8 | 15 889 |
| Work in progress 30 April 20*9 | 18 550 |

*Required:*

A summarised manufacturing account for the year ended 30 April 20*9 for James John.

*Solution:*

James John summarised manufacturing account for the year ended 30 April 20*9

|  | £ |
|---|---|
| Prime cost | 506 781 |
| Factory overheads | 307 374 |
|  | 814 155 |
| Add work in progress 1 May 20*8 | 15 889 |
|  | 830 044 |
| Less work in progress 30 April 20*9 | (18 550) |
| Cost of goods manufactured transferred to income statement | 811 494 |

**work not yet certified:** similar to *work in progress* in a manufacturing business. As a *contract* progresses there will be work completed that a valuer has not yet been asked to certify. The contractor will make a valuation of this work at the financial year end and carry it forward in the *contract account* to start the next financial period's contract account.

**Do you need revision help and advice?**

Go to pages 259–72 for a range of revision appendices that include plenty of exam advice and tips.

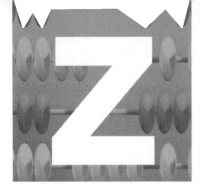

**zero-based budget** questions each activity as if it were new and before any resources are allocated towards it. Each plan of action has to be justified in terms of total costs involved and total benefits to accrue, with no reference to past activities.

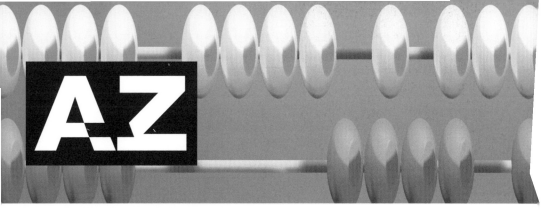

# Accounting revision lists

## Using A–Z Online

In addition to the revision lists given below, you can use the A–Z Online website to access revision lists specific to your exam board and the particular exam you are taking. Log on to **www.philipallan.co.uk/a-zonline** and create an account using the unique code provided on the inside front cover of this book. Once you have logged on, you can print out lists of terms together with their definitions, which will help you to focus your revision.

## Main topics required for success in accounting examinations

The topics outlined below are the elements commonly examined in most accounting examinations. To use the lists, select a topic that you wish to revise and look up the terms listed. This may lead you to cross-references which will build up to give a comprehensive answer.

When answering any written section in an examination, always make a plan as this will ensure that you do not repeat yourself and thus waste time. It will also allow you to organise your points into a logical, sensible format. Remember **IDA**: always **I**dentify the point you wish to make, **D**iscuss it in general terms and then **A**pply the point to the question being asked.

1  Concepts
2  Marginal costing
3  Basic bookkeeping
4  Partnerships
5  Limited companies
6  Incomplete records
7  Statement of cash flows
8  Standard costing
9  Ratio analysis
10  Capital investment appraisal
11  Inventory valuation
12  Social accounting
13  Costing
14  Budgets

# 1 Concepts

Accruals concept

Business entity concept

Consistency

Dual aspect concept

Going-concern concept

Materiality

Money measurement concept

Prudence

Realisation concept

# 2 Marginal costing

Break-even analysis

Break-even charts

Break-even point

Contribution

Contribution pricing

Contribution/sales ratio

Fixed costs

Limiting factor

Make or buy decisions

Penetration pricing

Special-order pricing

Variable cost

# 3 Basic bookkeeping

Bad debts

Balance sheet

Bank reconciliation statement

Books of prime entry

Control accounts

Correction of errors

Extended trial balance

Income statement

Manufacturing accounts

Provision

Provision for doubtful debts

Provision for depreciation

Reserves

Suspense accounts

Trial balance

# 4 Partnerships

Garner v Murray (1904)

Goodwill

Partnership Act 1890

Partnership agreement

Partnership capital accounts

Partnership current accounts

Partnership dissolution

Partnership income statement

Partnership salaries

Realisation account

Retiring partner

Structural changes

# 5 Limited companies

Auditors' report

Bonus issue

Capital reserves

Called-up capital

Calls in advance

Calls in arrears

Current assets

Debentures

Directors

Directors' report

Equity

Forfeiture of shares

Issue of debentures

Issue of ordinary shares

Non-current assets

Paid-up share capital

Preferred shares

Provisions

Published accounts

Redemption of shares

Reserves

Revenue reserves

Rights issue

# 6 Incomplete records

Adjustment accounts

Club accounts

Income and expenditure account

Life membership funds

Receipts and payments account

Single entry bookkeeping

Statement of affairs

# 7 Statement of cash flows

Bonus issue

Cash and cash equivalents

IAS 7

Revaluation reserve

# 8 Standard costing

Direct labour variances

Direct material variances

Flexible budgets

Management by exception

Overhead variances

Sales variances

Standard hour

Standard minute

Standard setting

Variance analysis

Variances

# 9 Ratio analysis

Credit control

Gearing

Liquidity ratios

Profitability ratios

Users of financial statements

Working capital cycle

## Formulae for the calculation of accounting ratios

Acid test ratio
$$\frac{\text{current assets} - \text{stock}}{\text{current liabilities}}$$

Current ratio
$$\frac{\text{current assets}}{\text{current liabilities}}$$

Dividend cover
$$\frac{\text{profit after tax and interest}}{\text{ordinary dividend paid}}$$

Dividend yield
$$\frac{\text{dividend per share}}{\text{market price per share}} \times 100$$

Earnings per share (EPS)
$$\frac{\text{earnings in pence}}{\text{number of issued ordinary shares}}$$

Gearing
$$\frac{\text{fixed cost capital}}{\text{total capital}} \times 100$$

Interest cover
$$\frac{\text{profits before interest and tax}}{\text{interest payable}}$$

Margin
$$\frac{\text{gross profit}}{\text{sales}} \times 100$$

Mark-up
$$\frac{\text{gross profit}}{\text{cost of sales}} \times 100$$

Net margin
$$\frac{\text{net profit}}{\text{sales}} \times 100$$

Price/earnings ratio (P/E)
$$\frac{\text{current market price of a share}}{\text{earnings per share}}$$

Rate of inventory turnover
$$\frac{\text{cost of sales}}{\text{average inventory held}}$$

Return on capital employed (ROCE)
$$\frac{\text{profit before interest and tax}}{\text{capital employed}} \times 100$$

Return on owner's equity
$$\frac{\text{profit before interest and tax less preference dividends}}{\text{issued ordinary share capital plus all reserves}} \times 100$$

Trade payables' payment period
$$\frac{\text{trade payables}}{\text{credit purchases}} \times 365$$

Trade receivables' collection period
$$\frac{\text{trade receivables}}{\text{credit sales}} \times 365$$

# 10 Capital investment appraisal

Accounting rate of return

Capital budget

Capital expenditure

Cash flows

Cost of capital

Discounted cash flow

Internal rate of return

Net present value

Opportunity cost

Payback

Time value of money

# 11 Inventory valuation

AVCO

Consistency

FIFO

Net realisable value

Periodic inventory

Perpetual inventory

Prudence

# 12 Social accounting

Social accounting

# 13 Costing

ABC costing

Absorption

Allocation of overheads

Apportionment of overheads

Direct labour costs

Direct material costs

Factory overhead expenses

Indirect expenses

Over-absorption of overheads

Overheads

Prime cost

Under-absorption of overheads

# 14 Budgets

Budgetary control

Cash budget

Cost centre

Flexible budget

Master budget

Management by exception

Production budget

Trade payables budget

Trade receivables budget

Variance analysis

Variances

Zero-based budget

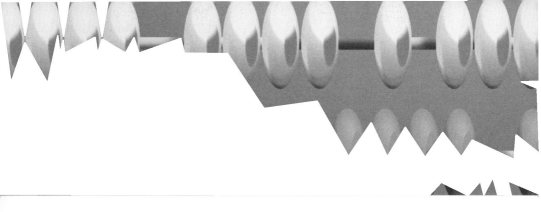

# A* grade revision lists

For candidates wishing for high grades in their AS and A2 examinations, the following terms are all-important. Make sure you revise them carefully, giving yourself time to discuss each of them with a tutor or fellow student, if anything is unclear.

## AS topics

Bank reconciliation statements

Budgeting and budgets

Concepts and conventions of accounting

Control accounts

Manufacturing accounts *(not AQA)*

Provisions

Ratios and ratio analysis

Reserves

Subsidiary books

Suspense accounts

Value-added tax *(not AQA)*

## A2 topics

ABC costing

Absorption costing

Capital investment appraisal

Financial statements of limited companies

Incomplete records

International Accounting Standards

Manufacturing accounts *(AQA)*

Marginal costing

Methods of inventory valuation

Partnership accounts

Standard costing

Statement of cash flows IAS 7

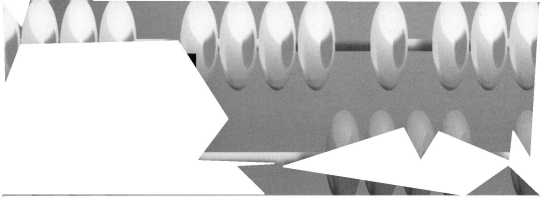

# Hints for exam success

The most obvious advice here is to be well prepared for the day of the examination — undertaking a thorough programme of revision is critical for success. Revision must be started in plenty of time to allow you to identify any aspects of your specification that you do not fully understand. If you have done this early enough, you will have the time to work through the sections where you are weak and to ask for further help and guidance from your tutor if necessary.

Revision is helped by a revision plan or timetable. This can be as simple as creating a checklist of topics that you can tick off when you have read through your notes, and perhaps tick again when you have worked through some questions, for example:

| Read notes | Re-write notes in brief | Test with past questions |
| --- | --- | --- |
| Concepts | | |
| Partnerships | | |
| Club accounts | | |
| Inventory valuation | | |
| Social accounting | | |

By doing this, you can see that you are making progress. Many students experience the feeling that they are 'not getting anywhere' or they 'will never understand all this' during their revision. Using a checklist and ticking off the topics can help to reassure yourself that your revision programme is well under way.

Try to work out which time of day suits you best to do your revision. If you are still at school or college, try to make the best possible use of your free time. Most importantly, try to develop a routine for your studies; it then becomes much easier to discipline yourself to get down to work.

Students revise effectively in many different ways. If you begin to lose your concentration during one of your revision sessions, try switching to another method – a change is as good as a rest. You must take regular breaks too. Different revision methods include:

- reading aloud
- asking a friend to question you
- practising test questions
- summarising your explanations/answers
- answering questions within a limited time

- explaining a topic to someone who doesn't study accounting — if you don't feel you can do this, then perhaps you need to study that topic a little more

Some people revise to music and your tutors will probably tell you to use whichever method suits you best, but remember that you will have to complete your examination under examination conditions, which do not include music, so make sure that you are able to concentrate under those conditions too.

## Examiners' terms

Another way to improve your chances of success is by making yourself familiar with the terms that examiners might use in your examination papers and therefore how they will expect you to respond. What follows is not an exhaustive list of terms, but it includes the ones most commonly used, together with an explanation of the type of approach you will be expected to take.

**Advise:** this instruction usually requires you to consider the information given in a question or calculated by yourself and then to use it to arrive at a business decision. This can be based on financial and/or non-financial considerations.

**Analyse:** this word is used when a written answer is required. You will be expected to discuss as many aspects of the topic in question as possible, bearing in mind that you must retain focus on the question. You should provide an argument which outlines the potential advantages and disadvantages of a given situation or decision.

**Assess:** this instruction is asking you to weigh up information both for and against a stated action or situation. It requires you to give an evaluation (a justified conclusion).

**Calculate:** find the answer mathematically without necessarily preparing a detailed statement. For example, you might be asked to calculate the profits of a business. This can be done by making a comparison between the opening and closing capitals and then making an adjustment to take into account any capital introduced into the business during the year and any drawings made by the proprietor(s) during the year. A detailed income statement is not required, but do remember to show your workings.

**Comment:** weigh the results and evidence given or calculated in the first part(s) of a question in order to reach your conclusion. When such an instruction is given, the examiner expects you to demonstrate a deeper understanding of the topic in question. Your comments must be consistent with your results.

**Comment critically:** weigh up the pros and cons of the information given or deduced from a question in order to reach your conclusion. Remember that a critique considers the positive aspects of a problem as well as the negative aspects.

**Define:** give an explanation of the word or term given in the question. Remember that an example is not an explanation, although it may earn you further development marks after you have provided your definition.

**Describe:** provide a detailed outline of the steps involved in a financial transaction or the characteristics of a financial document.

**Discuss:** this means that both sides of a problem have to be outlined and considered before you reach a conclusion. It is important that you reach a conclusion based on your discussion and one which is consistent with the information that you present and with the instruction given in the question.

**Draft:** a preparatory statement or document which may need to be altered later in the light of further information becoming available.

**Evaluate:** this requires you to consider all the information given in the question and to reach a decision based on the facts outlined. It requires a personal judgement so do not be afraid to express your own opinion.

**Examine:** this requires you to discuss the facts relevant to the situation given in the question.

**Explain:** this term is designed to give you the opportunity to show that you have developed a clear understanding of the facts outlined in the question. You can do this by giving a clear and precise definition and then enlarging on points made. A relevant example may help you to gain further marks. Once again, it must be emphasised that an example is not an explanation in itself but it can help to add some clarity to your answer.

**Explain the difference between:** this requires you to compare alternatives; it does not require you to reach a conclusion or to make a recommendation. However, you must make comparisons rather than just make two lists. For example, if a question asks you to explain the difference between preferred shares and ordinary shares, you could say that preferred shares pay a stipulated dividend whereas ordinary share dividends may vary from year to year. Notice the use of the word 'whereas' to show that you are considering the differences.

**Extract:** show the appropriate part of a financial statement. For example, you might be asked to calculate an inventory figure and then show how it would appear in the balance sheet. Your answer could look something like this:

**Balance sheet extract at 31 October 20*9**

Current assets

Inventory £32 900

Note the use of the word 'extract' in the heading.

**Formula:** same as model.

**Identify:** name examples asked for in the question. Generally, your answer would take the form of a list.

**Illustrate:** use an example taken from the information given in the question or derived from your own answer and explain its relevance within the question.

**List:** itemise the components briefly without any attempt to explain.

**Model:** generally, another name for the formula that you have used to calculate your answer. When calculating ratios you should always show the model that your calculations are based on, for example:

$$\text{mark-up} = \frac{\text{gross profit}}{\text{cost of sales}} \times 100$$

**Outline:** give a brief explanation. Candidates are often unsure how much to write when given this instruction; the length of response should always be governed by the mark allocation.

**Prepare:** present the required answer from the information given in the question.

**Quality of written communication:** in recent years marks have been awarded in A-level examinations for communication skills such as layouts, working, spelling, punctuation and grammar. Candidates will also need to demonstrate the ability to present ideas and information in an appropriate manner and demonstrate that they can argue with clarity and in a logical structure.

**Statement:** a presentation of the relevant facts in a format suitable for the reader. The format could be a memorandum, or it could take the form of a report, but do not fall into the trap of thinking that statements are necessarily written presentations – they can take the form of an income statement or a series of adjustments to a draft profit figure. Remember that the term 'statement of affairs' has a presentation very similar to the conventional balance sheet.

**Recommend:** after considering all the facts outlined in the question and/or your answer, you must advise on a course of action: for example, 'based on the information outlined above I would advise Rebecca to invest in Gavington plc'.

**Reservations:** outline any doubts that you may have on the course of action determined after due consideration of the facts outlined in the question.

**State your assumptions:** this phrase allows you to tell the examiner why you have pursued a certain line of thought in your answer. Your actions must be based on a logical line of thought to gain marks.

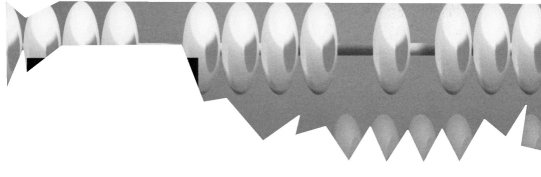

# International standards terminology

The following table is included to help you to become familiar with the recent changes in terminology.

| Old UK term | International term |
| --- | --- |
| Accruals | Other payables |
| Bank and cash | Cash and cash equivalents |
| Cost of goods sold | Cost of sales |
| Creditors | Trade payables |
| Creditors' amounts falling due within 12 months | Current liabilities |
| Creditors' amounts falling due after more than one year | Non-current liabilities |
| Debtors | Trade receivables |
| Final accounts | Financial statements |
| Fixed assets | Non-current assets |
| Goodwill etc. | Intangible assets |
| Interest payable | Finance costs |
| Interest receivable | Investment revenues |
| Investments | Investment property |
| Land and buildings | Property |
| Loans repayable within 12 months | Bank overdraft and loans |
| Loans repayable after 12 months | Bank (and other) loans |
| Long-term liabilities | Non-current liabilities |
| Net profit ✓ | Profit for the year ✓ |
| Prepayments | Other receivables |
| Sales | Revenue |
| Share capital and reserves | Equity |
| Stock | Inventory |
| Sundry expenses | Other operating expenses |
| Sundry income | Other operating income |
| Trading and profit and loss account | Income statement |

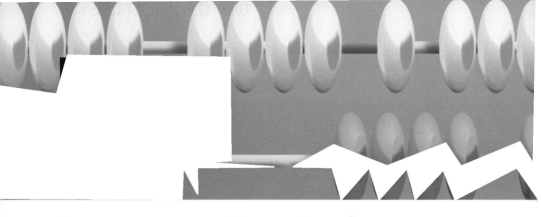

# Some common abbreviations

| | |
|---|---|
| AAT | Association of Accounting Technicians |
| ABC | activity-based costing |
| ACA | Associate of the Institute of Chartered Accountants in England and Wales |
| ACT | advance corporation tax |
| AGM | annual general meeting |
| AIM | alternative investment market |
| APR | annual percentage rate |
| ARR | accounting rate of return |
| AVC | additional voluntary contributions |
| AVCO | weighted average cost |
| b/d | brought down |
| b/f | brought forward |
| c/d | carried down |
| CD-Rom | compact disc read only memory |
| CE | chief executive |
| CEO | chief executive officer |
| c/f | carried forward |
| CFS | cash flow statement |
| CGT | capital gains tax |
| CIF | carriage insurance and freight |
| CIMA | Chartered Institute of Management Accountants |
| CIPFA | Chartered Institute of Public Finance and Accountancy |
| c/o | care of |
| Co. | company |
| COD | cash on delivery |
| COGS | cost of goods sold |
| COS | cost of sales |
| CPI | consumer price index |
| CPU | central processing unit |
| Cr | credit |
| CT | corporation tax |

| | |
|---|---|
| CVP | cost-volume-profit |
| DCF | discounted cash flow |
| Dept | department |
| Dr | debit |
| DTI | Department of Trade and Industry |
| e&oe | errors and omissions excepted |
| ECGD | Export Credits Guarantee Department |
| ED | exposure draft |
| EMS | European Monetary System |
| EOQ | economic order quantity |
| EPOS | electronic point of sale |
| ERM | exchange rate mechanism |
| EU | European Union |
| FA | Finance Act |
| FAS | financial accounting standards |
| FCA | Fellow of the Institute of Chartered Accountants |
| FCMA | Fellow of the Institute of Management Accountants |
| FIFO | first in first out |
| Footsie | 100 Financial Times share index (of 100 leading companies) |
| FOB | free on board |
| FRS | financial reporting standard |
| FT | Financial Times |
| FTSE | Financial Times share index |
| HP | hire purchase |
| IAS | International Accounting Standard |
| IASB | International Accounting Standards Board |
| ICAEW | Institute of Chartered Accountants in England and Wales |
| ICAI | Institute of Chartered Accountants in Ireland |
| ICAS | Institute of Chartered Accountants in Scotland |
| IFRS | International Financial Reporting Standards |
| IMF | International Monetary Fund |
| IOU | I owe you |
| IPO | initial public offering |
| IRR | internal rate of return |
| ISA | individual savings account |
| IT | information technology |
| JIT | just in time |
| LIFO | last in first out |
| LSE | London Stock Exchange |
| Ltd | Limited |
| Memo | memorandum |
| MIRAS | mortgage interest relief at source |
| MIS | management information systems |
| MLR | minimum lending rate |

| | |
|---|---|
| MMC | Monopolies and Mergers Commission now known as the Competition Commission |
| NAV | net asset value |
| NBV | net book value |
| NIC | National Insurance contribution |
| NIFO | next in first out |
| No. | number |
| NPV | net present value |
| OFT | Office of Fair Trading |
| P&La/c | profit and loss account now known as income statement |
| p.a. | per annum |
| PAYE | pay as you earn |
| PBIT | profit before interest and tax |
| PDB | purchases day book |
| P/E | price/earnings |
| PEP | personal equity plan |
| PER | price/earnings ratio |
| PIN | personal identification number |
| plc | public limited company |
| PRDB | purchases returns day book |
| PV | present value |
| R&D | research and development |
| R/D | refer to drawer |
| ROA | return on assets |
| ROCE | return on capital employed |
| ROE | return on equity |
| ROOE | return on owners' equity |
| RPI | retail prices index |
| RPM | resale price maintenance |
| SAYE | save as you earn |
| Sch | schedule |
| SDB | sales day book |
| SI | statutory instrument |